A Political
Theory Primer

A Political Theory Primer

Peter C. Ordeshook

ROUTLEDGE

New York   London

Published in 1992 by

Routledge
An imprint of Routledge, Chapman and Hall, Inc.
29 West 35 Street
New York, NY 10001

Published in Great Britain by

Routledge
11 New Fetter Lane
London EC4P 4EE

Copyright © 1992 by Routledge, Chapman and Hall, Inc.

Printed in the United States of America on acid free paper.

Library of Congress Cataloging in Publication Data

Ordeshook, Peter C., 1942–
    A political theory primer / Peter C. Ordeshook.
      p. cm.
    Includes bibliographical references and index.
    ISBN 0-415-90240-1 (hb.)—ISBN 0-415-90241-X (pbk.)
    1. Political games. 2. Political science—Mathematical models.
  3. Game theory. I. Title
  JA74.074   1992
  320'.01'51--dc20   91-32883
                                                     CIP

British Library Cataloguing in Publication Data also available

Contents

Acknowledgments

Several persons read preliminary versions of the text, and on this score I would like to single out Brian Roberts, Richard Boylan, Yan Chen, Peng Lian, Mikhail Filippov, and Emerson Niou. Arthur (Skip) Lupia, who acted as my TA for a number of years (and who consistently scored higher than me on student evaluations), contributed to the formulation and refinement of a number of exercises. Finally, I would like to thank the many Caltech undergraduates who offered their suggestions and critical comments, even though they had to tolerate drafts replete with typographical errors and homework assignments (hopefully now suitable revised) that were not always solvable in finite time.

Introduction

V.O. Key, in his introduction to elementary statistics, wrote: "Most political scientists, accustomed as we are to other modes of analysis, bristle at the sight of even the most common statistical symbol."[1] This reaction no longer characterizes our discipline since nearly all serious researchers appreciate or have grown accustomed to the principles of hypothesis testing, regression analysis, simultaneous equations estimation, and multivariate scaling, and the terminology and notation of R-squares, F tests, Durban-Watson statistics, and maximum likelihood estimators are commonplace in our journals. However, Key's characterization rings true if we substitute the words "the notation and concepts of formal political theory" for "statistical symbol," because few political scientists are comfortable with ideas such as Nash equilibrium, extensive form, stationary strategy, separable utility, multidimensional issue space, or repeated game.

This fact is unfortunate, because these concepts and their attendant mathematical notation, properly used, augment our reasoning with tools that allow us to detect inconsistencies and ambiguities in our thinking. Unfortunately, the language of mathematics and, thus, the language of political theory, is too often inaccessible to those who have entered the discipline not to understand mathematics but instead to understand and perhaps influence politics. However, those who are interested in understanding the inner logic of politics cannot forever ignore the opportunities for augmenting their thinking with formal constructs. Such constructs constitute too powerful an instrument of logical reasoning, and politics is too important a subject to leave its study to the often imprecise and logically flawed world of intuition, "wisdom," and verbal analysis—to a domain in

---

[1]V. O. Key, *A Primer in Statistics for Political Scientists*, New York: Crowell Co., 1954.

1

which the well turned word or eloquent phrase, however imprecise or illogical, carries the argument and dictates policy.

Of course, mathematical notation alone cannot supply us with understanding any more than entering random numbers into some well-constructed computer can produce something other than nonsense as output. In order to put mathematics meaningfully to work we must operate within an explicitly defined paradigm—a view of the world that guides both our intuitive reasoning and our use of mathematical ideas. In short, we must find a way to use notation and formal argument in an efficient way—in a way that ensures learning something about politics and not merely something that might be taught more effectively in a mathematics department.

This volume offers an introduction to one view of the world—**the paradigm of rational choice**—and to the part of that paradigm, game theory, that is of special significance to politics. Thus, this volume seeks to communicate the logical structure of a set of ideas that allow us to think about and to model a diverse range of political phenomena by using a single set of principles about individual decision making when those decisions are made in the context of institutions that we choose to call political.

Because this is an introductory text, we will not dwell on formal niceties. Indeed, we want to avoid the error made by too many practitioners in the field who become overly enamored of notation and who judge their colleagues' contributions by the skill with which that notation is manipulated rather than by substantive import. Thus, rather than survey the literature on political theory, we will focus instead on those ideas that point the way to key theoretical insights about some specific political processes. In particular, we provide an introduction that examines answers to such questions as:

1. How should the two major parties in a plurality-rule election system respond to the threat of entry by a third-party candidate?

2. Why do the plurality rule procedures of U.S. elections yield, in general, competition between only two major parties?

3. Are low levels of turnout necessarily symptomatic of something amiss in a democracy?

4. Should parties always prefer to control as many seats as possible in a legislature?

5. Does a poorly informed electorate create an inherent policy bias favoring those who can afford to secure good information about government policy?

6. Can social outcomes appear irrational even though everyone in the society satisfies nearly anyone's definition of rational?

7. Why is it that Congress often devotes more time and effort to debating procedures than it does to debating the actual legislation under consideration?

8. Are the votes legislators cast always good indicators of their assessments of their constituent's preferences, even among legislators whose primary goal is to win reelection?

9. What kinds of legislation are likely to induce legislators to trade votes across issues—to vote-trade (logroll)?

10. Does the committee system of Congress lead to outcomes that differ in a consistent way from the outcomes that would prevail if the Congress as a whole debated each and every measure?

11. Why is tax reform such an especially problematical form of legislation to consider, especially in an election year?

12. Why are congressional incumbents so frequently reelected despite the fact that Congress as an institution is held in low esteem by the public?

13. Should we attribute conflicts between a president and members of Congress merely to a clash of personalities, or are there explanations that derive from the fact that presidents and members of Congress are elected in different ways?

14. Aside from their general distrust of voters, what theoretical rationale is there for the indirect democracy bequeathed us by the Framers of the U.S. Constitution—in particular, for a bicameral legislature?

15. Why does the government regulate the rates charged by taxicab drivers and interstate moving companies, while at the same time it fails to regulate the prices of automobiles and most other major consumer purchases?

16. It is often asserted that "special-interest groups" buy politicians and control politics, but what of the view that campaign contributions correspond to politicians expropriating from interest groups?

17. When is it advantageous to commit to a decision before others and when is it more advantageous to hold off making commitments?

18. What are the conditions under which international systems will be stable, and how has the contemporary technology of nuclear weapons affected these conditions?

19. When everyone knows that everyone else is capable of deception, is it ever the case that a strategy of deception is more likely to succeed in achieving specific aims in international politics than a strategy of truthfulness?

20. What is the underlying structure of nuclear deterrence, what are the conditions under which such deterrence can be expected to work, and when can it be expected to fail?

21. Are the seeds of arms races and international conflict sown in human nature?

22. What role does verifiability play in strategic arms-limitation talks, and what degrees of verifiability are sufficient to ensure a "workable" arms-reduction treaty?

However, before proceeding, we would like to offer several special notes of caution. First, it will become apparent that modeling political processes frequently requires the imposition of a great many assumptions in order to render an analysis analytically tractable and intuitively understandable. We raise this issue here to confront directly the mistaken belief that, owing to such assumptions, formal theory is more limited than "informal" theory. It is certainly true that by making assumptions explicit, we reveal the limitations of our analysis. However, it is hardly the case that an analysis is more general if its assumptions are obscure, and we should discount the weight given to an argument to the extent that it cannot be shown to follow logically from a set of explicit assumptions about well defined primitive variables. Those who dismiss an idea, moreover, because its initial form imposes severe assumptions should be cautioned about failing to understand the processes whereby theory is developed. If, after establishing an initial representation of a situation, we deem that representation promising—either because it offers an unanticipated insight or because we did not appreciate beforehand the opportunity to model the situation in precisely the way shown—we can begin to weaken or generalize the initial assumptions. Hopefully, a general pattern in the analysis will emerge so that eventually a wholly general result can be established as a "first principle."

Related to this argument is a second note of caution, which is that it is incorrect to believe that the process of generalizing results will eventually lead to "complete" models of political processes. Indeed, only the naive student believes that we can understand most of politics merely with a sustained effort at formal modeling and game-theoretic analysis. Such a goal remains out of reach even in the natural sciences, which is why we distinguish between science—the discovery of first principles—and engineering—the application of those principles, in combination with experiment, experience, and common sense, to specific "real world" problems. In a primitive sense (primitive, because our theory is far from complete), the material covered in this volume concerns first principles, and the models we offer (as well as those offered in the literature) should not be interpreted as wholly satisfactory descriptions of any specific ongoing political process or institution. Instead, they are merely a piece of the puzzle, and the insights that contemporary political theory offers must be combined in an artful way with a substantive understanding of the problem at hand gained through experience. Unfortunately, we cannot communicate either art or experience here, and thus, the approach we introduce cannot preclude the necessity for learning about politics in other ways.

Another reason for not assuming that formal modeling can solve all of our problems is that a great many first principles remain to be discovered. For example, we are only beginning to understand how to model cooperative action (coalitions and the enforcement of agreements) and how to incorporate the incomplete information that pervades most decision-making situations into our game-theoretic models. Similarly, we often hear it said that the "rational choice" view of the world is flawed because it is self-evident that people are not rational—that their actions are often random or self-defeating, or, worse still, that the limited capacity of the brain itself and of people's abilities to make sense out of their environment limits their ability to function in accordance with the mathematical precision of formal theory. All of this may be true, but it ignores the fact that we cannot yet offer an unambiguous definition of rationality and that we can interpret the fundamentals of theoretical inquiry as being concerned precisely with this definition. Thus, although clever verbal argument coupled with a crude familiarity with bits and pieces of theory may win a coffee-table debate on the paradigm's pros and cons, such a debate is what we want to avoid in favor of a clear understanding of issues already well articulated in the literature.

One of our goals, then, will be to reveal some of the ambiguities that characterize research. Understanding these ambiguities will give us some insight into what we might expect from those who work at the forefront of theoretical developments, and it will also tell us what to demand of them so that their efforts will provide us with a better understanding of reality. This appreciation opens our eyes to topics that we imperfectly understand but which fuzzy or informal thinking has heretofore obscured from view.

1

Representation of Political Processes

1.1 The Basic Perspective

We begin with the assertion that all of politics concerns the actions of people whose fates are interdependent, where the nature of that interdependency is determined in significant part by institutions we choose to call political.

Such a characterization of politics may appear obvious or redundant, but it has profound consequences for the way we think about our subject. It implies that explanations of events focusing on the actions of a single individual, although perhaps contributing to our understanding, cannot provide a scientifically valid, causal explanation for those events. Arguing that the absence of a key legislator from a vote "caused" some bill to pass or fail ignores the fact that this absence is decisive only if the votes of others, as registered through specific institutional procedures, render that legislator's vote pivotal. Attributing electoral defeat to a candidate's stand on some issue ignores the fact that the defeat requires preferences among voters of a particular sort, it requires that voters be cognizant of the candidate's position, it requires that the candidate's opponent not be associated with an equally untenable position, and it presumes the existence of electoral procedures that allow more profitable campaign tactics. Judging an event such as the assassination of a national leader as the cause of a war commits the error of failing to see that an assassination, although perhaps a necessary condition for the outbreak of conflict, cannot be a sufficient condition: leaders must still decide between war and peace in light of their ultimate objectives, taking account of the responses of others to their actions, both in the international arena and domestically. The event may reveal new information about an adversary or an ally, or it may change military capabilities and make conflict more or less attractive for one side or another, but we cannot attribute cause until we understand the interdependent context of events.

These examples of things political reveal that our study must take account of three things: (1) the responses of decision makers to the fact of interdependent choice, (2) the role of institutions in determining the nature of that interdependence, and (3) the goals of individual decision makers as they are expressed through action in the context of specific institutions.

1. Notice that it is not sufficient that we as analysts understand that political outcomes are dictated generally by the actions of two or more decision makers. We must also accommodate the possibility that political decision makers themselves understand and react to this fact. And once we make this accommodation, seemingly intuitive expectations about outcomes are readily questioned. Consider, for example, a scenario in which a star quarterback is injured and is replaced with someone who is known to be far less proficient at passing. In this instance we might predict that the offense will pass less frequently. However, notice that it also seems reasonable to suppose that the defense is aware of this situation, and that it can anticipate fewer passing plays and more running plays, in which case it will devote more attention to a running defense. But now we have a new problem: if the offense anticipates this response on the part of the defense, then it might reasonably choose to pass more frequently with its inferior quarterback. But then again, if the defense anticipates this response, then perhaps it should reassess its decision to defend primarily against running plays.

   We are saying two things with this example. *First*, explanations for individual decisions that take the form "actor i chose action Y over Z because i preferred Y to Z" are not wholly satisfactory. Instead, we must consider propositions of the form "i chose Y because i believed that the other relevant actors, j, k, etc., would choose B, D, etc., and given these choices, action Y led to a better outcome for i than did other alternative actions. (Y is i's best response to B, D, and so forth.)" Although this restatement may appear to be only a modest revision in our thinking, once we accept it, as our football example reveals, we must also understand that we cannot fully explain final outcomes until we utter a parallel statement for person j (as well as for every other relevant decision maker)—that j chose B because, if i, k, etc., choose

Y, D, etc., respectively, then B led to the best outcome from *j*'s perspective. The *second* implication of our example is that after formulating such sentences, we necessarily confront the problem of higher orders of thinking. If what *i* chooses is a function of what *i* thinks that *j*, *k*, etc., will choose, and if what *j* chooses is a function of what *j* thinks *i*, *k*, etc., will choose, and so on, then how does each decision maker resolve the problem that all decisions are determined simultaneously—that what *i* does depends on what he believes *j* believes about him, and so forth?

The relevance of game theory is that it seeks to disentangle this simultaneity and to discover the choices people might reasonably be expected to make in such contexts. That is,

Game theory models individual decision making when people's fates are interdependent, when people are aware of their interdependence, and when each person tries to accommodate his or her awareness and the fact that others are aware as well.

2. Our characterization of things political and subsequent examples serve to emphasize the importance of institutions and the necessity to understand how institutions influence individual actions. A legislator's vote is pivotal only if a specific voting rule is employed, and an issue, as well as the candidates' stands on it, is relevant to an election's outcome only if those who care about the issue are enfranchised to vote and if their votes can be pivotal. Even in international systems that we might model as being anarchic because they are governed by little more than the rule that nations with greater military capability can overcome those with less, if we want to understand why they remain anarchic—why various institutions are not used to regulate interstate action—we must attempt to understand the choices that people might be compelled to take if these institutions were to be implemented.

3. There is a final feature of our characterization of politics that is implicit in our previous examples—namely, that decision makers are goal directed. Before discussing this assumption in detail, however, we should first dispense with a potential ambiguity about the identities of these decision makers. Perhaps because of linguistic convenience, discussions of politics commonly refer to the actions that various groups or collectivities take and to the goals they pursue. However, language such as "interest groups lobby," "the legislature

prefers," "the court decides," and "the union supports" commits the error of anthropomorphic reasoning. Groups and collectivities cannot act or choose. Actions may be taken in the name of groups, and the members of some collectivity may all have to act in concert for an action to gain the weight of group attribution, but only individuals can sign a check, push a voting lever, state a judicial opinion, or utter an endorsement. Of course, we too will find attributing actions to groups an irresistible linguistic convenience, but when succumbing to such conveniences we must keep in mind that ultimately the only valid explanation for a political event is one that explains the decisions of the individuals we judge germane to the event.

Having thus characterized politics as the study of individual interdependent choice in the context of institutions, the additional assumption that people's actions can be interpreted as directed toward the attainment of identifiable goals renders the rational choice paradigm the appropriate vehicle with which to study politics. Admittedly, though, attributing goals to people can be a difficult task. Goals are often obscure, such as when we do not understand fully the weights a Soviet premier places on long-term economic vitality, short-term national security, and personal survival or when we cannot judge when a legislator will act on the basis of a personally held policy preference as against the desire to be reelected. Similarly, we may have difficulty in understanding the goals of citizens who appear more likely to vote when elections are close than when they are landslides, since the probability that a vote is decisive remains, for all practical purposes, zero in even close elections. At other times goals may be readily apparent, such as when we believe that an election candidate cares little about policy and is interested merely in winning, or when experience tells us that if corporate leaders fail to strive for greater profits, their jobs if not their firms will disappear.

Whether goals are obscure or self-evident, the assumption that goals motivate people's actions is the engine driving our explanations of political events, and it is this assumption that leads us to explore the applicability to politics of the formalism associated with the rational choice paradigm. However, given the difficulties that often accompany the identification of a person's goals, we should ask how we are to proceed with our analyses and modeling of politics. In addition, we should also ask how we can mute this criticism—that the assumption of goal-directed behavior verges on becoming a tautological explanation for events, since we can always assert that a person's goal is to do precisely what we observe him or her to be doing.

The assumption of goal-directed action is given meaning by joining it to specific hypotheses about the content of goals. Because we want to explain as much as possible with as little as possible, one method is to conceptualize people in terms of the measurable things that might guide their actions. Thus, for legislators, we might assume that their primary objective is to win reelection and that policy preferences are secondary; for voters, we might assume that they are concerned solely with their personal income, or with some specific set of political issues; for international leaders, we might assume that they are motivated to increase their country's welfare, to maintain their nation's sovereignty, or simply to remain in power. As our models of specific processes mature, we can consider more complicated goals and allow for trade-offs between competing objectives. We can, for example, let legislators give some weight to personally held policy preferences as well as to the desire to be reelected. And as we become more sophisticated in the construction of our models, we can try to determine which of our results depend on the details of goals and which results remain valid for more general descriptions about goals. We must always keep in mind, however, that formal theory gains substantive meaning only through the careful attribution of goals to the people whose actions we are modeling.

1.2 Essential Components of a Game

To illustrate the sorts of questions we must ask and answer as we try to understand specific political events, consider the following news item pertaining to the hostilities that arose between the United States and Iran in the Persian Gulf in 1988:

> The precise rules of engagement [for U.S. naval forces] remain classified. [House Armed Services Committee Chairman] Aspen said it is necessary to keep the rules of engagement secret so the Iranians do not know which ships will be defended by U.S. forces and which will not be. "We are trying to deter the Iranians from violent action in the gulf . . . When they know what the rules of engagement are, they can work around them." (*The Los Angeles Times,* April 23, 1988)

Without delving deeply into the events surrounding this report, notice that we can evaluate the policy it describes only if we supply some additional facts. First, we must grapple with the fact that it is not "Iranians" who are to be deterred, but those who make decisions about the deployment and actions of the Iranian military. It probably matters little if Iranian Kurds near the Soviet border feel deterred if, at the same time, no one in Teheran feels the same. Thus, we must ask: Who are the relevant decision makers, and what options for action are they likely to perceive—what actions are they likely to be deterred from and what actions will they presumably choose instead? Answering this question requires some understanding of Iran's domestic politics and the institutions mediating conflict there. Second, we should ask why the decisions of these Iranians might be expected to be a function of their information about U.S. rules of engagement. What features of American strategy are likely to intervene between Iranian actions and outcomes? This question can be addressed only if we understand the goals of those decision makers and how those goals are served by particular outcomes. We should also be concerned with the courses of action the Iranians perceive as being available to them. And, naturally, to fully understand this policy's logic, we must also understand the goals of those decision makers in Washington who established it, as well as their assessment of Iranian goals and the likely Iranian response to this and alternative policies. In short, then, an analysis of this situation requires, at a minimum, a specification of the following seven items:

1. A list of relevant decision makers,
2. The goals (policy objectives) of these decision makers,
3. The actions available to each decision maker,
4. A list of feasible outcomes,
5. The relationship between actions and outcomes,
6. The relationship between outcomes and goals,
7. Each decision maker's perceptions of items 1–6, as well as each decision maker's perceptions of the perceptions of others.

Finally, after having specified items 1–7 as they pertain to our example, we should determine whether or under what circumstances the implied ambiguity of U.S. policy can be unraveled by careful analysis. Can an Iranian strategic planner deduce the choice emanating from Washington, and can a strategic planner in Washington deduce the best choice for Iran, aware of the fact that his counterpart in Iran is doing the same?

All of the questions we have asked about this news item should occur to any competent strategic planner. What good policy analysis requires, though, is a general structure that forces us to these questions and ensures that we have not overlooked any important consideration. In other words, we require a structure that tells us "automatically" whether the linkages between goals, outcomes, alternative actions, and institutional constraints in an environment of interdependent choice have been adequately specified. Only then can we begin to answer the last question we posed concerning our prediction about actual decisions.

For another example that illustrates how we intend to proceed, consider the seemingly perpetual lament about the level of voter turnout in U.S. presidential elections. Time and again we are reminded that few citizens exercise their franchise, presumably because they fail to perceive great differences in policy between the candidates. The implication is that such perceptions and the accompanying low turnout are symptomatic of something wrong with our democracy. However, consider this argument: In large electorates, pluralities (the differences in vote totals between pairs of candidates) in even close presidential elections generally exceed tens of thousands of votes. Thus, the probability that any one vote is decisive is infinitesimal, if not zero. In addition, if the candidates fail to offer distinct policy choices and if voting is costly (in terms of time), then we should ask instead: Why do so many vote?

To answer this question, we must construct an election model that fills in the details of items 1–7. First, limiting our model initially to two-candidate elections, the relevant decision makers are voters and the two candidates. Second, each voter must vote for one candidate or the other, or abstain, whereas as an initial simplifying assumption, we can suppose that the set of actions available to each candidate consists of alternative policy promises. For purposes of constructing a "well defined" model, we can represent these alternative promises as points on a line that might correspond to a "liberal-conservative" or to a "left-right" continuum. Third, the goal of each voter, presumably, is defined in terms of the public policy that eventually prevails as a result of the election. Specifically, we can suppose that each voter has a most preferred policy and that the further one moves from this policy, the less satisfied that voter becomes. And, as an initial assumption, we can suppose that candidates are motivated primarily by the desire to win. Fourth, outcomes are denoted by the identity of the victorious candidate, in conjunction with some final policy. Fifth, the final outcome is determined, presumably, by the actions of voters and the choices of the candidates in the obvious way. Sixth, the extent to which each voter's goal is satisfied is a function of how "far" the policy advocated by the victorious candidate is from that voter's most preferred policy. Finally, we can suppose that all voters and candidates are aware of this election scenario.

Having specified such a model, we can then address a variety of subsidiary questions: What is the relationship, if any, between individual decisions to vote (and, thus, turnout) and the actions of candidates and their parties? What is the relationship, if any, between a citizen's preference for one candidate or another and the citizen's likelihood of voting? Is it necessarily the case that it is in a candidate's interest to offer policy choices distinct from the opponent so that turnout might increase? Do our electoral institutions differ in systematic ways from the institutions of other countries so as to induce lower turnout either directly by their influence on citizens or indirectly by their influence on the strategies pursued by candidates and political parties? Do candidates and voters respond to our institutions in such a way that campaign platforms and public policy differ from those induced by systems in which nonvoting is fined or voting is subsidized? What assumptions are implicit in the presumption that low turnout is symptomatic of something amiss?

So, before we can draw any conclusions about the meaning of turnout rates, we must understand the interrelationships of electoral institutions, candidate campaign tactics, public policies implemented by incumbents, and citizen choices. And once again, the answers to such questions require that we explore the model constructed when we filled in the details of items 1–7 outlined previously.

1.3 The Extensive Form

Constructing a model of a particular political process in a way that allows us to apply what we learn from it to the study of other processes and events requires the development of some general conceptual constructs. This, in turn, suggests that we also require some convenient mathematical notation with which to represent those constructs. Beginning with what it is we want to explain—the actions of individuals—consider once again our example of conflict in the Persian Gulf. Since we have not yet presented the tools required to model domestic politics, suppose for the moment that a single decision maker, 1, sets Iranian policy, and that another such person, 2, chooses the U.S. action. Suppose person 1 can choose one of the following actions:

a_1: *Do nothing*
a_2: *Attack non-U.S.-flagged shipping*
a_3: *Attack any target of opportunity, including U.S.-flagged shipping*

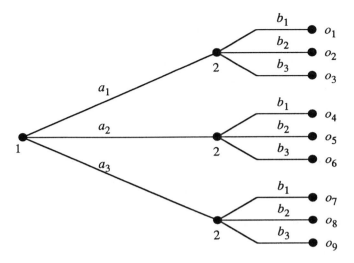

Figure 1.1   Persian Gulf Crisis Extensive Form

Suppose person 2 must choose one of these actions:

b_1: *Do nothing*
b_2: *Attack Iranian ships*
b_3: *Withdraw*

Because what one person decides may depend on what others do, we must identify the actual sequence of decisions and the outcome that follows from each feasible sequence. Presently, we have in mind a situation in which 1 moves first, and 2 responds to 1's initial choice. Figure 1.1 offers an especially convenient representation of this scenario, which we call **the extensive form**. Reading this figure from left to right, it states that 1 chooses first from the set of actions $\{a_1,a_2,a_3\}$, and then 2 chooses from the set $\{b_1,b_2,b_3\}$. Further, if person 1 chooses a_1 and 2 chooses b_1, the status quo (denoted o_1) prevails and no shipping is harmed; if person 1 chooses a_1 and 2 chooses b_2, we can assume that the Iranian navy suffers considerable damage but the United States is condemned by other nations (an outcome denoted by o_2); and so on. For convenience, we enumerate all possible outcomes by the notation $o_1, o_2, \ldots,$ and o_9, and we leave it to the reader to imagine what outcomes o_3 through o_9 might entail.

It is not our intention yet to analyze this situation and to offer predictions about actions—in fact, our model is far too simple to yield meaningful implications. Rather, our purpose is to illustrate a way to represent the situation that, upon refinement and elaboration, might prove to be a useful tool for arriving at substantively meaningful predictions or policy recommendations. We also want to demonstrate the flexibility of this approach for representing decision situations of considerably greater complexity. Hence, let us examine the four essential components of Figure 1.1, which are:

1. **Decision nodes**, which identify who it is that must decide at a particular stage in the decision-making sequence,
2. **Branches**, which connect one node to another, and which thereby indicate which decision node, if any, follows another as a consequence of the selection of a particular action,
3. A **labeling of lines** so as to denote the particular actions to which they correspond,
4. **Specification of the outcomes** that prevail after everyone acts

We impose two constraints on branches and outcomes. First, we do not want to leave open the possibility that people might act in ways disallowed by our model and we want to identify actions unambiguously, so we require that the branches radiating from any node correspond to exhaustive and exclusive alternatives. Exclusivity requires that one and only one branch (alternative action) can be chosen at each node. Requiring that actions are exhaustive assures us that decision making proceeds down at least one path toward a final outcome; requiring exclusivity assures us that at most one path is pursued, and, therefore, that only one outcome ultimately prevails. Second, the requirement that actions are exclusive and exhaustive implies that outcomes are also exclusive and exhaustive. Thus, if $O = \{o_1, o_2, \ldots, o_n\}$ denotes the set of all outcomes portrayed in an extensive form, then at least one and only one outcome in O must ultimately prevail. Nodes labeled by an outcome are called **terminal nodes**.

At this point we note that, although our example fails to illustrate this possibility, one of the "decision makers" can be Nature. However, unlike a human decision maker, nature is not assumed to pursue any goal—it is neither deliberately malevolent nor benevolent, nor is it an entity that acts in anticipation of what other decision makers choose. Thus, decision nodes can be of two types:

1. Those denoting a decision point for one of the decision makers we have identified as relevant to the problem at hand,
2. Those representing random moves by nature, **chance nodes**

The branches from Nature's nodes are labeled p_1, p_2, and so forth to identify the probability that one branch or the other is "selected." Chance nodes can occur anywhere in an extensive form, but since nature's choices must also be exclusive and exhaustive, the sum of the probabilities assigned to the branches at any such node must equal 1.

In addition to allowing chance moves by nature, extensive forms need not be limited to representing the decision problem confronting two persons; nor are we required to suppose that decision makers can act only once in a situation. People can choose sequentially— first one, then another, then the first again—and, indeed, who chooses can be made dependent on the actions others take.

> **Example:** Suppose each chamber (H and S) of a bicameral legislature consists of a single member (never let it be said that theorists do not know how to simplify a problem in the name of tractability) and that both legislators must pass a bill (choices p and f) before it goes to the president (P), who can approve (a) or veto (v) it. If the president vetoes, the two chambers must vote to override (o) or sustain (s) the veto. If we suppose further that H moves before S, Figure 1.2 portrays the extensive form of this situation. Notice that we allow chamber S to vote even though it knows that chamber H has already killed the legislation. This assumption, of course, allows us to accommodate the possibility that legislators treat the failure outcomes differently, depending on who can be held responsible for killing the measure. The U.S. Senate's passage of Contra aid in 1988, despite the House's prior rejection of the proposal, illustrates this possibility.

One possibility that we have not considered is that people choose in ignorance of what others have done. Referring to our Persian Gulf example, suppose the United States (player 2), prior to 1's initial decision, can secretly choose between increasing (c_1) and maintaining its current forces (c_2). Consider Figure 1.3's representation of this situation, which merely offers two versions of Figure 1.1, depending on 2's initial action. However, we have drawn a dashed "envelope" around 1's decision nodes to indicate that, since 2's first move is secret, 1 does not know which node it is at when it is time to act. No envelopes are drawn about 2's nodes, since 2 knows what secret action it took.[1] We refer to envelopes such as the one in Figure 1.3

---

[1] To ensure a consistent mathematical notation, we can suppose that such envelopes surround all decision nodes but that some such envelopes merely encompass one node.

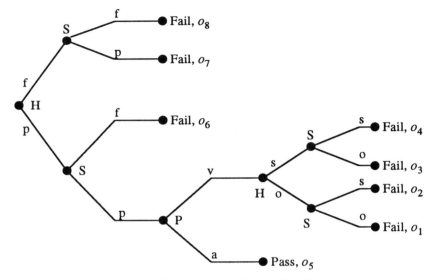

Figure 1.2 Legislative Extensive Form

as **information sets**, and we can not understate their importance. With them, for example, we can not only represent secret moves but simultaneous moves as well, or, equivalently, moves by several decision makers that remain secret for awhile. Suppose, for example, that our legislative example is modified to require that both chambers of the House always vote simultaneously rather than sequentially (admittedly, a curious and difficult requirement to implement). Figure 1.4 shows the modifications of Figure 1.2 required to represent this institutional change.

Notice that in the event of simultaneous or secret moves it should not matter who we identify as the first to act and who the last; we could just as easily suppose that S moves first and that the information sets in Figure 1.4 pertain to H's decision nodes. For the same reason the two extensive forms in Figure 1.5a and 1.5b are equivalent. Although 1.5a draws person 1's decision node first, and 1.5b draws person 2's first, the subsequent information sets model a situation in which neither player knows the choice of the other when it is that person's "turn" to choose.

In addition to secret or simultaneous moves, information sets allow us to model other diverse types of situations. For example, there is nothing in the rational choice paradigm that presupposes that decision makers have perfect memories. Thus, Figure 1.6a illustrates

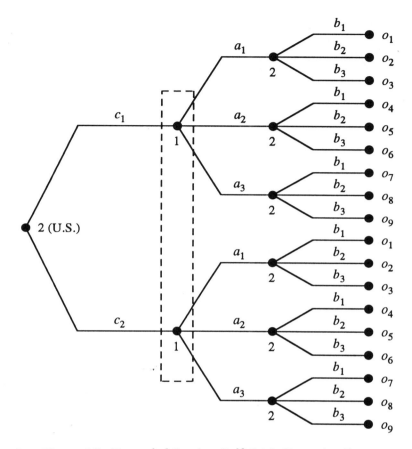

Figure 1.3 Expanded Persian Gulf Crisis Extensive Form

a situation in which persons 1 and 2 alternate in making binary choices, where each observes the choices of the other, but person 1 can only recall the last decision and person 2 can recall only the last two. Because 2 has the better memory, 2's information sets are more detailed and, thus, more numerous than are person 1's. For a final example of the flexibility that information sets allow, we note that the structure of a person's information can be modeled depending on the actions that person or others take as the situation unfolds. To illustrate this possibility, Figure 1.6b portrays a situation in which one person's information depends on what another person chooses. In this example, person 2 learns whether or not 1 chose a_1, but if a_1 is not chosen, 2 cannot tell whether 1 has selected a_2 or a_3.

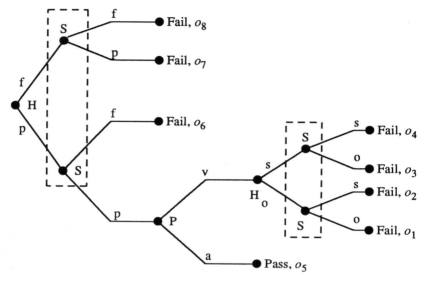

Figure 1.4 Legislative Extensive Form With Simultaneous Moves

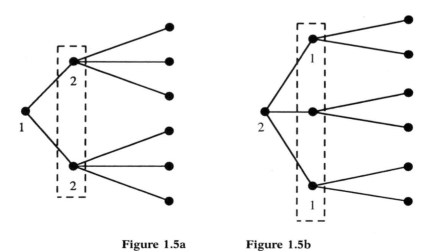

Figure 1.5a   **Figure 1.5b**

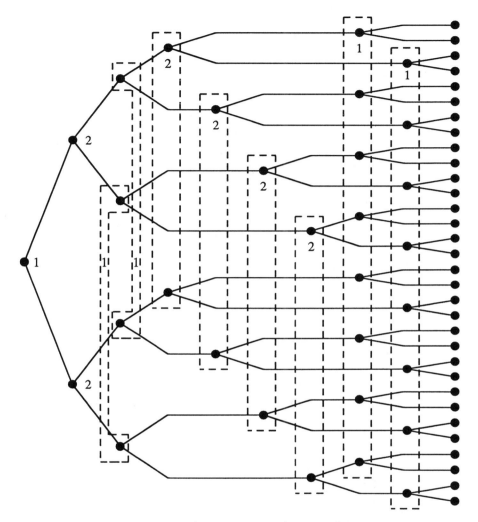

Figure 1.6a Extensive Form With Limited Memory

More generally, information sets allow us to distinguish between two general classes of interdependent choice situations—games with perfect versus imperfect information.

*In a game with **perfect information**, all information sets encompass a single decision node. Such games correspond to situations in which all decision making is sequential and all decision makers know the choices that they and others made any time in the past. In a game*

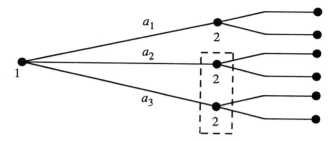

Figure 1.6b

with **imperfect information**, *at least two decision nodes are in the same information set for at least one decision maker. Such games correspond to situations in which at least one decision maker is unaware of the choices made by another decision maker.*

Although information sets increase the applicability of extensive forms, certain rules must be adhered to when we use them. Specifically,

1. All decision nodes contained in an information set correspond to the same decision maker. An information set describes what a decision maker knows about earlier decisions when it is his or her turn to act and, thus, each information set describes something about a specific person.

2. Each node in an information set has the same number of branches emanating from it; otherwise the decision maker can identify which node he or she is at by the number of alternative actions.

3. For the same reason, the labels attached to the branches at each node must be matched by the labeling of branches at any other node in the same information set.

Finally, we will impose two additional restrictions on extensive forms. First, we will suppose that the branches connecting nodes cannot "double back" to some previous node. Later we will accommodate the possibility that some branches may require that the people replay all or part of the game, such as when they fail to reach agreement in some bargaining session and must try again, until an agreement is reached. For now, however, it is easier to consider situations in which such possibilities are excluded. A second and related assumption is that all branches lead eventually to some outcome. That is, we suppose that the time allowed to play a game is finite. As with repetition, we later consider situations that, in principle at least, allow for the possibility of infinite play.

1.4 Preference and Utility

The preceding examples of extensive forms merely scratch the surface of possibilities, and thus they do not reveal the ambiguities we will encounter as we use such forms to model various events and processes. However, before we explore some of these problems with additional examples, we must develop a notation for representing goals. After all, we seek to portray the alternative actions of people because we want to predict which choices follow from their goals, and to make such predictions we must find a convenient way to represent goals.

We begin with the assumption that goals manifest themselves as preferences over the outcomes that an extensive form identifies as feasible, and we use two more specific assumptions to summarize the logical form of preferences, regardless of the goals rationalizing them. First, we assume that preferences are **complete**. This assumption requires that for any two outcomes in the set O of outcomes thought to be feasible, a person either prefers one outcome to the other or is indifferent between them. That is, if given a choice between o_i and o_j, a person will either make a definitive choice or be indifferent. Second, and perhaps more controversial, we assume that preferences are **transitive**. That is, if o_i is preferred to o_j, and if o_j is preferred over or equally preferred to o_k, then o_i is preferred to o_k.

The assumption of transitivity, then, precludes the confusion that those of us, untrained in the subtleties of art, are likely to exhibit in an art museum. If required to state a preference between successive pairs of paintings, this author would almost certainly generate a great many intransitive choices. And, in addition to supposing that people cannot be confused, the assumption of transitivity supposes that people's perceptual abilities are perfectly formed—which is almost certainly not true in many situations. For example, if a person prefers unsweetened to sweetened coffee, then transitivity requires that that person prefer a cup of coffee with no sugar to a cup containing one grain of sugar, a cup containing one grain to a cup containing two grains, and so on. No one, though, is likely to be able to detect the difference of a single grain, so although indifference prevails across a long series of paired comparisons, transitivity is violated by the strict preference between the first and last alternatives.

Although we can imagine circumstances under which either the completeness or transitivity assumption might fail to describe a person's revealed preferences, and although we can impose weaker requirements on preference for many of the results we review in this volume, as abstractions they are nevertheless especially convenient. In particular, they imply that the relation of individual preference between pairs of outcomes orders the outcomes in O in an unambiguous way from best to worst in much the same way that we order numbers from great to small. Indeed, completeness and transitivity imply that we can summarize preferences by such numbers—assigning a large number to an outcome that ranks high on a person's preference order, a small number to one that ranks low, and the same number to any two outcomes if the person is indifferent between them. In particular, suppose we denote by $u_i(o)$ the number assigned to outcome o for person i such that for any two specific outcomes, o_j and o_k, $u_i(o_j) > u_i(o_k)$ if and only if o_j is preferred to o_k. Then we refer to u_i as person i's utility function—in particular, u_i is i's **ordinal utility function**, because it orders the outcomes in O. Notice that if o_1 is preferred to o_2, which is preferred to o_3, then assigning the numbers 5, 2, and 0 respectively conveys the same information as the assignment 10,000,000, 5, and -1. All we require of an ordinal utility function is that its value increase as we consider outcomes that stand higher on a preference order.

Having thus represented individual preferences over outcomes, it is useful to consider whether we can do the same for collectivities of people, since politics is concerned with the decisions rendered by different types of groups such as legislatures and committees. However, consider the following example:

The Condorcet Paradox: To this point we have conceptualized people as black boxes into which we feed alternatives or outcomes and out of which complete and transitive preferences emerge. Suppose we try to conceptualize a group in a similar way—as a box that transforms individual preferences into a group preference. Unlike people, though, we can look inside this box and record the procedures whereby the group performs this transformation. So suppose that the group in question uses simple majority rule to order alternatives, and suppose we feed these three complete and transitive preferences into the box:

A preferred to B preferred to C

C preferred to A preferred to B

B preferred to C preferred to A

What emerges from the box, however, is quite unlike the preferences we fed into it. Rather than a transitive order, we get a **cycle**: A is socially preferred to B (A defeats B), B to C, and C to A. Thus, the **social preference order** under simple majority rule can be intransitive. This possibility, known as the **Condorcet Paradox**, shows how groups differ from the people that comprise them.

Barring further developments, we could, of course, assume that the Condorcet Paradox is but an anomalous, albeit unanticipated, characteristic of majority rule. This paradox might merely cause us to question the reverence that is sometimes associated with outcomes chosen "democratically" by majority rule principles. However, a profoundly important theorem, **Arrow's Impossibility Theorem**, tells us that this paradox is not anomalous or confined to majority rule procedures—it is possible to observe "irrational" social preferences under almost any social process:[2]

> *An intransitive social ordering of outcomes can characterize a group that uses nearly any procedure for ordering alternatives (short of a dictatorship in which one member's preference is decisive).*

Later we will grapple with the full consequences of this theorem, which is one of the most important in political theory. However, here we merely want to emphasize the special role played by the transitivity and completeness assumptions in modeling people and the fact that these assumptions cannot play an equivalent role in our discussions of groups. That is, although it is often convenient to

---

[2]Briefly, Arrow offers these axioms as a characterization of reasonable social decision mechanisms:

1. The social ordering is complete and transitive,

2. No individual preference order over the feasible outcomes is a priori excluded as a possibility,

3. The social ordering of the outcomes in O depends only on individual preferences over O,

4. If one or more persons raise some outcome in their orders and no one else lowers that outcome, then, *ceteris paribus*, that outcome should not fall in the social order,

5. No individual should be everywhere decisive—a dictator.

Arrow's theorem establishes that these five assumptions are inconsistent—that if we want, for example, to maintain the first four axioms, we can do so only if we admit a dictatorship. See Kenneth Arrow, *Social Choice and Individual Values*, 2nd ed., New Haven: Yale University Press, 1963.

attribute motives to groups in the same way that we attribute motives to individuals (with such terminology as "the electorate prefers," "the interest group lobbied for," "the government chooses,"
and so on), such linguistic shortcuts are not generally valid. Thus,
although we may choose to use such shortcuts to convey general
meaning, we must keep in mind that any theoretically valid explanation for social processes and outcomes must rest ultimately on an
assessment of the preferences and actions of individuals.

However, even if we limit our representation of preferences to individuals, the two assumptions of completeness and transitivity and
the concept of an ordinal utility function are not generally sufficient
to represent preferences in a wholly convenient way. Recall that our
conceptualization of extensive forms allows the possibility that nature makes moves in accordance with chance, in which case particular actions need not yield definitive outcomes—they may yield lotteries over outcomes instead. Briefly, letting p_j denote the probability
that outcome j prevails, then

> $p = (p_1, p_2, \ldots, p_n)$ *is a lottery over the set of outcomes* $O =$
> $\{o_1, o_2, \ldots, o_n\}$ *if* $0 \leq p_j \leq 1$ *for* $j = 1, 2, \ldots, n$, *and* $p_1 + p_2 + \ldots +$
> $p_n = 1$.

The particular difficulty with lotteries is that if, for instance, a person orders three outcomes from best to worst o_1, o_2, o_3, if one action
leads with certainty to the middle-ranked outcome o_2 whereas another leads to a lottery between o_1 and o_3, then we cannot say which
action the person will choose—we do not yet know how a person
orders lotteries over these outcomes. Indeed, we cannot even say that
a person will choose his most preferred outcome in lieu of choosing
a lottery between his second and last choices, although such a decision, even for persons who love gambles, seems only reasonable.

We have two choices. The first is to suppose simply that person
i's utility function u_i is defined over lotteries just as it is over pure
outcomes (pure outcomes being those "degenerate lotteries" that assign a probability of 1 to one outcome and 0 to the rest). However,
although there is nothing improper with this approach, it necessitates carrying a great deal of baggage in order to explain or to predict choice in an uncertain world—namely, we must know (or at
least pretend that we know) utility functions that not only order the
outcomes in O but that also order all lotteries over O. The particular
disadvantage of this approach is that even if the set of pure outcomes, O, is finite, there exist an infinite number of possible lotter-

ies, which implies that acceptance of this option dashes any hope of learning preferences by observing choices.

A second approach is to suppose that assumptions in addition to completeness and transitivity hold—assumptions that allow us to deduce preferences over lotteries in a more convenient way from preferences over outcomes. In particular, suppose there are n outcomes in O, and let $p = (p_1, p_2, \ldots, p_n)$ and $q = (q_1, q_2, \ldots, q_n)$ denote two lotteries over O, where p_j and q_j denote the probability that outcome o_j prevails if p and q, respectively, prevail. Notice now that an especially convenient summary of preferences over lotteries pertains if we can say that

> the lottery p is preferred to the lottery q (that is, $u_i(p) > u_i(q)$) whenever the **expected utility** from p exceeds the expected utility from q—that is, whenever

$$p_1 u_i(o_1) + p_2 u_i(o_2) + \ldots + p_n u_i(o_n) >$$
$$q_1 u_i(o_1) + q_2 u_i(o_2) + \ldots + q_n u_i(o_n).$$

The advantage of this relation between preference and expected value is that it allows us to deduce the relative standing in a person's preference order of a particular lottery from the probabilities that characterize the lottery and from the utility numbers we assign to the pure outcomes. However, if we accept this formulation then, first, we must be more careful in our assignment of utility numbers. Second, we must be willing to accept some additional assumptions about preference and the way in which people treat probability, with the understanding that not all preferences or choices need be consistent with these assumptions.

To see first that our earlier method of assigning utility numbers is inadequate if we wish to deduce preference over lotteries, suppose again that o_1 is preferred to o_2 and that o_2 is preferred to o_3. If we are not concerned with lotteries, then assigning ordinal utility numbers such as 3, 2, and 1 or 1, $\frac{1}{5}$, and 0, respectively, to o_1, o_2, and o_3 suffices to summarize preferences. Suppose, however, that the person in question is indifferent between an even-chance lottery between o_1 and o_3 and securing o_2 with certainty. In other words, suppose

$$u((.5, 0, .5) = .5 u_i(o_1) + .5 u_i(o_3) = u((0, .5, 0)) = u_i(o_2).$$

But now if we set $u_i(o_1) = 1$ and $u_i(o_3) = 0$, it must be the case that $u_i(o_2) = .5$. In other words, the expected-value equation establishes a constraint on utility numbers such that the assignment of two numbers determines the third. Because not every ordinal assignment of numbers suffices in this instance, in order to distinguish it from utility numbers that merely summarize the ordering of pure outcomes, we refer to a utility function that satisfies the expected value equation as **cardinal utility**.

However, we are not done. Having assigned the numbers 1, .5, and 0 to the three outcomes, we should ask: What guarantee do we have that these numbers permit us to deduce person i's preferences over lotteries other than the one we have considered? If, for example, we consider the lottery q = (.3,.4,.3), which, with the current assignment of numbers, yields the same expected utility as the lottery p = (.5,0,.5), what assurances do we have that the person will be indifferent between p and q? The answer, of course, is NONE, unless we impose some assumptions about the way people treat probabilities.

We will not discuss those assumptions, aside from stating that a sufficient condition for establishing such an assurance is that people treat probabilities in the same way as we treat them in introductory statistics or probability texts.[3] For example, then, suppose that subjective probabilities across an exhaustive and exclusive set of outcomes sum to 1; that if A and B are independent events, then the probability of "A or B" is merely the sum of the "probability of A" and the "probability of B"; and that if the expected value of the lottery p is the same as q's, then we can freely substitute p for q in the description of outcomes without altering a person's preferences.

---

[3]In addition to supposing that preferences over the set of outcomes O are complete and transitive, the assumptions we require are that

1. Preferences over lotteries are complete and transitive,

2. A person is indifferent between any two lotteries that yield the same probabilities over O—people have no taste for especially simple or complex lotteries if they generate equivalent probabilities over O,

3. If a person strictly prefers the most preferred outcome in O to the least preferred outcome in O, then between any two lotteries that place weight only on these two outcomes, the person prefers the lottery that renders the most preferred outcome more probable.

4. If a person is indifferent between the lottery p and the certain outcome o in O, then that person is indifferent if we substitute p for o in any other lottery.

These assumptions are sufficient to ensure the validity of the **Expected Utility Theorem**, which asserts that there exists a cardinal utility function over O such that the utility function summarizing a person's preferences over lotteries corresponds to the expected utility calculation.

Example: The supposition that people subjectively treat probability as in an introductory statistics text, however, is not without pitfalls and we can easily generate some contrary empirical evidence. Consider these three outcomes:

o_1: *$5 million*

o_2: *$1 million*

o_3: *nothing*

Presumably, most people prefer more money to less, so we can assume that $u_i(o_1) > u_i(o_2) > u_i(o_3)$. But imagine being confronted with the necessity to choose between the lotteries $p = (0,1,0)$ and $p' = (.10,.89,.01)$. Thus p awards $1 million with certainty, whereas p' offers a meaningful chance of $5 million, but at the expense of some small chance of winning nothing at all. Although many people might choose p' over p, there are those who, reasoning that a "bird in the hand is worth two in the bush," would choose p. Now, however, consider the two lotteries $q = (0,.11,.89)$ and $q' = (.10,0,.90)$. In our experience, when asked to carry out this thought experiment, people nearly unanimously choose q' over q. But consider this: for those who chose p over p', the expected utility hypothesis requires $u(o_2) > .1u(o_1) + .89u(o_2) + .01u(o_3)$, or equivalently,

$$.11u(o_2) > .1u(o_1) + .01u(o_3).$$

On the other hand, choosing q' over q implies that $.10u(o_1) + .90u(o_3) > .10u(o_1) + .90u(o_3)$, which is equivalent to

$$.11u(o_2) < .1u(o_1) + .01u(o_3).$$

These two inequalities, though, are contradictory, so no assignment of utility numbers to the pure outcomes is consistent with the expressed preferences over lotteries.

One source of this inconsistency is the failure to treat probabilities in accordance with probability theory—if, in particular, people treat the .01 probability difference of receiving nothing between p and p' differently than the mathematically equivalent difference between q and q'. Moving from p to p' makes the undesirable event of winning nothing possible, whereas moving from q to q' merely makes it more probable. Probability theory regards these .01 differences as equivalent, but we cannot preclude the possibility that subjective evaluations of probabilities depend on the context of decisions.

Such possibilities do not require abandoning the notion of cardinal utility. Even if this notion is only approximately correct, it offers a greatly simplified structure for the representation of preferences. For this reason we assume the validity of the cardinal utility idea, keeping in mind that it is at best an approximation of reality and not an inviolate axiom about people and their choices.

Example: We conclude this section by introducing a representation of preferences that is an important part of a great many models of politics. Imagine that an outcome, o, can be characterized by the values of two variables, x and y, so that $o = (x,y)$. In economics, where the key decision makers are consumers, x and y are interpreted as the amounts of two goods that can be purchased in the market, and it is assumed that the consumer chooses x and y so as to maximize utility $u(o)$, subject to some budget constraint, say B. To simplify matters, we suppose that x and y can, in principle at least, assume any positive value (including fractional amounts), in which case the set of alternative outcomes—commodity bundles—can be represented by the positive quadrant of a 2-dimensional (Euclidean) coordinate system. However, rather that represent the utility function $u(x,y)$ with a third dimension, economics introduces the idea of an *indifference curve*. Briefly, an indifference curve connects all outcomes over which a consumer is indifferent. Two such curves— u' and u''—are illustrated in Figure 1.7a. The curve u', then, implies that the consumer in question is indifferent between o' and o''. However, assuming that the consumer wants as much of x and y as possible, the consumer prefers both of these outcomes to o'''—thus, we say that the curve u' is higher than u''. The downward slopes of these curves indicate that as y is decreased, remaining at the same level of utility requires that we compensate the consumer by increasing x.

If we suppose now that p_x and p_y denote the per-unit prices of x and y, then the consumer's budget constraint is $xp_x + yp_y = B$, which corresponds to line B in Figure 1.7a. Notice in particular that u' is the highest feasible indifference curve that our consumer can reach without exceeding his budget, and thus the outcome o^* is the solution to this consumer's utility maximization problem.

Now let us change this problem's description in an important way. Instead of assuming that x and y are purchased in the market, suppose they are supplied by government—rather than assuming that x and y can be purchased at a shopping mall, suppose that their values are set by some political process in which our consumer is a participant. And instead of interpreting $xp_x + yp_y = B$ as the consumer's budget constraint, suppose it corresponds to the government's budget constraint (which we temporarily assume is fixed), so positions on line B denote alternative feasible government policies—in this instance, a policy is the emphasis the government gives to spending on good x (e.g., defense) versus good y (e.g., education).

If our consumer were dictator, he would, of course, choose $o^* = (x^*,y^*)$ as the government's policy. However, we can no longer assume that any one person has dictatorial control over final outcomes, and indeed, we should not even suppose that o^* will be considered. If the final outcome is the one selected by a victorious candidate in a two-candidate election, if positions on the budget constraint line correspond to alternative election campaign platforms, and if our consumer is merely one of many voters, we cannot suppose a priori that o^* corresponds to any candidate's campaign promise. Thus, to learn how our consumer might vote, we must know preferences over all alternative government policies—over all positions on the government's budget constraint line. Fortunately, we can learn these preferences from Figure 1.7a. Notice that as we move from o^* to the left or right along B, we necessarily move to lower indifference curves. Thus, if we lay out the line B horizontally and add a vertical dimension to represent preference, we get the curve in Figure 1.7b, which for obvious reasons we refer to as a *single-peaked preference curve*.

The key property of a single-peaked preference curve is that its ordinal features are characterized by two things—an ideal policy, o^*, and the statement that utility declines as we move away from o^*—which allow us to extend our development to more complex policies. For example, if the government must choose x, y, and, through selection of a tax rate, B, then a geometric depiction of government policy requires two dimensions—one specifying the relative weight given to x versus y, and a second representing the relative size of the government. Rather than add a third dimension to represent utility, however, we can use the economist's trick to represent preference in this policy space. Specifically, if we continue to assume that preferences are characterized by an ideal policy and by preferences that decline as

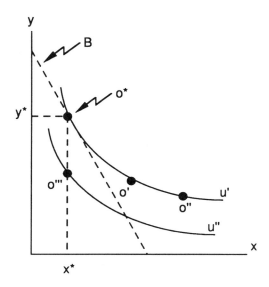

Figure 1.7a   Indifference Curves

we move in any direction from this policy, then we can represent indifference curves by circles, ellipses, or some other equivalent form. Thus, for the special case of circular indifference curves, Figure 1.7c portrays several of these curves, where circles of greater radius correspond to lower levels of preference.

Preferences like those in Figure 1.7c are called *spatial preferences*, and they are used extensively to model a variety of political processes. And aside from allowing us to conceptualize matters geometrically, they link political models to classical economic models of markets, and, thus, they are an important part of the reintegration of political and economic theory. Specifically, because we can derive spatial preferences from "economic" ones, we can begin the comparative analysis of public versus private supply of goods and services.

1.5 The Decision to Vote

Using utility numbers to summarize preferences allows us to complete an extensive form and positions us to use that form to predict choices. However, before we tackle prediction, let us first consider one additional example of a situation that concerns a single decision

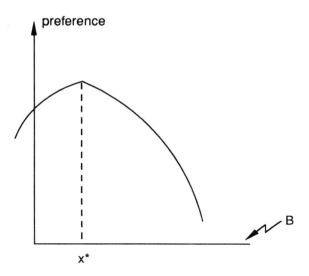

Figure 1.7b Single-Peaked Preference

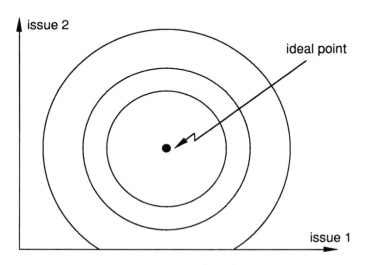

Figure 1.7c Spatial Preferences

maker. Specifically, consider the simple act of voting and suppose a person must choose between voting for candidate 1 (act a_1), for candidate 2 (act a_2), or abstaining (act a_0). And although many of us may base our evaluations of candidates on how others tell us they will vote, in large electorates using a secret ballot, it is not always the case that we want to try to explain this decision by assuming that not only do citizens condition their choices on what other citizens do but that they also condition on what they think others think they in particular will choose. Hence, it is more convenient to treat the remainder of the electorate as "nature," and to suppose nature selects one of five "actions" as follows:

s_1 (s_2): *If the citizen abstains, candidate 1 (2) loses by more than one vote,*

s_3 (s_4): *If the citizen abstains, candidate 1 (2) loses by one vote,*

s_5: *If the citizen abstains, the candidates tie.*

Clearly, the likelihood that nature chooses s_3, s_4, or s_5 is small—a probability reasonably approximated by zero. Nevertheless, if our citizen is not concerned with the magnitude of a candidate's victory, but merely with who wins and who loses, this classification of nature's actions identifies the contingencies that determine the consequences of choice. Under s_1 or s_2, the decision is irrelevant to the determination of the eventual outcome; under s_3 the citizen can create a tie by voting for candidate 1 whereas under s_4 he can create a tie by voting for 2; and under s_5, a vote is decisive for determining the winner. Letting p_i denote the probability that nature chooses s_i, Figure 1.8a portrays this situation's extensive form. However, notice that instead of associating terminal nodes with outcomes, we instead identify the utility payoff to our decision maker at each node, where u_j is the benefit from candidate j's victory, C is the cost of voting, and $(u_1 + u_2)/2$ is the expected utility from a tie, which we suppose is broken by a coin toss.

Because we assume nature chooses blindly, without regard to our citizen's actions, we do not bother to draw an information set about nature's choices, although inclusion of such a set would not affect our subsequent analysis. If, on the other hand, we had supposed that nature "moved first," followed by our citizen's choice, then the inclusion or exclusion of an information set that encompasses all five decision nodes is not irrelevant because, unlike nature, a person can condition his or her decisions on this information. Assuming, then, that nature moves first, Figure 1.8b shows a representation of the

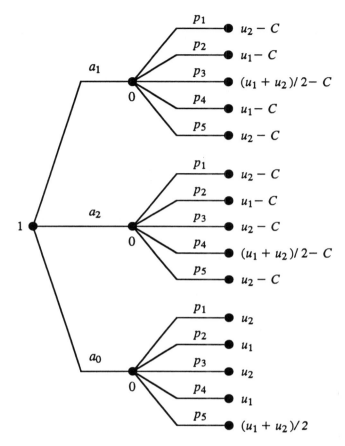

Figure 1.8a Decision Tree for Voting

situation that is equivalent to the one in Figure 1.8a. Inclusion of the information set in this figure implies, of course, that the citizen does not know with certainty how others vote and thus the ultimate consequence of actions, so as before only probabilities can be assigned in accordance with the probabilities associated with nature's actions. Elimination of this set, on the other hand, models a situation in which the citizen knows the consequences of actions with certainty. Thus, the first circumstance is referred to as **decision making under risk** whereas the second is referred to as **decision making under certainty**.

What we want to emphasize now is that although extensive forms with a single decision maker are a special case of the situations we

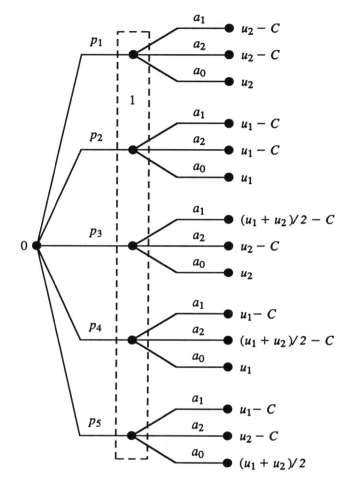

Figure 1.8b   Equivalent Form of Figure 1.8a

want to consider in this volume, we should not suppose that the analysis of such cases cannot raise interesting questions. Because nature has no goals and merely "chooses" a state without anticipating what our citizen chooses, we modeled the citizen as a person who merely forms subjective estimates of the probability that each of nature's states prevails. This, in turn, implies that each action is a lottery, and our prediction is that the citizen chooses the lottery with the greatest expected utility. In our example, this assumption yields the conclusion that a person should never vote in a two-candidate race for a second choice—if u_1 exceeds u_2, then $u(a_1) > u(a_2)$.[4] Whether or not a person should vote in the first place, however, depends on the values of parameters. Specifically, some simple algebra establishes that $u(a_1)$ exceeds $u(a_0)$ if and only if[5]

$$(p_3 + p_5)(u_1 - u_2)/2 - C > 0.$$

The implications of this expression point to some difficulties in modeling political processes. In large electorates, the probabilities p_3 and p_5 are quite small, and so it seems irrational to vote unless $u_1 - u_2$ is large enough to offset infinitesimal values of $p_3 + p_5$ and to allow the first term of the expression to offset the cost of voting. But if $p_3 + p_5$ is essentially zero, $u_1 - u_2$ must exceed nearly any reasonable estimate to render voting rational. It appears, then, that people vote only because they overestimate the efficacy of their vote or because the C is not a cost at all, but a benefit (and thus is negative).

Letting C be a benefit supposes that voting is a consumptive act rather than an instrumental one—that voting is valued by citizens in its own right and that people vote because they have been socialized to do so. Some people might be bothered by the idea, because it renders voting rational by assumption. However, this discussion merely serves to emphasize that at some point, we must take the preferences that people bring to a situation as exogenous to the analysis. Although we can often derive a preference order over one set of outcomes from an order over another set, at some point we must take preferences as exogenously determined. Because we want our analysis of voting to be simple, we might wish that only preferences over candidates and readily apparent costs determine actions. But as is often the case in politics, we must contend with the

---

[4]The reader should confirm, on the other hand, that if three or more candidates compete, people should vote for a second choice candidate if their first choice has little or no chance of success and if the utility difference between a second- and first-choice candidate is not too great.

[5]Briefly,

$$u(a_1) = p_1[u_2-C] + p_2[u_1-C] + p_3[(u_1+u_2)/2-C] \\ + p_4[u_1-C] + [1-p_1-p_2-p_3-p_4][u_1-C],$$

whereas

$$u(a_0) = p_1u_2 + p_2u_1 + p_3u_2 + p_4u_1 + \\ [1-p_1-p_2-p_3-p_4][(u_1+u_2)/2].$$

Setting up the inequalities and canceling terms yield the asserted inequality.

	s_1 (p_1)	s_2 (p_2)	s_3 (p_3)	s_4 (p_4)	s_5 (p_5)
a_1	u_2-C	u_1-C	$(u_1+u_2)/2-C$	u_1-C	u_1-C
a_2	u_2-C	u_1-C	u_2-C	u_1+u_2-C	u_2-C
a_0	u_2	u_1	u_2	u_1	$(u_1+u_2)/2$

Figure 1.9 The Strategic Form of Figure 1.8

fact that many of the actions have a symbolic value that is every bit as important as their instrumental value vis-à-vis some more "objective" specification of outcomes. Later, we may wish to model the source of these symbolic values, but if we ignore them altogether, we can seriously distort our conclusions.

1.6 The Strategic Form

Whether they model a single decision maker or several, extensive forms are valuable aids in thinking about political processes and in identifying the decision sequence confronting people as well as what they know when making those decisions. Sometimes, however, this form is needlessly complicated, and an alternative representation— the **strategic form**—is more useful. Consider again the voting example portrayed in Figure 1.8a (or 1.8b), and consider the equivalent alternative representation in Figure 1.9. The rows of this table denote our decision maker's choices, the columns denote nature's decisions, and in the cells of this table we enter the utility numbers that summarize our decision-maker's preferences. Completing our description, we include the probabilities p_1 through p_5, which we suppose correspond to the decision-maker's subjective estimates that nature chooses s_1, s_2, and so on.

So as not to occasion any confusion about who moves first or second after depicting the situation in this tabular representation, as a convention we suppose that both nature and our citizen move simultaneously—our citizen chooses a row and nature chooses a column without one choice being revealed beforehand to the other. Although this might seem an odd restriction to impose universally, we shall see shortly that it is neither odd nor restrictive. In this instance, though, such an assumption is of little consequence, since Figure 1.8a supposes that the citizen moves before nature, and since we suppose nature does not condition its choice on the citizen's action.

Of course, the strategic form representation of a citizen's voting decision in large electorates is little more than a bookkeeping device—a way to keep track of the outcomes that follow from specific choices and states of nature. Note, however, that no new conceptual ideas must be introduced if we substitute a second decision maker for nature, provided that this additional decision maker is also presented with a simple choice, and provided that we can identify the outcomes that prevail (or lotteries over outcomes) for a conjunction of choices by the two decision makers. Indeed, we could elaborate matters further with three-, four-, and n-dimensional tables to accommodate any number of additional decision makers. However, at this point we should return to the assumption of simultaneous choice and consider how we contend with those situations in which a person is afforded the opportunity to choose after observing the choices of others.

To simplify matters, let us consider a situation in which there are just two decision makers, but in which one of them must make two choices—the first in anticipation of what the other decision maker will do and a second, subsequent choice in reaction to what that person has done. In particular, let us see how we can represent the decision situation shown in Figure 1.3 in strategic form.

The representation of 1's choices are simple since 1 must act without knowing what 2 has done. The particular difficulty here is that not all choices can be represented as simultaneous. Supposing, though, that person 2 is fully informed about the situation's extensive form, imagine 2's thinking prior to making the first move. This person knows he will make a second choice after seeing what 1 has done. Thus, the assumption that 2 is fully informed about the extensive form is sufficient to ensure that 2 has sufficient information to formulate a contingent plan of action, called a **strategy**. Briefly,

> *Strategy: A strategy is a plan of action that specifies what a player will do at each of that player's information sets.*

With respect to our example, a strategy for 2 could look as follows: Choose c_1, and if 1 then chooses a_1, choose b_2; if 1 chooses a_2, choose b_3; and if 1 chooses a_3, choose b_1.

The point we want to make about strategies and the strategic form is that without any loss of generality we can suppose that people choose their strategies before any initial move is made, and we can suppose further that all persons choose their strategies simultaneously (or, equivalently, in ignorance of what strategies others choose).

Of course, it might seem strange to presume in our example that 2 chooses a plan that takes him through the entire form without waiting to see what person 1 does. After all, we might ask, doesn't such preplanning restrict 2's flexibility and limit the opportunity to modify decisions as events unfold? In fact, no such restriction is implied by the notion of a strategy. We must keep in mind that every possible contingency and everything that person 2 might learn about the situation is represented already in the extensive form and all contingencies are planned for by a strategy. In particular, the only fact that 2 learns in our example is 1's choice, and a strategy already allows a person to make a decision contingent on what information set is reached as the situation unfolds—on the choice that 1 takes. Thus, we can suppose that both 2 and 1 choose their strategies simultaneously and beforehand.

Later, as we consider more complicated possibilities in which people may have estimates about the probability that they are in one information set or another—estimates that they may want to revise as a situation unfolds—we will want to allow for more complicated strategies. In our current example, however, person 1 has only one information set and thus his strategies (contingent decisions) are simply the three choices a_1, a_2, and a_3. In contrast, person 2 has many strategies. Specifically, 2 has two initial choices, and then must plan for three contingencies—three possible information sets. Since 2 has three choices at each of these information sets, person 2 has $3^3 = 27$ strategic options after its and person 1's initial choices. Thus, the total number of strategies for person 2 is 27 (the number of possible plans for handling the contingencies that follow 1's choice) times 2 (the number of initial choices), or a total of $2 \times 27 = 54$ strategies.

This situation's strategic form, then, is a 3×54 matrix (person 1's 3 strategies × person 2's 54 strategies), and were we to construct it we would begin by observing that the choice of a strategy by each person yields a determinate outcome. For example, if 1 chooses "a_2," and if 2 chooses "c_1, and if 1 chooses a_1, choose b_1; if 1 chooses a_2, choose b_3; but if 1 chooses a_3, choose b_2," then a unique path (c_1, then a_2, then b_3) is traced through the extensive form to the outcome o_{15}. The strategic form corresponding to this situation, then, will look like the one shown in Figure 1.9, with two exceptions. First, it will be considerably larger. Although it will contain only three rows for 1's strategies, it must contain 54 columns to denote all of 2's strategies. Second, it will not be accompanied by any probabilities for 2 or 1's choices that parallel the probabilities we associate with nature's choices in Figure 1.9—such probabilities must be deduced from hypotheses we offer later as to how people respond to interdependent choice situations. Beyond this, however, Figures 1.9 and the strategic form representation of Figure 1.3 will look quite similar.

Because the concept of a strategy and the strategic form is so important in game theory, let us consider a second example.[6]

Example: Suppose three legislators, A, B, and C, must vote alphabetically in a roll-call ballot (A, then B, then C) on whether to increase their own salaries. Each legislator, with expenses of public service being what they are, prefers to receive the pay raise even if he or she must vote for it. However, constituents, an aggregation of ungrateful wretches, will punish their legislator for voting in this way. Thus, from each legislator's point of view, there are four possible outcomes, which we order from most to least preferred:

o_1:   *The raise passes, but the legislator votes against it.*

o_2:   *The raise passes, and the legislator votes for it.*

o_3:   *The raise fails, and the legislator votes against it.*

o_4:   *The raise fails, but the legislator votes for it.*

Using utility numbers to summarize preference, for legislator i we let

$$u_i(o_1) = 2, u_i(o_2) = 1, u_i(o_3) = 0, \text{ and } u_i(o_4) = -1.$$

Figure 1.10 portrays this situation's extensive form, where terminal nodes are associated with a payoff 3-tuple—the utility to legislator A, B, and C, respectively, of that node.

To construct the situation's strategic form, notice that legislator A's strategies are quite simple because this legislator cannot condition his or her actions on any prior actions. Thus, legislator A has two strategies:

a_1:   *Vote **for** the raise.*

a_2:   *Vote **against** the raise.*

Legislator B has more complicated strategies since B can formu-

---

[6]This example is taken from Peter C. Ordeshook, *Game Theory and Political Theory*, New York: Cambridge University Press, 1986.

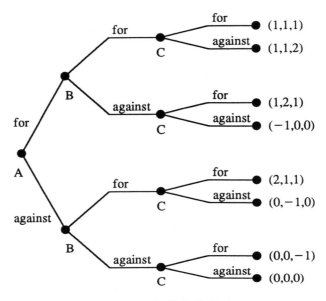

Figure 1.10 Roll-Call Voting

late a plan that conditions on A's decision—B has two information sets:

b_1: *If A votes* **for**, *then vote* **for**;
 and if A votes **against**, *then vote* **for**.

b_2: *If A votes* **for**, *then vote* **for**;
 but if A votes **against**, *then vote* **against**.

b_3: *If A votes* **for**, *then vote* **against**;
 but if A votes **against**, *then vote* **for**.

b_4: *If A votes* **for**, *then vote* **against**;
 and if A votes **against**, *then vote* **against**.

Finally, C's strategies are more complicated since C can condition on what A and B do. C has four information sets, and a strategy must specify what C does at each one, so a typical strategy reads as follows:

If A and B vote **for**, *then vote* **for**,

if A votes **for** *and B votes* **against**, *vote* **for**,

if A votes **against** *and B votes* **for**, *vote* **against**,

if A and B both vote **against**, *vote* **for**

We are not arguing that this is a good strategy (it is a poor one); but notice that in this instance we can represent this strategy for C by the 4-tuple (f,f,a,f) to indicate the choices it implies at each of C's four information sets. Notice, moreover, that since C can do one of two things at each information set, C has a total of $2^4 = 16$ strategies. So this situation's strategic form is the $2 \times 4 \times 16$ matrix (2 strategies for A, 4 for B, and 16 for C) in Figure 1.11.

To illustrate Figure 1.11's construction, consider the cell corresponding to $(a_2, b_2, (a,f,a,f))$. In this instance A votes against. Acting in accordance with b_2, B also votes against. Finally, since both A and B vote against, (a,f,a,f) dictates that C vote for. Ordering the payoffs (player C, player B, player A), the final outcome, in terms of utility, is $(-1,0,0)$, and, thus, we enter this utility vector in the corresponding cell of Figure 1.11.

The reader may wonder what advantage a $2 \times 4 \times 16$ matrix has over the picture in Figure 1.10. Although we cannot answer such questions at this point, we note that one of the benefits of a strategic form is that it allows the efficient use of mathematical notation. Recall that a mathematical function is a mapping from one set (its domain) to another set (its range). A function such as $f(x,y) = xy$ takes values of x and y and maps these values into their product. Strategic forms perform an equivalent task—they take strategies and map them to payoffs, or, if we have not yet assigned payoffs to outcomes, to descriptions of the outcomes themselves. Generally, then,

A **strategic form game** *consists of three elements:*

1. *A list of decision makers*

2. *A specification of the strategies available to each decision maker*

3. *Functions that map strategies to individual payoffs*

Letting $N = \{1,2,. . .,n\}$ denote the set of decision makers; x_i denote the strategies available to person i, with x_i a generic element of x_i; and $u_i(x_1,x_2,. . .,x_n)$ be the mapping of strategies to i's payoff, $(N, x_1, . . ., x_n, u_1, . . ., u_n)$ provides a complete description of a game in strategic form.

Identifying the x's and u's when we model a situation is not always easy, especially if we want these entities to assume a form that allows for analysis. But these same problems confront us when we specify an extensive form, and once we have that form, the strategic form is well defined. This fact leads to two questions about strategic and extensive forms. First, noting that the extensive form in Figure 1.3 yields a strategic form with $3 \times 54 = 162$ cells, is it generally true that strategic forms are more complicated than their associated

C:	Player A chooses a_1 Player B chooses:				Player A chooses a_2 Player B chooses:			
	b_1	b_2	b_3	b_4	b_1	b_2	b_3	b_4
f,f,f,f	1,1,1	1,1,1	1,2,1	1,2,1	1,1,2	−1,0,0	1,1,2	−1,0,0
f,f,f,a	1,1,1	1,1,1	1,2,1	1,2,1	1,1,2	0,0,0	1,1,2	0,0,0
f,f,a,f	1,1,1	1,1,1	1,2,1	1,2,1	0,−1,0	−1,0,0	0,−1,0	−1,0,0
f,f,a,a	1,1,1	1,1,1	1,2,1	1,2,1	0,−1,0	0,0,0	0,−1,0	0,0,0
f,a,f,f	1,1,1	1,1,1	0,0,−1	0,0,−1	1,1,2	−1,0,0	1,1,2	−1,0,0
f,a,f,a	1,1,1	1,1,1	0,0,−1	0,0,−1	1,1,2	0,0,0	1,1,2	0,0,0
f,a,a,f	1,1,1	1,1,1	0,0,−1	0,0,−1	0,−1,0	−1,0,0	0,−1,0	−1,0,0
f,a,a,a	1,1,1	1,1,1	0,0,−1	0,0,−1	0,−1,0	0,0,0	0,−1,0	0,0,0
a,f,f,f	2,1,1	2,1,1	1,2,1	1,2,1	1,1,2	−1,0,0	1,1,2	−1,0,0
a,f,f,a	2,1,1	2,1,1	1,2,1	1,2,1	1,1,2	0,0,0	1,1,2	0,0,0
a,f,a,f	2,1,1	2,1,1	1,2,1	1,2,1	0,−1,0	−1,0,0	0,−1,0	−1,0,0
a,f,a,a	2,1,1	2,1,1	1,2,1	1,2,1	0,−1,0	0,0,0	0,−1,0	0,0,0
a,a,f,f	2,1,1	2,1,1	0,0,−1	0,0,−1	1,1,2	−1,0,0	1,1,2	−1,0,0
a,a,f,a	2,1,1	2,1,1	0,0,−1	0,0,−1	1,1,2	0,0,0	1,1,2	0,0,0
a,a,a,f	2,1,1	2,1,1	0,0,−1	0,0,−1	0,−,0	−1,0,0	0,−1,0	−1,0,0
a,a,a,a	2,1,1	2,1,1	0,0,−1	0,0,−1	0,−1,0	0,0,0	0,−1,0	0,0,0

Figure 1.11 Payoffs Are Ordered: Player C, Player B, Player A

	A for		A against	
	B for	B against	B for	B against
C for	1,1,1	1,2,1	2,1,1	0,0,−1
C against	1,1,2	-1,0,0	0,-1,0	0,0,0

Figure 1.12

extensive forms? Second, is it possible to lose information when we move from an extensive form to the corresponding strategic form?

In answering these questions, it is important to keep in mind that several of the hypotheses we offer later about interdependent choice apply only to extensive forms. Thus, our discussion of the strategic form at this point does not mean that we intend to abandon the extensive form. Rather, the strategic form is introduced for purposes of analytic convenience, and if, for whatever reason, we believe that it does not serve that purpose, we should return to the extensive form. With respect to the issue of complexity, notice that the number of strategies depends on opportunities to make contingent decisions, and, thus, on whether each player has many information sets or only a few. To illustrate the dependence of this complexity on the structure of information, consider our pay-raise example again, but suppose that the legislature, instead of voting by roll call, votes by secret ballot—in which case legislator B cannot condition on legislator A, and legislator C cannot condition on legislator A or B. Indeed, the strategies of B and C are now identical to A's—to vote for or against. Thus, the strategic form reduces to the one shown in Figure 1.12, which is considerably simpler than that shown in Figure 1.11 and no more difficult to describe than the extensive form.

Another response to our question about the relative complexity of strategic forms compared to extensive forms is provided by noting that many situations that concern us do not have readily apparent extensive forms or their forms are so complicated that we prefer the immediate simplification offered by the strategic form. Consider, for example, the task of modeling a two-candidate election. We know, of course, that even if we limit our attention to the sorts of things candidates do during the formal campaign process, elections are exceedingly complex events. Suppose, however, that we are concerned with what types of policies simple majority rule elections engender. We might be interested in such questions as:

What are the characteristics of policy positions that the candidates might find especially attractive as campaign promises? Will the candidates offer the electorate distinct choices on the issues or will they advocate identical policies? If incumbents must choose their position first, does the challenger have any advantage? Will the candidates have any incentive to offer ambiguous policy positions?

Rather than model an election in detail (an impossible task), we can begin with a representation designed to "get a handle" on such questions. Suppose the election concerns one issue and the positions on it can be scaled and represented by numbers between 0 and 1. Supplying some notation, let X denote all such numbers, with x denoting a generic element of X, so if the candidates choose their platforms (positions on the issue) simultaneously, then we can let x_i represent candidate i's strategy, $i = 1, 2$. If lurking in the background is a model of voters telling us how many voters prefer x_1 and x_2 for all possible values of these two variables, then we can calculate candidate 1's proportion of the vote as a function of x_1 and x_2, denoting this function by $V_1(x_1,x_2)$. Of course, 2's proportion of the vote is simply $1 - V_1(x_1,x_2)$. Finally, if each candidate's utility increases as his or her proportion of the vote increases so that we can let $u_i(x_1,x_2) = V_i(x_1,x_2)$, then this function, in conjunction with the characterization of strategies as numbers in the interval [0,1], is a strategic form model of an election. This notation does not, of course, complete the analysis, since we must still consider the relationship between espoused policy and voter choice. Nevertheless, the analysis resulting from such a description, although it skips directly to a strategic form representation, allows us to begin an inquiry into the questions about elections we posed earlier.

Now, however, we must consider our second query—whether moving from the extensive form to the strategic form preserves all the relevant information about a situation. Unfortunately, our answer to this query is that some information may be lost in the transition, and, therefore, we must treat strategic forms with care. To illustrate this possibility, consider the following scenario:

Example: A legislature, L (which we treat as a single decision maker) can either pass a currently pending bill (action B) or refer the bill back to committee (action R), at which time the committee, C (which we also treat as a single decision maker), can either kill the bill (action K), or, after revisions that everyone can anticipate, send it back to the floor (action F), at which time the legislature can either pass the amended bill (action AB) or so emasculate it by amendment that it becomes equivalent to

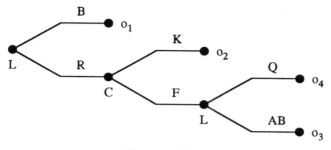

Figure 1.13a

the status quo (action Q). This situation's extensive form with terminal nodes denoted by the outcomes o_1 through o_4, then, is the one depicted in Figure 1.13a.

Turning now to the strategic form that Figure 1.13a implies, notice first that the legislative committee has but two strategies, F and K, whereas the full legislature has three:[7]

x_1: *B (pass the bill)*

x_2: *R and if C chooses F, choose AB (pass the revised bill)*

x_3: *R and if C chooses F, choose Q (defeat the revised bill)*

The strategic form, then, is the one in Figure 1.13b, but notice that the cell (x_1,K) makes no sense—it specifies an action for the committee whereas the choice of x_1 implies no role for it.

If we look at Figure 1.13b alone and ignore the corresponding extensive form, we might in fact draw an incorrect inference about decisions. It may, of course, turn out that this ambiguity is a curiosity with no substantive significance, but we should be alert to such possibilities since later we want to examine whether our hypotheses about action are affected by the form we use to represent a situation.

Before we conclude this section, we want to emphasize that although some persons believe that the strategic form is restrictive because it presupposes simultaneous choice and some try to circumvent this "problem" by allowing for sequential choice, this view and this method of analysis are incorrect. The **only** correct interpretation

[7]Actually, since a strategy is defined to specify a choice at every possible information set for a person, the full legislature has four strategies—"B then AB," "B then Q'," "R then AB," and "R then F." However, the first two strategies are equivalent since they imply choices which preclude the legislature from ever reaching its second information set, and so we collapse them to the single strategy, "B."

	F	K
x_1	o_1	o_1
x_2	o_3	o_2
x_3	o_4	o_2

Figure 1.13b Strategic Form of Game in Figure 1.13a

of a strategy is a plan on how to play an extensive form, so the strategic form is no more or less restrictive than any alternative. And to analyze a strategic form by assuming that one player chooses before the other is to violate that form's meaning and purpose.

1.7 Voting Trees

Portraying extensive or strategic forms that involve as few as six or so people can yield a serious paper shortage. However, to illustrate how we can sometimes proceed, suppose there are n people, whom, because of the symmetry of the situation, we distinguish only by the index labels we attach to them. Making use of symmetry, we can try to model the strategic form payoff function of an individual decision maker, leaving the decisions of the remaining $n-1$ persons as a parameter of that function. The strategic imperatives this analysis reveals will, by symmetry, apply to the remaining $n-1$ persons, and this fact may be sufficient to allow us to infer everyone's eventual choice.

Example: Suppose each of n (odd) legislators must choose between (act X) introducing a pork barrel bill for his or her district (where the benefit to the district is B and the cost, which is borne equally by all n districts is C) and (act ~X) opposing all such legislation. If a majority chooses ~X, then no such legislation passes, and everyone's payoff is zero. However, if a majority of legislators choose X, then the districts of legislators choosing act X each receive a benefit of B minus their share of the total cost of the legislation passed, whereas those districts not represented by such a legislator receive no benefit but must nevertheless pay their share of the cost of the m pork barrel projects. So if the number of legislators choosing X is m, and if $m > (n+1)/2$, then those choosing X receive $B-mC/n$ whereas those choosing $\sim$X receive $-mC/n$. Assuming that an individual legislator's utility equals the net benefits accruing to the district he or she represents, letting $(X,m-1)$ denote introducing a pork barrel bill when $m-1$ others follow suit, and letting $(\sim X,m-1)$ denote not introducing such a bill when $m-1$ others choose a, then

$$u(X,m-1) = 0 \qquad \text{if } m < (n+1)/2,$$
$$u(X,m-1) = B - mC/n \qquad \text{if } m > (n+1)/2,$$
$$u(X,m-1) = 0 \qquad \text{if } m-1 < (n+1)/2, \text{ and}$$
$$u(X,m-1) = -(m-1)C/n \qquad \text{if } m-1 > (n+1)/2$$

describes each legislator's payoff as a function of what that legislator and all other legislators choose. These four expressions, then, form a convenient summary of the situation that is equivalent to the strategic form, and, as we see later, they are sufficient to yield the conclusion that if C isn't too big (but not necessarily less than the benefit B), then all legislators choose X.

The preceding example is, of course, a specific and special example of how we can simplify a situation. An important and more general class of n-person decision situations concerns developing a simpler representation of formal voting procedures in a legislature. Consider again the example in Figure 1.2, and recall that we simplified the presentation there of the extensive form by supposing that each chamber of Congress has but one member, since if we assumed that the House has 435 members and the Senate 100, drawing the corresponding extensive form would entail a considerable waste of time. Alternatively, though, we could interpret the decision nodes at H and S in this figure as the "decisions of the House and of the Senate." This interpretation threatens to commit the error of attributing goals and rationality to groups, but if we are careful, and if, when analyzing this form, we keep in mind that such nodes merely represent the joint decisions of a great many people, then such a figure, in combination with a statement of how decisions are actually made within each chamber, can prove quite convenient. However, to remind ourselves that it is not individual decisions that are being represented at every node, we can refer to figures such as 1.2 as **voting trees** rather than as extensive forms.

Example: Consider the formal voting procedures described by a **legislative agenda**, which specifies the order of voting among alternatives when a legislature must select a single alternative

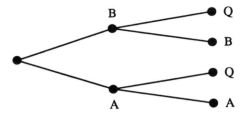

Figure 1.14a

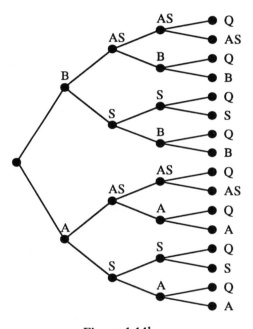

Figure 1.14b

from a list containing (usually) three or more alternatives. Suppose, in particular, that the committee confronts three alternatives: a bill as reported out of committee (B), an amended version of the bill (A), and the status quo (Q). Suppose, as is common, that the legislative agenda first calls for a vote between B and A and then requires a vote for final passage, which is equivalent to taking the winner of the first vote and pairing it against the status quo, Q. The voting tree in Figure 1.14a portrays this agenda.

Example: Figure 1.14b summarizes the usual procedures of Con-

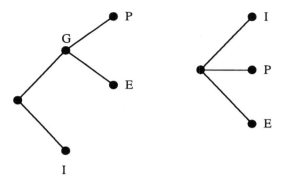

Figure 1.14c and d

gress when it confronts a bill (B), an amended bill (A), a substitute bill (S), an amended substitute (AS), and the status quo
(Q). Congress first pairs B against A and then S against AS. Then
it pairs the winners of these two votes, and, in a vote for final
passage, it pairs the survivor against the status quo Q.

Example: So as not to convey the mistaken impression that voting trees have application only to legislative decisions, the tree
in Figure 1.14c portrays the usual scenario of Western court pro-
ceedings in which a jury first decides a person's innocence (I) or
guilt (G). If found innocent, the suspect is set free; but if found
guilty, the jury (or judge) then chooses the form of punishment—in this instance, execution (E) or imprisonment (P). The
tree in Figure 1.14d, on the other hand, models a single (non-
binary) plurality vote between execution, imprisonment, and
being set free. One question the reader should try to answer is:
Which tree should a person prefer if he or she is the alleged
criminal, and how does this preference depend on the beliefs
and preferences of the jury?

To see that we might not want to move beyond a representation
such as the ones that Figure 1.14a-d offers, we note with respect to
Figure 1.14a that even if this legislature has only three members,
the extensive form depicting this situation has sixty-four terminal
nodes (the first vote leads to $2^3 = 8$ such nodes, each of which leads
to a second vote with $2^3 = 8$ nodes). Thus, a legislative agenda with
six votes (seven motions) and 100 legislators yields a tree with 6
times 2^{100} terminal nodes—a number equal approximately to 15 times
10^{30}—and it seems silly to suppose legislators can analyze something we cannot even draw. Clearly, Figure 1.14a-d is considerably

more efficient than its extensive form counterparts, but we must keep in mind that the nodes of such trees represent a rather messy extensive form in which all individual choice nodes are enveloped by information sets that model the assumption that all ballots are secret or simultaneous. Fortunately, in subsequent chapters we show that a diagram such as Figure 1.14a is all that we need to analyze agenda voting if every vote in the agenda is taken by secret ballot but if the aggregate result of each ballot is announced prior to the next vote.

1.8 The Task Ahead

It might seem that our next task is to model more complex and substantively interesting processes than we have thus far considered in our examples. We have tried to show, however, that even simple processes can yield complex extensive and strategic forms, so before we pursue the possibility of developing simplified representations of other, more realistic situations we must first develop some theoretical ideas that allow us to utter predictions about choice. Such ideas can then be used to assess the value of the representations we already possess and to guide us to efficient representations of more complex interactive decision-making scenarios.

To develop such ideas, however, it is imperative that we appreciate fully the fundamental difference between an analysis that assumes interactive decision making and one that models each person as making decisions against opponents who cannot respond fully to a situation's strategic environment. Recall our analysis of voting in section 1.3. The "trick" there that allowed us to proceed without the necessity for developing any new ideas, aside from the hypothesis that people maximize expected utility, is the supposition that nature's probabilities of choice are determined exogenously—that the citizen in question enters the problem with a fixed guess about probabilities and does not suppose that nature is trying to anticipate his actions. However, although this assumption is reasonable in a large electorate, if we suppose that the electorate contains but a few potential voters or if we replace nature with one or more other thinking, rational decision makers who are aware of the mutual dependence of their actions, such an assumption is not appropriate. Specifically, if "nature" is one or more other decision makers like the citizen in our example, then those probabilities—if, in fact choice is probabilistic—are endogenously determined.

However, to analyze interdependent decision making requires one

	C	D
A	4,1	2,3
B	1,4	3,2

Figure 1.15

additional assumption—that of **common knowledge**. To this point we have only accommodated variations in people's information by introducing the concept of an information set. But implicitly we have assumed that decision makers are aware of the extensive and strategic forms characterizing their choice environments, and thus we have assumed that they are aware of the information that others possess as the situation unfolds. Thus, the only uncertainties that can arise, aside from not knowing precisely what others have chosen, come from nature's probabilistic moves. Indeed, until chapter 4, we will impose the assumption that all people share the same view of the game they are playing—they are all equally informed about the game's extensive or strategic form, including the preferences of all players. Actually, though, we will make an even stronger assumption. Specifically, we will assume that a situation's extensive form is common knowledge—that is, we assume that everyone is aware that everyone else knows the extensive form, everyone knows that everyone knows the extensive form, and so on, ad infinitum.

The importance of the common knowledge assumption cannot be understated. It models people who can think whatever it is that others are thinking, and each person knows that others can anticipate whatever it is that they think. No person in our analysis has reason to reject the hypothesis that all other decision makers can anticipate whatever it is that he or she thinks.

To see where this assumption leads, consider the 2×2 strategic form in Figure 1.15, where the first entry in each cell corresponds to person 1's (row chooser's) utility and the second corresponds to person 2's (column chooser's) utility.

Once we assume common knowledge we can imagine the following thought process for person 1 as he contemplates his options:

> *I think that I should choose A, because it offers me my best choice and provides a better guarantee than does B (a minimum payoff of 2 versus 1). But then . . . if person 2 reasons as I do, he will infer that I will chose A, in which case he will choose D, in which case I should choose B (since I prefer a payoff of 3 to a payoff of 2). But then . . .*

if person 2 reasons as I do further, he will infer my decision to switch to B in response to his choice of D, in which case he will conclude that C is his better choice, in which case I ought to choose A. But then again, if he anticipates my reasoning, he will conclude that I will choose A, in which case he will respond with D . . . and so on.

Of course, such "he-thinks-that-I-think" reasoning will also characterize person 2's thinking. So suppose that person 1, exasperated and perplexed, concludes that person 2 will choose between C and D with equal probability. In this instance, the expected value from A equals $4/2 + 2/2 = 3$, whereas the expected value from B equals $3/2 + 1/2 = 2$. Person 1, then, might decide to choose A. But again, if person 1 believes that 2 will anticipate the tentative speculation that 2 will choose randomly, 1 should also anticipate that 2 can infer 1's choice of A, in which case 2 will not choose randomly at all and will instead choose D, because it is a best response to A. But once again, if 1 anticipates this reasoning himself . . . and so on and so forth.

If our example seems too abstract, consider the agony of a compulsive football fan when cheering his team to victory in the waning seconds of a close game: It's fourth down on the opponent's four yard line, and trailing by five points, there is time for his team to try one more play. Should the play be a run or a pass? Running has averaged a mere two yards per attempt thus far, and passes have been successful more than half the time. The anxiety is occasioned by the fact, however, that everyone knows that the defense knows that the run has been relatively unsuccessful, and thus it is especially dangerous to assume that a running defense is certain. But then, a running play works well against a defense primed for a pass. Of course, the defense will know that the offense will think that the defense will concentrate on the pass, and thus it should concentrate on the run instead, . . . and so on.

Game theory tries to sort out this thinking, specifying actions that, from each person's perspective, represents an "appropriate" response to the situation. In this way, game theory tries to define what we mean by rational choice, and by imposing the assumption of common knowledge, it supposes that the definitions of rationality it offers are common knowledge as well. That is, not only is a situation's structure common knowledge, but our operant hypothesis by implication is that the rationality of all decision makers is also common knowledge.

The fundamental question before us, then, is: What strategies will be chosen in light of one's goals, in light of the goals of others, and in light of a mutually recognized strategic interdependency? If I can anticipate your thoughts, and if I know that you know this, and so on, what should I do if your goals in a situation do not correspond to mine? More complicated still, what if the things you believe about me are a function of what I do, if what I do partially determines my ultimate utility payoff, and if I know that you know that I am aware that you will be making inferences of various sorts from my actions? And does the problem reach an impossible level of complexity when I know that equivalent strategic concerns also confront you?

We have, then, come full circle and back to the problem that introduced this chapter—namely, that the "rational" selection of strategies entails solving a simultaneous decision problem on the part of each and every decision maker. What we want to emphasize, though, is that such problems are not the invention of our paradigm—they permeate politics. As in our original Persian Gulf example, formulating good policy requires ascertaining the choices a president should make when confronting an adversary, when that adversary's actions are known to be conditioned on what it thinks will be the strategy that emerges from Washington, and when that adversary is known to know that the president is attempting to anticipate all strategic responses. Similarly, predicting a president's choice requires an understanding of his perceptions of the strategic environment. The same modeling task confronts us, moreover, if we ask about the strategy the minority leadership in Congress might pursue in attempting to manipulate an agenda when it knows that the majority party leadership is also plotting strategy in anticipation of the minority's course of action. How should a bureaucrat deal with a congressional committee if he or she seeks to maximize an agency's budget, where both the members of the committee and the bureaucrat know beforehand that everyone is aware of the bureaucrat's goal. Into what type of institutional structure should Congress imbed some program when it knows that members of the executive branch, who will administer that program, have different goals than members of Congress? What will be the responses of candidates to some interest group when they know that such groups can contribute valuable resources to a campaign, but also know that voters will use the interest group's actions as a source of information about the candidates' policy prejudices. Establishing a methodology for posing such questions in a more coherent and rigorous form so we can answer them is the task to which we turn in the next chapter.

Suggestions for Further Reading

The classic general introduction to game theory is provided by R. Duncan Luce and Howard Raiffa, *Games and Decisions*, New York:

Wiley and Sons, 1957. P.C. Ordeshook, *Game Theory and Political Theory*, New York: Cambridge University Press, 1986, and Herve Moulin, *Game Theory for the Social Sciences*, New York: New York University Press, 1986, offer introductions designed for students who are especially interested in political theory. Other useful introductions to game theory's modeling philosophy include Steven Brams, *Paradoxes of Politics*, NY: Free Press, 1976, and Henry Hamburger, *Games as Models of Social Phenomena*, San Francisco: W.H. Freeman, 1979.

For additional examples of congressional agendas, see P.C. Ordeshook and Thomas Schwartz, "Agendas and the Control of Political Outcomes," *American Political Science Review*, 81 (1987):180–99. With respect to the general issue of the applicability of the rational choice paradigm to politics, the interested student should begin with V.O. Key's text, cited in our introductory chapter, whereas for a contrary view see the essays in Kristen R. Monroe, *The Economic Approach to Politics*, New York: Harper-Collins, 1990.

Exercises

1. If free competition reigns in an industry with two firms, each firm sells 20 million units of that industry's products at a net profit of $1/item. But if they collude to set a higher price, each sells 15 million units at a net profit of two dollars each. If one firm defects to the lower competitive price, its sales soar to 35 million units while the other firm sells nothing. Before each firm sets its price (which they do simultaneously) Senator Billie Bob proposes a licensing agreement whereby each pays a tax of $.20/item to produce the product at the fixed cartel price— ostensibly to insure that "destructive competition" does not "leave hard-working Americans unemployed." Construct this situation's extensive form, where each firm must first approve or disapprove of the licensing arrangement, which goes into effect only if both firms agree to it.

2. Assume there are three states (1, 2, and 3) of equal size, that the polls close first in state 1, then in 2, and then in 3, and that the election winner must capture a majority (two) of the states. Draw an extensive form representing the decision of a single citizen in state 3 who must decide whether to vote and for whom to vote in a two-candidate election. Assume that this person treats the decisions of all other voters and the outcomes of the

balloting in other states as probabilistic choices by nature. (Assume that ties within states never occur.)

3. Draw the extensive form of the agenda "A versus B, the winner against C" for a three-person legislature in which legislator 3 observes 1's choice, but in which no other legislator observes any other choices.

4. Suppose persons 1 and 2 make a sequence of binary decisions, first 1, then 2, then 1, then 2, and so forth, and suppose that all decisions are observed by both persons. Portray a minimal extensive form that allows you to represent a situation in which 1 has perfect memory, but 2 can only recall his last two moves and the last move of 1.

5. A defense department bureaucrat oversees two related programs, X and Y. Recent cost overruns force him to "bury" these costs in the accounting of one of these programs. Two agents from the government accounting office that you oversee will, at the end of the year, review his records. Each agent can be assigned to one of the following activities: (A) audit the personnel records of both programs; (B) audit the inventory of both programs; (C) audit the expenses of parts suppliers for both programs. If one of your agents detects the overrun you earn $+10$, otherwise you earn -10, whereas the respective payoffs for the bureaucrat are -10 and $+10$. The probability that an individual auditor detects the overrun given the focus of his audit and given the program in which the overrun is buried is as follows:

	X	Y
A	.5	.2
B	.3	.6
C	.1	.8

Assuming that you can allocate your two auditors as you choose and that the auditors otherwise act independently, portray this situation in extensive form.

6. Referring to problem 5, suppose you must make your decision

before the bureaucrat chooses the program in which to bury the cost overrun and that the bureaucrat can pay you two units to learn the assignment of one of your two auditors. Describe the extensive form for this situation.

7. Assume three people (1, 2, and 3) must choose one candidate from the list A, B, C, and D. Assuming that all persons observe all prior choices, draw the extensive form of a procedure in which first 1 deletes a candidate, then 2, and then 3, and in which the candidate that remains is elected.

8. Suppose that prior to making any choices, a fair coin is tossed to determine which of the following two strategic forms will describe you and your opponent's utility payoffs (the first number in each cell denotes your payoff—row chooser—whereas the second number denotes your opponent's):

	b_1	b_2		b_1	b_2
a_1	9,5	1,−3		3,0	9,−2
a_2	3,7	4,6		9,9	3,8

   a. Assuming that neither person observes the outcome of the coin toss and that both of you must choose simultaneously, portray the situation's extensive form.

   b. Portray the extensive form assuming that you can secretly pay three dollars to learn the outcome of the coin toss.

9. Portray the following situation in extensive form: You are searching through a stack of used textbooks for a book that most closely approximates a new text. However, you do not know the identity of the "best" text, nor its condition, and because time is costly, you think it is unreasonable to plan at the very beginning to look through the entire pile in order to identify the least-emasculated book. Thus, you look at one book at a time until you find a text that is "acceptable." To make this problem manageable, assume that there are only three texts and that anywhere from zero to three of them are acceptable.

10. Suppose the value of some object is $x_1 + x_2$, where both x_1 and x_2 are random variables that can each take on a value of 0 or

1. Suppose person 1 observes x_1 but not x_2, whereas person 2 observes x_2, but not x_1. Portray in extensive form an auction in which 1 and 2, after observing x_1 and x_2, respectively, bid .5 or 1.5 for the object by submitting their bids in sealed envelopes. Assume that the person submitting the highest bid wins the object, but must pay whatever he or she bid, and assume also that, in the event of a tie, a coin toss determines the winner.

11. Congressman Pork represents a district with a significant electronics industry that is in an economic slump because of foreign competition. Accordingly, he introduces a bill for a $100 billion federal subsidy for consumer electronics, but he knows that several committee members led by Congresswoman Pam Sonic are opposed to his bill. The bill will be debated next week and Pork can offer one of two arguments on behalf of it: (1) The United States needs the technology of consumer electronics for possible conversion to military use, in which case $50 billion would be appropriated. However, if Sonic anticipates this argument she can seek out expert witnesses to testify that such technology is irrelevant to defense needs, destroying Pork's argument and defeating the bill. (2) Pork could emphasize the jobs that the federal subsidy would provide for constituents of the majority of the committee members. In this case, he could get $40 billion. Sonic's counterargument mentioned above would have no effect on this approach, but Sonic could organize a letter-writing campaign of consumers against the bill. In this case, the committee would compromise at $25 billion. However, the letter-writing approach would have no effect if Pork's military security argument goes uncontested, since the committee feels that money is no object when it comes to national security. Portray this situation in strategic form by using a reasonable attribution of utility to the outcomes for both Pork and Sonic.

12. Referring to the legislative pay-raise example in section 1.6, portray the extensive and strategic forms for each of the following circumstances:

    a. Legislator C, but not B, observes A's choice.

    b. Legislator B, but not C, observes A's choice.

    c. Legislator C, but not A, observes B's choice.

13. Portray a congressional voting tree in which, with the alternatives B (bill), A (amended bill) and Q (status quo) already on

the agenda, a predesignated legislator must decide before the actual balloting whether to introduce a substitute bill S. Assume that, regardless of whether or not the substitute is introduced, Congress must first decide whether to amend the original bill B.

14. Imagine a binary voting tree with three alternatives and five legislators.

    a. How many terminal nodes does the extensive form representation of the situation contain?

    b. How many strategies does each voter possess (assuming that each voter cares only about the number voting for or against a motion as against knowing the identities of for and against voters)?

    c. Do our answers to (a) and (b) depend on whether voting occurs by secret ballot or by roll call vote? If so, how?

    d. How many terminal nodes does the extensive form contain if there are four alternatives?

2

Analysis of Extensive Form Games

2.1 Rationality

Because individual rationality is a presumed prerequisite to game theory's relevance, debates in political science over the application of that theory usually begin with the question: Are people **rational**? Of course, the word "rational" conjures up many meanings, depending on context and who uses it. For some analysts it means acting in accordance with goals that are deemed "reasonable." For others it means merely that people have discernable goals, whereas for others the concept of rationality is associated with a variety of normative prescriptions concerning equity, justice, and fairness. Indeed, so confusing are its definitions that it is tempting to ban the word from our lexicon. Nevertheless, if we use this word, a necessarily mistaken definition is implied by the presumption that our analysis applies "only if people are rational." Certainly, we have imposed some restrictions on the domain of our analysis with the supposition that people have connected and transitive preferences. These assumptions, though, are preliminary and do not define what we might mean by rational action. With them alone we cannot yet say what actions or strategies a person should choose in an interdependent-choice environment. Thus, because game theory's ultimate purpose is to formulate general rules of action in such choice situations, game theory does not assume that people are rational; rather, it attempts to define what we might mean by this concept. Put differently, game theory seeks to identify the decisions that people might be reasonably expected to make in interactive decision-making situations, and these decisions correspond to what we mean by rational action.

Our concluding discussion in the previous chapter presented in abstract form the specific problem that confronts us in analyzing a game and defining what we mean by "rational"—specifically, we must see how people might resolve the "he-thinks-that-I-think" regress that arises when choices are interdependent and when the character of this interdependence is common knowledge. To see this problem differently, suppose we are interested in learning about the policies that candidates might advocate during an election campaign or about how people might vote in a committee governed by parliamentary procedures. The specific questions we might ask are as follows:

1. In planning a campaign, what policies might a candidate advocate and what issues might he or she emphasize if the candidate knows that the opponent is trying to answer the very same question, and if the answer to the first question depends on how voters evaluate the policies advocated by all candidates?

2. If voting for a less-preferred alternative when voting in a committee agenda leads to a better outcome (because such a vote eliminates a truly despised alternative), how can one account for the possibility that all others in the committee might be thinking along the same lines, and that one's best voting strategy depends on what others decide, and vice versa?

These questions illuminate two facts. First, the components of extensive and strategic form games that chapter 1 outlines—including the assumptions we make about individual preferences—are themselves merely preliminary. These components require only that we think carefully about matters so that we can represent in a coherent way the environment confronting decision makers. However, neither extensive nor strategic forms alone (including our assumptions about preference) can provide answers to our questions, because we have yet to decide how to analyze those forms in order to predict decisions. Second, these questions establish the necessity to analyze decision making in interdependent choice situations differently than the way we analyze actions when only one person is involved. Rather than simply "maximize expected utility," the assumption of common knowledge requires that we must also "put ourselves in the heads of others" in order to see how they might act.

These questions also reveal the necessity for a careful consideration of what it means to think and act rationally. If the situation concerns a single decision maker, we can define rationality to mean simply that people act so as to maximize their expected utility. But in the interdependent choice contexts that frame our questions, even "putting ourselves in the heads of others" only takes us partway to a solution. Although we can continue to suppose that a person seeks to maximize his or her utility, if the consequences of actions depend on what others do, and if the game is common knowledge, then we must also take into account the fact that they are simultaneously "putting their heads into ours." The definition of rational choice, then, must specify how people think about how others think and how they might disentangle the simultaneity of these contemplations.

2.2 Working Backward Up Extensive Forms

To analyze extensive forms, we begin by taking advantage of the assumption that such forms end—that all sequences of choices lead ultimately to some identifiable terminal node. As we have already noted, this assumption is not unrestrictive since it precludes us from considering choices that yield a repetition of a part of the form. In principle, of course, a legislature could repeatedly report a bill back to committee and the committee could respond by repeatedly reporting the same measure to the full legislature. We consider such possibilities later, but presently we want to learn how to solve finite extensive forms—to identify unambiguously the choices people make and the outcomes that prevail.

Example: Consider again the perfect information game in Figure 1.1, which we introduced with a newspaper report citing the desirability of some degree of deception or ambiguity in U.S. strategic policy toward Iran in the Persian Gulf. To see whether such a policy makes sense, given our admittedly trivialized representation of the situation, suppose, for whatever reason, that 2 orders the outcomes from best to worst thus:

$$O_1, O_2, O_3, O_6, O_5, O_4, O_8, O_9, O_7$$

As portrayed, 2 knows, when it is his turn to choose, which decision node he is at—he is fully informed about 1's previous decision—in which case 2 should have little difficulty deciding what to do. Given 2's preferences, b_1 should be chosen if 1 chooses a_1, b_3 if 1 chooses a_2, and b_2 if 1 chooses a_3. That is, once 1 acts, person 2 is confronted with the trivial decision problem of taking the action that leads to 2's most preferred, available outcome. Now, however, our common knowledge assumption implies that just as we are able to anticipate 2's response to 1's choice, 1 should be able to anticipate this response as well. Thus, 1 should know that his choice of a_1 leads eventually to o_1 (via 2's choice of b_1), a_2 to o_6, and a_3 to o_8. Similarly, then, 1's task is reduced to a simple decision problem in which his choice is dictated by his preferences over the outcomes o_1, o_6, and o_8.

Example: Although it models the actions of three decision makers, we can apply the same procedure to the extensive form in Figure 1.2. Working from the bottom (right side) of this form to the top—from terminal nodes to the initial node—suppose first that the Senate, unlike the House, is controlled by the president's party and that it thereby prefers to sustain any presidential veto. The House, then, knows that its decision to override is irrelevant, but because it is controlled by the opposition party, it will nevertheless vote to override in the hope of establishing a position for the party for the forthcoming election. The president, then, must choose between signing the legislation and vetoing it. Suppose the president prefers passage, but only because he perceives the necessity to endorse the bill's general intent. Then, if the House passes the measure, the Senate must choose between eventual passage and being blamed for the bill's defeat. On the other hand, if the House fails to pass the bill and the Senate votes for passage, Senate members and the president are allowed to stake out a useful position for the forthcoming campaign, whereas a vote that matches the House's decision sends the bill and associated issues to obscurity. Suppose the Senate prefers passage to partisan conflict, and establishing contrary policy positions to obscurity. The House must then choose between passage (the Senate's preference if the House votes to pass) and allowing the opposition party to stake out new positions for the campaign (if the House chooses f). Thus, knowing the House's preference between these two outcomes terminates our analysis—the House and Senate will pass the measure, and the president will sign it.

Clearly, in any realistically complex extensive form, such reasoning might result in a massive confusion of "if . . . then . . ." propositions. And even for the simple example of Figure 1.2, readers almost certainly found the preceding example difficult to follow. However, we can simplify matters by making our reasoning more programmatic. First, let us introduce the notion of a decision node's strategic equivalent:

	1st							last
House	o_4	o_3	o_8	o_7	o_6	o_5	o_1	o_2
Senate	o_7	o_8	o_3	o_1	o_5	o_6	o_2	o_4
President	o_8	o_1	o_7	o_6	o_5	o_2	o_3	o_4

Table 2.1

a decision node's **strategic equivalent** *in an extensive form is the outcome that ultimately prevails whenever that node is reached.*

Returning now to our previous example,

Example (continued): Suppose, first, that the House, Senate, and president order the eight outcomes from first to last as shown in Table 2.1. (Notice that some of these preferences do not come into play since the relevant decision maker will not be afforded the opportunity to choose between them; nevertheless, for consistency, we assume a complete order.)

We can now "prune" our extensive form, substituting choice nodes with their strategic equivalents. Beginning at the end of the extensive form we substitute the predicted outcome at the nodes for which we can predict choices on the basis of individual preferences. In our example, we know that the Senate will vote to override the president's veto. Thus, eliminating the choice of s (Sustain) from the Senate's last move and substituting o_1 and o_3 as the strategic equivalents of S's decision nodes, we obtain the reduced tree in Figure 2.1a. Next, since the House prefers o_3 to o_1 in order to stake a position contrary to the opposition, we can eliminate the choice of s for the House and obtain the form in Figure 2.1b. Since the president prefers passage (o_5) to allowing the opposition to establish a contrary position, we eliminate the choice of a veto and obtain the form in Figure 2.1c. Continuing in this way, the Senate's preference for o_5 over o_6 and o_7 over o_8 allows us to reduce the extensive form to the one shown in Figure 2.1d, in which case we can easily see that the House will vote for passage. Hence, the bill passes.

Example: For another example of applying backward reduction in order to determine the strategic equivalents of decision nodes, consider again the pay raise example from the previous chapter

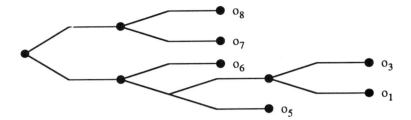

Figure 2.1a First Reduction

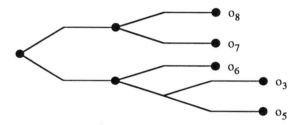

Figure 2.1b Second Reduction

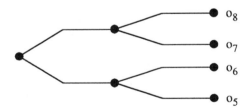

Figure 2.1c Third Reduction

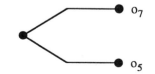

Figure 2.1d Fourth Reduction

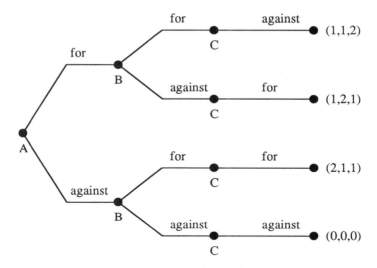

Figure 2.2a First Reduction

(section 1.6, Figure 1.10). Look first at the various decisions confronting legislator C at each of its four decision nodes:

1. If legislators A and B both vote **for**, then clearly C should vote **against**.

2, 3. If A and B vote differently, then C should vote **for** in order to secure the raise.

4. If A and B both vote **against**, then C would be a fool to vote **for**.

Thus, Figure 1.10 reduces to the one shown in Figure 2.2a. Legislator B, of course, can anticipate these responses and conclude that if A votes **for**, he or she should vote **against** (since this forces C to vote **for**), but if A votes **against**, then B and C must vote **for** to secure the raise. Thus, Figure 2.2a reduces to the form in Figure 2.2b. Finally, A can see that if he votes **for**, then B votes **against** and C **for**, whereas if A votes **against**, then B and C will ensure the passage of the raise. Hence, A, who moves first, can safely vote **against** and force B and C to shoulder the burden of voting **for**.

Example: For a final example of how we can work backward in an extensive form when information is perfect, consider this problem: Three committee members must pick one (and only one) candidate from a list of four. The preferences of the com-

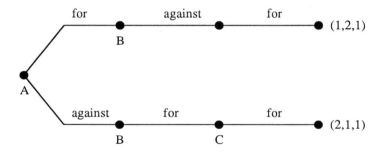

Figure 2.2b Second Reduction

mittee for the four candidates, A, B, C, and D, are given below, ranked from best to worst. The committee uses a procedure whereby member 1 first vetoes a candidate, then 2 vetoes a candidate from the remaining three, then 3 vetoes one of the two remaining candidates. The candidate who is unvetoed is elected.

member 1:	C	B	D	A
member 2:	B	C	A	D
member 3:	A	B	C	D

Figure 2.3a portrays this situation's full extensive form, where the branches label the alternative that the voter in question vetoes. Figure 2.3b shows the first reduction after 3's optimal responses are determined and Figure 2.3c reduces this form further by eliminating those branches that are not 2's optimal responses, in anticipation of what 3 will do. This last figure reveals that member 1 should first veto alternative B so that C ultimately prevails.

At this point the reader might be interested in learning some of the implications of our analysis for parlor games, such as tic-tac-toe and chess. First, consider tic-tac-toe. Were we to draw its extensive form (giving X the first choice with nine branches emanating from that node, giving O the second choice, with eight branches emanating from each of his or her eight nodes, and so on), we would produce a figure that differs from 1.1 and 2.1 only in complexity. There would be no information sets encompassing multiple nodes (since all moves are public and sequential), and every path through the form would lead to a well-defined outcome—either a victory for X, for O, or a draw. Thus, in principle at least, we could prune our tree (arbitrarily eliminating branches that yield the same outcome as some other branch) to arrive at a determinate outcome, and thereby learn

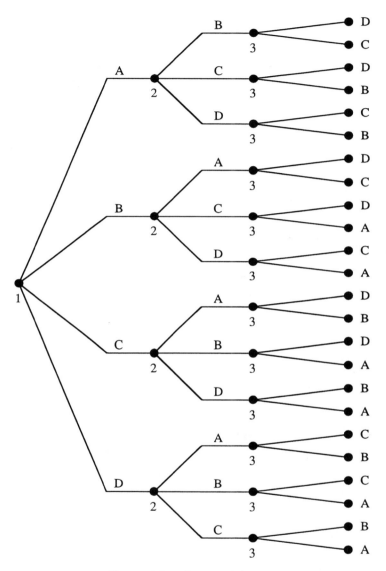

Figure 2.3a Sequential Veto

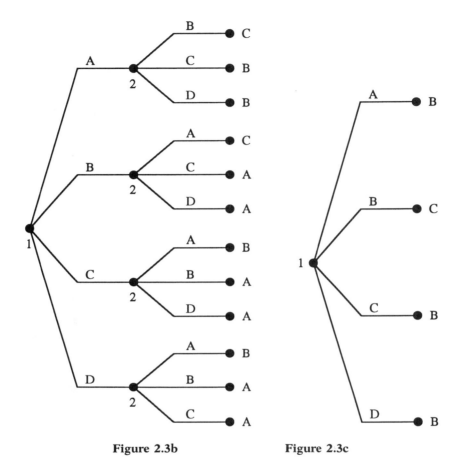

Figure 2.3b   **Figure 2.3c**

whether moving first necessarily confers an advantage. In principle, the same argument holds true for chess, except that the extensive form of this game is far too complex to draw. However, if we developed a computer capable of constructing and analyzing such a form, then chess would be "solved," because we could allow the computer to work backward on that form in order to determine our best choice at any point in the game. Indeed, all games would then be played identically (except, perhaps, at those nodes in which a player confronts choices that are equivalent in terms of final outcomes), at which point we suspect that sale of chess boards would decline precipitously.

These examples illustrate the approach we ought to take when beginning an analysis of an extensive form. Whenever possible, we should prune that form by seeing if there are any choices we can infer directly. At this point, however, the reader might object with the following argument:

> *What you have said is common sense. However, people typically must act without the opportunity to sit down and draw out extensive forms, in which case there is no guarantee that they will act as you have just described. Indeed, if only a single decision maker fails to act as assumed, your entire analysis is invalid.*

This objection is legitimate. But once again, we must keep in mind what the assumption of common knowledge implies—namely, that all persons are aware of the situation's strategic form. If for some reason a person's analytic capabilities are limited—if, for example, they cannot see the future, if they forget the past, or if they are uncertain about various aspects of the situation—then these facts ought to be represented in our extensive form description. Nevertheless, the reader is correct in believing that such common features of reality can undermine the validity of "working backward." For example, consider the extensive form in Figure 2.4, which is identical to the one shown in Figure 1.1 except now we encompass all of 2's decision nodes in a single information set. In this instance of a game of imperfect information we cannot say that if 1 chooses a_1, then 2 will choose b_1, because person 2 will not know what 1 has done. Indeed, Figure 2.4 not only models a circumstance in which person 2 is uninformed about what 1 does, but it also models the situation in which it is impossible for 2 to learn 1's choice because both persons choose simultaneously.

Aside from being a counter example to the idea that all extensive forms can be easily "pruned," Figure 2.4 also shows that our ability to prune depends as much on preferences as on the structure of information and choices. Referring again to this figure, notice that if preferences are changed so that person 2 orders the outcomes o_1, o_2, o_3, o_4, o_5, o_6, o_7, o_8, o_9, then choosing b_1 is best for 2 regardless of what 1 does. From the common-knowledge assumption, 1 can then infer that a_1 leads to o_1, a_2 leads to o_4, and a_3 leads to o_7, and person 1 is once again confronted with a simple decision.

The lesson we learn from these examples is that the meaning of rationality is clear if the sequence of moves is well defined, if every sequence of decisions leads to a clearly specified terminal node, if people have perfect information about past moves or if incomplete information is irrelevant to their decisions, and if the structure of the situation is common knowledge. We also want to make an observation that points the way to generalizing the ideas implicit in

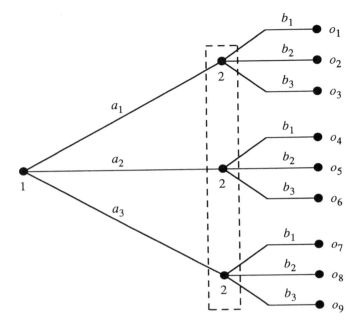

Figure 2.4 Simultaneous Choice

the method of working backward up an extensive form. If, in addition to identifying the strategic equivalents of nodes, we also kept a careful record of the implied choices, we could then describe strategies for action at each node that are in **equilibrium** in the following sense:

> *No person, after learning what any other person intends to choose, has any incentive to make a different choice at any decision node.*

That the sequence of choices that working backward up an extensive form reveals are in equilibrium follows from the fact that we have constructed the path from the first node to the predicted outcome by looking at each person individually when it is that person's turn to act and by retaining only those choices that are not inferior. Thus, these choices of all n people, taken together, are in equilibrium in the sense that, holding fixed the choices of any $n-1$ persons, the nth has no positive incentive to act differently. Later we will generalize this idea of an equilibrium so we can apply it to a wider class of extensive forms as well as strategic forms. However, we first turn to a class of situations that are of special significance to politics—voting by agenda—and for which we now have the tools for deducing some interesting conclusions about the manipulability of outcomes by persons who set agendas.

2.3 Agendas

Parlor games such as tic-tac-toe—games in which the extensive form is common knowledge, in which there are no chance nodes, and in which everyone's previous moves are known—have at least one equilibrium sequence of choices. However, owing to their special character, such games hardly serve as a basis for theorizing about politics. Furthermore, although the form in Figure 1.2 poses no analytic difficulties, we should keep in mind that our analysis is facilitated by the assumption that the House and the Senate each contain a single member or, flirting with the anthropomorphic error, that each chamber acts as a single decision-making entity with complete and transitive preferences.

On the other hand, the situation portrayed in Figure 1.2 illustrates one property that allows us to avoid the problem of intransitive social preferences. Specifically, the decision nodes for both chambers offer only **binary** choices—pass and fail, or sustain and override. And in the case of a binary decision, the problem of intransitivity cannot arise.

To use this fact, suppose both chambers vote by secret ballot and let us interpret Figure 1.2 as a voting tree rather than as an extensive form—that is, each decision node for the House and Senate actually corresponds to an extensive form in which 435 and 100 members, respectively, must simultaneously choose between p(ass) and f(ail) or between s(ustain) and o(verride). Notice now that if simple majority rule decides the issue at each such node, then at least for the last node in a binary tree it never pays to vote for one's second choice (unless one's vote counts negatively or unless the situation under consideration is imbedded in a larger game in which one's vote reveals something about one's preference that one prefers to disguise).

Example: For another example, consider again the voting tree in Figure 1.14a which models an agenda in which a bill, B, is first paired against an amended version of the bill, A, after which the winner of this vote is paired against the status quo, Q, in a vote for final passage. Suppose a majority of legislators prefer A to Q, a majority prefer Q to B, and a majority prefer B to A (a Condorcet cycle). Analyzing this tree from bottom to top, the left node pits A against Q, so in a simple pairwise vote everyone should vote in accordance with their preferences and A defeats

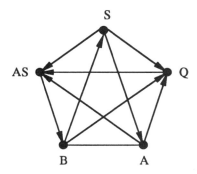

Figure 2.5a Majority Preference Relation

Q—A is the strategic equivalent at this voting node. But if B is paired against Q, Q is the strategic equivalent, which implies that the initial vote between A and B is, in fact, a vote between A and Q.

Thus, despite the fact that the nodes in voting trees summarize simultaneous choices, *we can prune the end branches of such a tree because each voter has an unambiguous best choice at each final node.* Now, though, because the assumption of common knowledge implies that everyone knows the strategic equivalent of each bottom node, after the majority winner (strategic equivalent) is substituted at each such node, we can, if there are several prior votes, repeat the pruning process at the new bottom nodes.

Example: To expand our example, consider again the congressional agenda in Figure 1.13b, which allows for five alternative outcomes—A, B, S, AS, and Q—and suppose the social ordering under simple majority rule implies that all alternatives but AS defeat Q; Q defeats AS; A defeats B and AS, but not S; B defeats S, but not AS; and S defeats AS. Figure 2.5a summarizes these majority relations. Figure 2.5b now shows the effect of pruning Q from all but the nodes that pair it against AS; Figure 2.5c shows the effect of pruning the tree in Figure 2.5b; and Figure 2.5d shows the pruning of 2.5c. Thus, given common knowledge of the agenda and of preferences, everyone should view the first vote as being between S and B, in which case B emerges as the eventual outcome.

The supposition in the preceding analysis that all voters ignore the labels of branches emanating from a voting node and vote in-

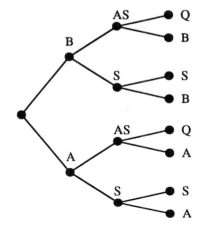

Figure 2.5b A Congressional Agenda, First Reduction

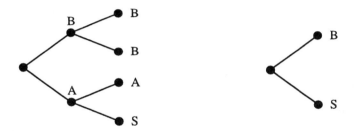

Figure 2.5c Second Reduction   **Figure 2.5d:** Third Reduction

stead on the basis of each branch's strategic equivalent is, of course, only one hypothesis about choice. An alternative hypothesis is that voters are naive (stupid?) and that they act merely on the basis of a myopic view of an agenda. We have, then, these two hypotheses:

> **Strategic voting:** *Voters ignore the labels of the motions currently under consideration and, focusing instead on the consequences of each decision, choose the alternative that yields the final consequence they most prefer,*
> **Sincere voting:** *Voters focus exclusively on the two alternatives currently up for a vote, and they vote sincerely for the alternative they most prefer.*

Given our assumption that all voters know the situation's extensive form (and thus its voting tree representation), and given that this fact is common knowledge, strategic voting is the only sustain-

1	2	3	4	5
A	B	C	D	A
A	D	B	C	C
C	C	A	C	B
D	A	B	A	D

Table 2.2

able hypothesis. Nevertheless, the empirical question is whether legislators, implicitly or explicitly, understand strategic voting and abide by its logic. We suspect, in fact, that they do, since this hypothesis supposes merely that legislators look ahead to the eventual consequences of their actions. If even novice chess players can look ahead several moves, it is foolhardy to suppose, a priori, that professional players in the game of politics cannot do the same. Indeed, it is not uncommon to learn that opponents of a bill have voted against an amendment that moves one or more of it provisions closer to their and a majority's view of an ideal bill. One reason for such voting patterns is that by making the bill more palatable, legislators only increase the chances of passing something they continue to prefer less than the status quo.

Example: This argument should not be interpreted to mean, however, that we cannot analyze situations in which voters are naive or in which some are strategic and others are naive. To illustrate this fact as well as the underlying logic of analyzing an agenda tree, consider a five-member legislature in which only legislators 1 and 2 are strategic voters, that uses the agenda "A versus B, the winner against C, the winner against D," and whose five members hold the preferences shown in Table 2.2.

Referring to Figure 2.6, which portrays the agenda, we know that everyone votes sincerely at the four final voting nodes. So, since D defeats A, C defeats D, and B defeats D, then D, C, B, and C are the strategic equivalents of these last four nodes.

Looking now at nodes 3, 2, and 1 in succession:

3. Voters 1 and 2, because they are strategic, know that A's victory on the second ballot leads ultimately to D whereas C's victory leads to C itself. Thus, if this node is reached, voter 1 votes for C and voter 2 votes for A. Voters 3, 4, and 5, however, are naive and vote on the basis of the immediate

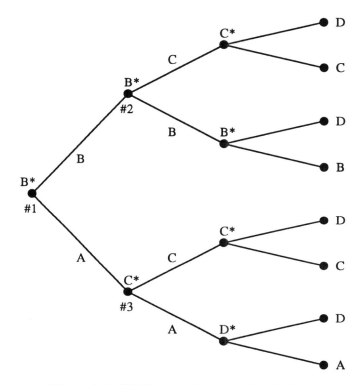

Figure 2.6 "*" Denotes Strategic Equivalent

    labels of the alternatives—A versus C—so 3 and 4 vote for C while 5 votes for A. Thus, if this node is reached, C wins and ultimately prevails.

2. Voters 1 and 2, although they are strategic, vote sincerely because a victory for B leads ultimately to B whereas a victory for C leads ultimately to C. And with all voters voting sincerely, B defeats C and B ultimately prevails if this node is reached.

1. Voters 1 and 2 know that, despite the labels of the alternatives, a victory for A leads ultimately to C, whereas B's victory allows B to prevail ultimately. Hence, both voters vote for B. Voters 3, 4, and 5, however, once again vote on the basis of labels, so 3 votes for A, 4 for B, and 5 votes incorrectly for A.

Since voters 1, 2, and 4 all vote for B on the first ballot, B is the final outcome from this agenda.

It is useful to keep in mind that agendas are embedded in a larger game—in a game in which it is reasonable to hypothesize that the ultimate aim of legislators is to be reelected. This fact opens up two possibilities. First, some legislators may be unable to act strategically, because they believe that a strategic vote will be misunderstood by constituents. Second, we should explore the possibility that some legislators will find it in their interest to attempt to convince their colleagues that they cannot vote strategically, because it is sometimes advantageous to appear dumb or otherwise constrained. Looking first at the second possibility, consider this example:

Example: Suppose a three-member legislature confronts four alternatives, A, B, C, and D; suppose it abides by the agenda "A versus B, the winner against C, the winner against D"; and suppose preferences are as follows:

Legislator 1:	*A*	*C*	*B*	*D*
Legislator 2:	*B*	*A*	*D*	*C*
Legislator 3:	*D*	*C*	*B*	*A*

Backward reduction reveals that if everyone is strategic, then B prevails; but this argument supposes that legislator 1 votes for B over C in the second ballot since C eventually leads to D. Suppose, however, that 1 can convince his colleagues that he cannot vote for B over C if B prevails on the first ballot. Legislators 2 and 3, then, will believe that the selection of B on the first ballot leads ultimately to D. This fact should convince 2 to vote for A rather than B on the first ballot—voting for B yields that legislator's third choice, D, whereas voting for A ensures A's eventual selection, legislator 2's second choice. Thus, by being or appearing to be constrained to vote sincerely, legislator 1 secures his first preference.

Whether 1 can, in fact, convince his colleagues that he cannot vote strategically is, of course, not part of our example—indeed, seeing the advantage a constraint confers on 1 should make legislators 2 and 3 suspicious of 1's motives. At the very least, though, this example does reveal the opportunities for deception and for feigning ignorance or the existence of exogenously imposed constraints on action.

Example: We should not interpret the previous example to mean, however, that it is necessarily advantageous to have one's actions constrained. For a specific example, suppose an amended version of a bill, A, which incorporates some welfare provision into an otherwise popular appropriations package, B, is introduced by opponents of the bill because they hope to weaken the bill's attractiveness. Suppose the legislature consists of three groups of legislators of approximately equal size with the following preferences, where group 2 consists of those legislators who introduce A:

Group 1:	*A*	*B*	*Q*
Group 2:	*Q*	*B*	*A*
Group 3:	*B*	*Q*	*A*

If the legislature uses the agenda "A versus B, the winner against Q"—denoted (A,B,Q)—and if everyone votes sincerely, then B prevails since it defeats both A and Q in pairwise votes. And although group 2 may try to thwart the will of the majority by strategically voting for A on the first ballot (so as to lead to a final vote between A and Q), if everyone votes strategically, B again prevails. Group 1 in particular should see that a vote for A on the first ballot is, in fact, a vote for Q and that they should thereby join with group 3 in assuring that B prevails over A in the initial ballot. At this point, then, the introduction of A seems to have been an ineffective strategy because it has little effect on the final outcome. In many real-world instances, however, legislators may fear that their constituents will not understand strategic voting. Thus, if the legislators from, say, group 1 have this concern with respect to a strategic vote for B on the first ballot, and if they thereby feel compelled to vote sincerely for the amendment, then, with everyone else strategic, A wins on the first ballot and Q prevails. So in this instance, group 2's introduction of A has the intended effect.

The preceding example establishes the strategic importance of procedures such as open and closed rules—rules that allow or exclude amendments to bills within a legislature—and the power someone can exercise if they control those rules. In fact, the simple example of the Condorcet cycle illustrates dramatically the potential power of those who set agendas.

Example: Suppose alternatives A, B, and C cycle so that A defeats B, B defeats Q, and Q defeats A in a majority vote. Backward reduction reveals that the agenda (A,B,Q) yields B as the final outcome, the agenda (A,Q,B) yields A, and the agenda (B,Q,A) yields Q. Thus, for this example at least, if a single person controls the order of voting, then that person is a dictator.

Hence, it is unsurprising to learn that legislatures and other committees commonly devote as much if not more attention to procedural matters than they do to the substance of the measures before them. Moreover, given the established procedures of the U.S. Congress for determining the order of voting as a function of the labeling of alternatives, we can now see the importance of the labels attached to various alternative measures. For example, we have already seen that if we use the agenda in Figure 1.14b (which corresponds to the usual procedures of Congress) to vote over A, B, S, AS, and Q, then for the preferences summarized in Figure 2.5a, B prevails. But if the legislature first pairs B against S, the winner against A, the winner against AS, and the winner against Q, then S emerges as the eventual winner. And such a manipulation can be achieved by using a congressional agenda if we merely relabel AS as the bill as originally reported out of committee, and if we call B, S, and A perfecting amendments. In this way, control of the committee overseeing the legislation in question, as well as control of who is recognized to offer amendments and substitutes, is decisive for choosing between B and S.

2.4 Agendas and Condorcet Winners

The preceding discussion establishes our ability to formulate examples of strategic manipulation, to analyze agendas by backward reduction, and to show the power of agenda setters, but we should also try to apply these lessons to establish some substantive conclusions. Thus, looking more closely at the ability of agenda setters to manipulate outcomes, consider again the Condorcet cycle in which A defeats B, B defeats C, and C defeats A, so that the agenda (A,B,C) yields B, (C,A,B) yields A, and (B,C,A) yields C. What we want to emphasize here about this situation is that the reason each agenda leads to a different outcome is that, although the cycle renders these three alternatives essentially indistinguishable (each defeats one alternative and each is in turn defeated by one alternative), an agenda necessarily creates an asymmetry by requiring that one of the three alternatives enter the voting only at the last stage. Suppose, however, that the social ordering of the alternatives already is asymmetric in the sense that it contains a Condorcet winner, where

> An outcome is a **Condorcet winner** if, under majority rule, it alone
> stands first on the social preference order, because it defeats every other
> alternative in a pairwise majority vote.

It is relatively easy to establish the following result:

> *In binary agenda voting processes characterized by complete information and common knowledge, Condorcet winners necessarily emerge as the eventual outcome.*

To see why this result is true, consider an agenda over any set of alternatives that contains alternative A, which we assume is a Condorcet winner. Since A must enter the agenda at some point, there is at least one path leading to it as the final outcome. Most agendas will contain many such paths, but if we choose one arbitrarily, notice that regardless of what we pair A against at the last vote, because it is a Condorcet winner, A defeats that alternative and is the strategic equivalent of the corresponding node in the initial pruning of the voting tree. This argument, however, applies to the next pruning, and so we can repeat it any number of times, thereby establishing the fact that A must be the strategic equivalent of at least one of the two initial branches of the agenda. But then a majority of voters will prefer and choose that branch over the other (unless the strategic equivalent of the other is also A), so A must emerge as the eventual winner.

Notice, though, that our argument for the eventual selection of Condorcet winners supposes that all voters are strategic—pruning a voting tree backward and determining strategic equivalents makes sense only if all voters look ahead to the eventual consequences of their actions. If they do not do so, then we can imagine agendas in which Condorcet winners do not prevail. (For example, if voters are not strategic and if A defeats B, then even if it defeats A and B, the alternative C is not selected in the agenda "first pair A against B and select A as the final outcome if it wins in this ballot; but pair B against C if B wins".) We can conclude, then, that if we observe people in a voting situation trying to manipulate outcomes by manipulating the order in which the several motions on the floor are to be brought to a vote, then either of two things must be true: (1) no outcome on the floor can defeat all other feasible alternatives in a majority vote—there is no Condorcet winner—or (2) some subset of voters, for whatever reason, are unable to act strategically.

On the other hand, if everyone is strategic and if there is a Condorcet winner, then we can anticipate that one of two things will happen. First, we should anticipate relatively simple agendas—perhaps those that merely entail a vote between it and the status quo or, in the event that the status quo itself is a Condorcet winner, no vote at all. Or second, those opposed to the Condorcet winner might try to invent and to introduce a new alternative that defeats such a winner.

This second possibility introduces an idea that we have not yet considered in any detail—namely, the processes whereby motions are introduced to form an agenda. Admittedly, though, we do not yet know much about such processes, in part because they do not always proceed in accordance with well-defined rules and are often-times idiosyncratic to the committee under consideration. Never-theless, if we return once again to a spatial conceptualization of preferences, we can illustrate some possibilities.

Example: Five committee members, 1, 2, 3, 4, and 5, have pref-erences over a two-dimensional Euclidean policy space of the sort introduced in section 1.4 that depend only on distance from ideal points, so that indifference contours in this space are cir-cles. Suppose those ideal points are as follows:

$$x_1 = (5,0)$$
$$x_2 = (10,0)$$
$$x_3 = (5,10)$$
$$x_4 = (0,10)$$
$$x_5 = (5,5)$$

Let the status quo, Q, be the point (30,30), and assume that, for any sequence of motions put on the floor $(A_1, A_2, \ldots, A_m)$, where A_i is the ith introduced motion, the committee first pairs A_1 against A_2, the winner against A_3, . . . and so on, with the sur-vivor paired against Q.

Consider, now, the location of the final outcome if each voter can each propose a motion of his choosing (an alternative in the issue space). To see that the ideal point of voter 5 prevails as the final outcome and to see, in fact, that 5's ideal prevails re-gardless of the order with which the voters are allowed to make their motions, notice first that the status quo is sufficiently oner-ous that nearly any reasonable proposal can defeat it. Thus we can ignore it in the analysis.

The second important fact is to notice that the ideal points are configured so that voter 5's ideal, x_5, is a Condorcet winner. To see this, the reader should first plot the five ideal points on a sheet of paper. Next, consider any point other than x_5, say x^*, and draw a line connecting x_5 and x^*. Finally, draw a second line that bisects the first line and that is perpendicular to it.

There are two things to notice now about this second line. First, regardless of how we choose x^*, there are more ideal points on x_5's side of this line (including x_5) than there are on x^*'s side. Second, owing to its construction, all ideal points on x_5's side are closer to x_5 than they are to x^*. These two things, in conjunction with the assumption that each voter's utility declines as we move away from that voter's ideal point, imply that in a simple majority voter between x_5 and x^*, x_5 wins. Thus, x_5 is a Condorcet winner.

It follows, now, that whenever 5 can make a motion, its dominant strategy is to propose its ideal, because our result about Condorcet winners ensures that once x_5 is placed on the agenda, it prevails eventually.

At this point it is useful to pause for a moment in our analysis of agendas and consider what it is that we have just established about Condorcet winners when outcomes and preferences have a spatial representation. The first thing the reader should ask, of course, is whether our example is special or whether every ideal point configuration gives rise to such winners. The answer to this query is that our configuration is special—notice that if we consider an ideal point other than x_5, we can pair that point with another ideal such that the line connecting these two points passes through x_5. As the following result states, the somewhat surprising feature of majority rule is that a Condorcet winner exists in the spatial framework if and only if points can be paired in this fashion:

> If the number of voters is odd, if at most one voter most prefers the point x^*, and if each voter's utility for a policy x is a function of the simple distance between x and that voter's ideal point, then x^* is a Condorcet winner if and only if all voters with ideal points not equal to x^* can be paired such that the lines connecting their ideals pass through x^*.

Although this result can be generalized to other types of spatial preferences—to preferences that give rise to indifference curves other than circles—the importance of this result is due to the fact that it does not merely state a sufficient condition for the existence of a Condorcet winner but also specifies a necessary condition. Thus, this result reveals that the existence of Condorcet winners with spatial preferences is extremely sensitive to the way in which preferences are distributed over a policy space. Put differently, Condorcet winners are rare.[1]

Later we will use this fact to infer things about electoral competition, cooperative committee processes, and political stability. For the present, though, we merely note its existence and we return to our example of agenda formation.

Example (continued): Thus far we have seen that if there is a Condorcet winner and if a person who most prefers that winner is allowed to enter motions onto an agenda, then that winner prevails as the eventual outcome. Now consider what happens when voter 5 is precluded from making a motion. First, if only voters 1 and 3 (or if only 2 and 4) can make motions, notice that 1 and 3 have diametrically opposite preferences with respect to x_5. So if voter 1 proposes a motion on the line between x_1 and x_2, voter 3 can secure a better outcome by proposing a motion that lies to the other side of x_5, but closer to x_5 than is 1's motion. Thus, the best outcome that voter 1 can secure—the best outcome that cannot be defeated by a motion by voter 3—is the Condorcet winner, voter 5's ideal.

If we had asked instead what prevails if only voters 1 and 2 can propose motions, then the analysis is a bit trickier, and depends on the order in which the voters move. (At this point, the reader may want to draw a picture in order to be able to reproduce the argument that follows.) Suppose voter 2 has the first move. What we want to show is that the eventual outcome is 1's ideal point. First, let 2 make the motion A. There are now two possibilities:

1. A is further from x_5 than is 1's ideal point,

2. A is closer to x_5 than is 1's ideal.

In case 1, since anything closer to x_5 defeats A, voter 1 will offer his own ideal as a motion, which defeats A and the status quo. In case 2, 1 will offer a motion that is slightly closer to x_5 than is A and that lies between x_1 and x_5. Of those points that lie between 1 and 5's ideals, however, voter 2 most prefers 1's ideal. Thus, voter 2 should propose 1's ideal directly—x_1 is the final outcome.

Now consider what happens if voter 1 is authorized to make a

---

[1]If the situation involves only a single issue—if the ideal points line up on a straight line—then the conditions of the result are necessarily satisfied and a Condorcet winner exists. Later, in chapter 3, we will illustrate this result directly.

motion before voter 2. If 1 again tries to secure x_1 by proposing this point, then 2 can find a great many points on the line connecting x_2 and x_5 that defeat x_1 and which voter 2 prefers to 1's ideal. (Thus, we see directly that 1 prefers that 2 have the first move since as we have just established, this gives 1 his ideal as the final outcome.) The best outcome that 1 can secure on the line between x_2 and x_5, then, lies midway between these two ideal points, because, from the location of voter ideal points, this is the point between 1 and 5's ideals that is closest to x_1. So voter 1 can either propose this outcome directly, or 1 can propose an outcome on the line connecting x_1 and x_5 that is the same distance from x_5 as is this midpoint.

Our result about Condorcet winners does not exhaust research on agendas, and later we consider what occurs when people do not have perfect information about each other's preferences. We conclude this section, however, with an example that demonstrates that at least in the context of agenda voting, "political power" is not always what it appears to be.

Example: Suppose you are offered the choice between being able to break tie votes in a committee unilaterally versus having ties broken by a coin toss. It might seem that you should prefer the opportunity to be decisive. Such an assumption, though, ignores the interdependent nature of choice and, in particular, it ignores the actions others might take in anticipation of your actions. Suppose an eight-member committee uses the agenda "A versus B, the winner against C," and that its members have these preferences:

you	2	3	4	5	6	7	8
A	A	B	B	C	C	A	B
C	B	A	C	B	B	B	C
B	C	C	A	A	A	C	A

Assuming that you can break tie votes, if A wins on the first ballot, then A prevails as the final outcome: the strategic equivalent of voting for A on the first ballot is a tie between A and C, which, presumably, you break in favor of A. But the strategic equivalent of B is B itself since B defeats C. Since B defeats A five votes to three, B wins on both ballots and you get your last choice.

Suppose, on the other hand that ties are broken by a coin toss and that voters 2, 5, 6, and 7 prefer a lottery between A and C to the certainty of their second choice, B—that is, for these voters let $u(A)/2 + u(C)/2 > u(B)$. Since you clearly prefer this lottery as well, a majority of voters (2, 5, 6, 7, and yourself) would vote for A, and you thereby secure a lottery between A and C rather than B with certainty. Being empowered to break ties, then, is disadvantageous, because a majority will act to prevent the use of this authority; but if ties yield lotteries, that majority vanishes and you can secure either your first or second preference.

Although our example is simple, it illustrates an important principle. Accustomed as we are to thinking of matters in simple decision-theoretic terms, we are often inclined to believe that additional resources, votes, or any of the presumed components of political "power" are beneficial. Indeed, most operationalizations of power found in the literature make this assumption. But game theory makes us sensitive to the possibility that others may react to our accumulating such "things" in such a way as to bring about outcomes that are less to our liking than if we had not accumulated them. We will give additional examples of such possibilities later, but for now it is sufficient to use our example merely to reemphasize the difference between decision-theoretic thinking and game-theoretic thinking.

2.5 Subgames and Subgame Perfect Equilibria

Agendas, of course, represent only one class of games, but the useful conclusions we arrive at with them by using backward reduction suggests that we should try to generalize this process so that we can apply it more broadly. To this end, we introduce the concept of a subgame.

> *Beginning at a decision node, a* **subgame** *is a part of an extensive form that is itself an extensive form and that, when detached from the original form, does not divide any information sets.*

A subgame, then, begins at a particular node and includes all branches and nodes that follow it in the original extensive form and that by some path are connected to that node. Next, we introduce the notion of a subgame perfect equilibrium which, as we argue subsequently, formalizes the essential ideas behind working backward up an extensive form.

> A **subgame perfect equilibrium** *is an n-tuple of strategies such that,*
> *when we look at any subgame, it yields an equilibrium in that subgame.*

Terms such as subgame and subgame perfect equilibria might seem
as far removed from politics as any mathematical jargon. However,
the preceding two sections are concerned with precisely these topics—*pruning a voting tree from its end to its beginning is equivalent*
to finding a subgame perfect equilibrium. To see this, notice first that

> *A node corresponding to any final vote in a binary agenda tree is a*
> *subgame. Although we require a great many information sets to por-*
> *tray this part of the agenda's extensive form if each vote is taken using*
> *a secret ballot, isolating this part of the tree does not divide any of*
> *those sets, provided that all voters know the results of prior votes.*

Second,

> *Since everyone possesses a well-defined best choice at each final de-*
> *cision node of a voting tree (as a consequence of the assumption that*
> *the agenda is binary), the only choice that can be part of a subgame*
> *perfect equilibrium is voting for one's preferred outcome or alternative*
> *from the pair of outcomes offered at that node (ignoring the modest*
> *complication that voters might be indifferent between the alternatives).*
> *That is, the simple majority preference relation determines the strategic*
> *equivalent of any node corresponding to a final vote in an agenda.*

Since a subgame perfect equilibrium must have voters voting optimally in every subgame, we can replace all final nodes with their
strategic equivalents. But this same argument now applies to any
node that precedes the two final nodes. Hence, a subgame perfect
equilibrium requires that voters choose optimally between strategic
equivalents at such nodes, and so pruning a voting tree back and
substituting strategic equivalents for voting nodes determines the
subgame perfect equilibrium.

Example: Referring once again to Figure 1.14b, the only subgame
perfect equilibrium strategy for a voter who prefers B to S to Q
to AS to A is one that specifies voting for Q if A and Q are paired
at that node, for S if S and Q are paired, and so on. A similar
argument now establishes that the extensive form represented
by the vote between A and S (as well as between A and AS, between B and S, and between B and AS) and all subsequent votes
is also a subgame. Thus, since our illustrative voter can foresee
the consequences of all decisions, the only subgame perfect equilibrium strategy for him is one that specifies voting for S over
A if S and A are paired in the next to the last vote, for AS if A
and AS are paired (since this yields Q), and so forth. But now

the entire extensive form is also a subgame, and we can repeat our argument.

This example, then, illustrates the following fact:

> *A subgame perfect equilibrium requires that all voters vote for the strategic equivalent ranking highest in their preference order, and this is precisely what we assume when we suppose voters are strategic and we prune a voting tree from bottom to top, substituting strategic equivalents for eventual outcomes.*

The reader should be able to see that the preceding argument applies not only to binary trees but to any extensive form that models a game of complete information—a game in which no two decision nodes share the same information set. But we can also see that we must supplement the notion of a subgame perfect equilibrium if we are to solve more general classes of games. In particular, notice that the binary nature of the tree in Figure 1.14b is critical to our ability to use backward reduction.

Example: Instead of using a binary voting procedure, suppose three voters (1, 2, and 3) use a single secret ballot vote and plurality rule to choose a final outcome from the set {A,B,C}. If, in addition, voter 1 is allowed to break ties if each of the three alternatives receives one vote, then Figure 2.7 describes the extensive form. Next, suppose these voters rank the three alternatives from first to last thus:

voter 1:	A	B	C
voter 2:	C	B	A
voter 3:	B	C	A

Clearly, voter 1 should always choose A, since doing so ensures the selection of A if voter 2 votes for A or if 1 and 2 disagree. But because 1 is decisive if all three voters choose differently, and because voter 3 wants to avoid allowing voter 1 to dictate the selection of alternative A, voter 3 does not have a strategy that is best under all circumstances. In particular, if 2 votes for B, then 3 should vote for B, but if 2 votes for C, then 3 should vote for C. For the same reason, voter 2 does not have a uniformly best choice.

Applying backward reduction is straightforward if all decision makers have unambiguous best choices at every decision node. But, as we have just seen, even the simple procedure of plurality voting over three alternatives can preclude such a choice. Thus, we require

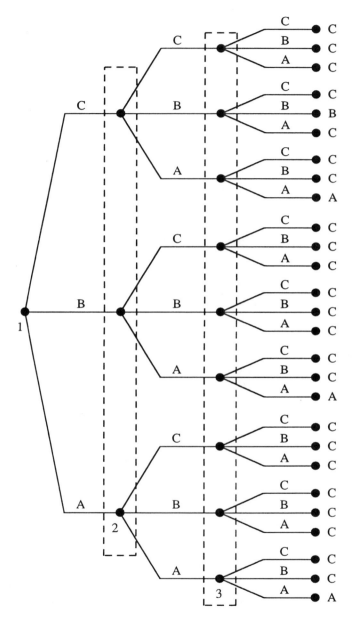

Figure 2.7 Plurality Voting With Secret Ballot

something in addition to the notion of subgame perfection to prune non-binary voting trees or to prune any extensive form for which we cannot identify uniformly best choices at each person's information sets. The development of such an idea is the focus of our next chapter.

Suggestions for Further Reading

For examples of the manipulation of outcomes using agendas, see Charles Plott and Michael Levine, "A Model of Agenda Influence on Committee Decisions," *American Economic Review*, 68 (1978): 146–60; James Enelow and David Koehler, "The Amendment in Legislative Strategy: Sophisticated Voting in the U.S. Congress," *Journal of Politics*, 42 (1980): 396–413; and James Enelow, "Saving Amendments, Killer Amendments, and the Expected Utility Theory of Sophisticated Voting," *Journal of Politics*, 43 (1981): 1062–89. Ordeshook and Schwartz, cited earlier, survey many of the formal results about the ability of agenda setters to influence outcomes by choosing an agenda. The major open research issue that remains, however, concerns endogenous agenda formation. At present, there are few models of such processes, but for some initial studies, see Jeffrey Banks and Farid Gasmi, "Endogenous Agenda Formation in 3-Person Committees," *Social Choice and Welfare*, 4 (1987): 133–52, and David Austen-Smith, "Sophisticated Sincerity: Voting over Endogenous Agendas," *American Political Science Review*, 81 (1987): 1323–9.

Finally, although there is a considerable body of research on Condorcet winners and spatial preferences (see the references in the next chapter), we can attribute the result we offer about existence of a Condorcet winner to Charles Plott "A Notion of Equilibrium and its Possibility Under Majority Rule," *American Economic Review*, 57 (1967): 787–806.

Exercises

1. You are a member of a three-person committee that must choose one outcome from the list (A,B,C,D). Suppose the following preference orders describe the committee (from most to least preferred):

you:	A	B	C	D
member 2:	D	C	A	B
member 3:	C	B	D	A

Which of the following procedures would you prefer to see implemented if you believed that the other two members of the committee were sophisticated: (1) an agenda that first paired B against C, the winner against A, the winner against D; (2) an agenda that first paired C against A, the winner against D, and the winner against B; (3) an agenda that first paired B against D, the winner against C, the winner against A; or (4) you should not care which is chosen.

2. Assume the following preferences by a five-member committee:

1	2	3	4	5
A	B	C	C	B
B	C	A	A	C
C	A	B	B	A

What is the outcome of the agenda (A,B,C) if only voter 2 is strategic? If voter 2 can educate at most one other person to be sophisticated, whom should he or she educate, assuming that voter 1 is too dumb to ever catch on to what is required?

3. Suppose a majority of the legislature prefers A to B. If you are opposed to A, if A and B must be voted on first regardless of what amendments are introduced, and if everyone is a sophisticated voter, which alternative would you prefer to introduce: C or D? C creates the majority rule cycle "A preferred to B preferred to C preferred to A" while D defeats both A and B. Your preferences are "B preferred to D preferred to C preferred to A."

4. You are a legislative aid advising a committee chair, who must choose between reporting bill A or B out of committee. If A is reported, it is certain to lose to the status quo Q. If B is reported out, it will be amended on the floor (alternative C), and you will be able to offer a substitute bill, D. Suppose the remaining members of the legislature fall into one of three equally numerous groups, with preferences as follows:

group 1:	B	D	A	C	Q

group 2:	C	Q	A	D	B
group 3:	Q	B	C	A	D

You are a member of the second group. Suppose the legislature votes using the agenda: "substitutes against the amendment, the winner against the bill, the winner against the status quo." You are certain that as things stand, everyone but you votes sincerely. Suppose the dollar value to you of each alternative is: C = $2,000, Q = $1,500, A = $500, D = $0, and B = −$3,000. What is the upper limit on how much you would be willing to pay to have someone educate the legislature so you and everyone else votes sophisticatedly?

5. A legislature (which we assume has three members) can consider four motions, where each motion affects the amount of money going to a legislator's district. Let the amounts (in thousands) to each district from each motion be as follows:

	District 1	District 2	District 3
A (status quo)	300	0	−400
B (committee bill)	500	−600	0
C (possible amend.)	0	800	−900
D (possible amend.)	−900	400	450

Motions A and B are on the floor as proposals and you must decide whether to propose an amended bill. If you propose C, the agenda will be C versus B the winner against A; if you propose D the agenda will be D versus B the winner against A. If D and C are both proposed, the agenda is D versus C, the winner against B, the winner against A.

a. Suppose you are the representative from district 2. Which amendment should you propose—C, which pays your district $800,000 or D, which pays $400,000?

b. Suppose you are chairman (and dictator) of the relevant legislative subcommittee, and that you can report out of your subcommittee either B or C or D as the bill that the legislature must consider. But you are also certain that whatever alternatives you fail to report out will be introduced on the floor as amendments. Thus,

If you report B, the agenda is "C versus D, winner versus B, winner versus A."

If you report C, the agenda is "B versus D, winner versus C, winner versus A."

If you report D, the agenda is "C versus B, winner versus D, winner versus A."

What would you choose as your bill if you were the representative from district 2?

c. With respect to part (b), if majority rule is used by the subcommittee to choose whether to report B, C, or D, what will it report?

6. You, player 1, and your opponent, player 2, each have three horses. Let your horses' speeds be denoted by a_1, a_2, and a_3, and let your opponent's horses' speeds be b_1, b_2, and b_3. Suppose their speeds are as follows: $b_1 > a_1 > b_2 > a_2 > b_3 > a_3$. Suppose three races are to be run in sequence and that each of you must decide which horse to enter in each race (no horse can race twice). You are allowed to decide, though, which horse to enter after the previous race is run. You and player 1 must choose a horse simultaneously for the first race, but your opponent chooses first (and you observe this choice) for the second race. The person who wins two or more races wins the stake of $1,000. However, since your horses are known beforehand to be slower on average, you are paid $250 to participate. Portray the situation's extensive form and deduce equilibrium strategies. Is there a determinate final outcome?

7. Assume the following preferences by a five-member committee, all of whom are sophisticated voters.

1	2	3	4	5
A	B	C	C	B
B	C	A	A	C
C	A	B	B	A

You are voter 1. Each voter receives a payoff of $100 from his or her first choice, $50 from a second choice, and $0 from a last choice. You and voter 2 are competing to set the agenda, but who will do the setting depends on who can "buy" voter 4. You and voter 2 must announce how much of your winnings you will pay after which voter 4 will choose between you and 2 to be the setter. Because of your sterling character, an indifferent voter 4 will choose you. To simplify matters, suppose that you and 2 must each bid $75, $25, or $0.

    a. Assuming that money and utility are equivalent, what is your bid, and what is the final outcome?

    b. How does your answer to part (a) change if 4 chooses 2 when indifferent?

8. Consider the following preferences within two chambers (lower and upper houses) of a legislature:

Upper house legislator			Lower house legislator				
1	2	3	1	2	3	4	5
B	C	D	A	B	B	D	C
C	D	A	C	O	D	A	B
D	O	C	B	C	A	O	D
O	A	O	O	D	O	C	O
A	B	B	D	A	C	B	A

Suppose the president cares only that some bill pass to upset the status quo. To achieve this, he can submit a single agenda to both houses of the legislature. All members of each house of the legislature are strategic and the lower house must vote before the upper house. If both houses choose the same bill for the president to sign, he signs it. If the houses choose different bills, the outcome is "No New Law" (O). If the president is strategic, which of the following four agendas should he submit?

i.   (A,B,C,D)   ii.   (D,C,B,A)
iii. (C,D,A,B)   iv. (B,D,C,A)

where (x,y,z,w) means "x versus y, the winner against z, the winner against w."

9. You are a contestant on a game show. There are three doors, labeled A, B, and C. Behind two of the doors are prizes worth nothing, and behind the third door is a prize worth $10,000. The game show host knows which door contains the valued prize, but you don't. You get first move, at which time you must choose one of the three doors. The game show host gets the second

move, at which time he must open one of the doors that you didn't select, revealing the contents behind that door and leaving the other two doors unopened. You get the third move, at which time you can choose to stay with your initial choice or switch your choice to the remaining unopened door. After you make your final choice, the door you selected in move 3 is opened, and you win the prize behind that door. Your preferences are to maximize your expected dollar payoff, whereas the preference of the game show host is to keep the suspense going as long as possible. Under what circumstances, if ever, should you switch doors after the game show host opens a door?

10. Suppose two countries, 1 and 2, each have second-strike nuclear capabilities in that they can retaliate after suffering a first strike or they can launch a second strike after sustaining a retaliation. Nature picks a country at random, whereupon it, say 1, can launch a preemptive attack (p) against the other's military capabilities. If 1 attacks, 2 can retaliate (r) or capitulate (c). But if 2 retaliates, 1 can choose between launching (l) its second-strike (which 2 no longer has) that moves 2 back to the stone age or it can do nothing (~l). On the other hand, if 1 does not launch a preemptive attack (~p), then the first move is 2's, with 1 and 2's roles reversed. The game ends if neither country attacks, after one country capitulates, or after one country launches its second strike following a retaliation. Assign some "reasonable" payoffs to the outcomes and determine the eventual outcome. What are the preferences that make a preemptive attack inevitable?

3

Analysis of Strategic Form Games

3.1 Nash Equilibria

If a person's information is not perfect—if information sets encompass two or more decision nodes—then backward reduction works only if that (and every other) player has an unambiguous best choice at each such set. But if this requirement is not satisfied—as in the example of simple plurality voting that concludes the last chapter—the "he-thinks-that-I-think" regress reappears and confounds any attempt to reduce an extensive form by backward reduction. This does not mean, however, that the concept of rationality is ambiguous. Consider again our plurality rule example and notice first that although voter 1 should always choose A, voters 2 and 3 should never vote for this, their worst, alternative. Now suppose that both voters 2 and 3 are risk averse in the sense that if given a choice between securing their second-ranked alternative with certainty versus an equiprobable lottery over all three alternatives, they both prefer the certain outcome. Finally, suppose that voter 2 believes that 3 will vote for his or her most preferred alternative, B, whereas 3 believes that 2, preferring to avoid a three-way tie between A, B, and C, will vote for B also. Thus, B prevails as the final outcome. Notice, moreover, that given these beliefs, neither voter has an incentive to unilaterally change his or her vote, since a unilateral switch to A yields A, their least preferred outcome, whereas a unilateral switch to C yields the three-way tie.

Put differently, voting for B on 2 and 3's part terminates the "he-thinks" regress. For example, if 2 reasons that he should vote for B because 3 will vote for B, and if he believes that 3 can anticipate his reasoning, then he should conclude that 3 will in fact vote for B as originally conjectured.

The preceding discussion illustrates one of the most important concepts in game theory—that of a **Nash equilibrium**. Thus, to define this idea more formally so that we can apply it generally, recall that a strategic form consists of a set of decision makers, N, a set of strategies for each decision maker, $X_1, X_2, \ldots, X_n$, and a set of functions, $u_1, u_2, \ldots, u_n$, which takes any combination of strategies by all n persons and maps each combination to utility payoffs. Letting x_i be a generic strategy for person i, and letting $u_i(x_1, \ldots, x_i, \ldots, x_n)$ denote i's payoff from the outcome that results from the joint strategic choice of $x_1, \ldots, x_i, \ldots, x_n$, then,

> **Nash equilibrium**: *A particular n-tuple of strategies, say $(x_1^*, \ldots, x_i^*, \ldots, x_n^*)$ is a Nash equilibrium if the following is true for every person i in N and for every x_i in X_i:*

$$u_i(x_1^*, \ldots, x_i^*, \ldots, x_n^*) \geq u_i(x_1^*, \ldots, x_i, \ldots, x_n^*). \qquad (2.1)$$

Thus, the n-tuple of strategies $\mathbf{x}^* = (x_1^*, \ldots, x_i^*, \ldots, x_n^*)$ is a Nash equilibrium if, once at $\mathbf{x}^*$, no person has an incentive to shift unilaterally to some other feasible strategy.

Although our verbal definition conveys the general meaning of this idea, the formal definition of a Nash equilibrium shows that each individual strategy that is part of such an equilibrium is a **best response** to the equilibrium strategies of the remaining relevant decision makers—it is the strategy that leads to the most preferred outcome from among those outcomes made feasible by the strategies of the remaining decision makers. That is, if a person can infer the equilibrium strategies of these other persons—then the person's choice problem reduces to an elementary decision problem of choosing the best response. A Nash equilibrium, then, is a set of strategies—one for each player—such that each strategy in the set is a best response to all the others. Resurrecting the notion of utility maximization, a Nash equilibrium strategy maximizes each person's utility or expected utility, given that every other person is choosing a Nash equilibrium strategy.

The particular virtue of a Nash equilibrium, of course, is that it terminates "he-thinks-that-I-think" regresses. If (a^*, b^*) is such an equilibrium, and if I (person 1) think that my opponent will choose b^*, then I should choose a^* because it is my best response; and if my opponent believes that I will choose a^*, then he should in fact choose b^* because it is his best response. However, despite the fact that it is designed to resolve "he-thinks" regresses, we should be careful before we assert that a Nash equilibrium "solves" all of our problems, since this idea does in fact sweep a great many problems under the rug. Specifically, we should ask:

1. What of the possibility of multiple Nash equilibria? And if there is more than one equilibrium in a game, will we have difficulty deciding which equilibrium offers the most reasonable prediction about choices?

2. What guarantees the existence of a Nash equilibrium? Is it possible that we will need to broaden its definition in order to ensure universal existence?

3. Is the argument for focusing on such equilibria suggested by the preceding discussion—namely that they terminate a "he-thinks-that-I-think" regresses—compelling?

4. Throughout this discussion we have assumed that all persons share the same information about the situation—no information is private. What is the relevance of the notion of a Nash equilibrium when this condition is not satisfied?

We postpone looking at the last question, but clearly the answer to it as well as to question 3 depend on our answers to our first two questions.

3.2 Mixed Strategies

That Nash equilibria need not be unique is established by the trivial example in which every person's payoff is the same for every strategy n-tuple. In this instance, all strategy n-tuples are equilibria since, regardless of what n-tuple we select, no person has an incentive to choose some other strategy. Such a simple example, in fact, illustrates an important feature of a Nash equilibrium. Specifically,

> *The definition of an equilibrium does not suppose that a player has a positive incentive to choose an equilibrium strategy if all others are doing the same; rather, it supposes that no one has a positive incentive to choose otherwise.*

Nash equilibria in which people have strictly positive incentives to choose their equilibrium strategy—equilibria in which strict inequality holds in the formal definition so that unilateral defection necessarily results in a lower payoff for the defecting player—are called **strong equilibria**. To see, then, that non-uniqueness can arise even when all equilibria are strong, and to see the problems that non-uniqueness can create, consider the example in Figure 3.1 of a simple 2×2 game. (Recall that as a general convention we denote the row chooser's payoff by the first entry in a cell and the column chooser's by the second entry.) Notice in particular now that this

	b_1	b_2
a_1	2,1	0,0
a_2	0,0	1,2

Figure 3.1

game has two Nash equilibria—(a_1, b_1) and (a_2, b_2)—but despite the fact that we are assured of being able to terminate one kind of "he-thinks" regress, non-uniqueness here occasions another kind of regress. Recall our earlier supposition in analyzing a strategic form game that all persons choose their strategies simultaneously, because if they could communicate their intentions beforehand, that communication would be a strategy of the strategic form. Hence, unable to directly coordinate with 2, person 1, in contemplating our example, might reason, "I should choose a_1, because this yields the equilibrium I prefer. However, if 2 thinks the same way, he will choose b_2, and we will both get 0. Thus, I should choose a_2. But, if 2's thinking parallels mine, then he will conclude that he should choose b_1," and so on. So non-unique equilibria in this instance occasion a coordination problem that, unless somehow solved, can lead to a non-equilibrium outcome.

The reader should not believe, moreover, that such problems cannot arise in real-world circumstances. Recall again our plurality voting example, where we concluded that the strategy vector (A,B,B) is a Nash equilibrium. Notice, however, that the vector (A,C,C), which yields C as the final outcome, is also a Nash equilibrium—voter 1 cannot influence the outcome by unilaterally switching to B or C, whereas if voter 2 or 3 unilaterally defects to A or B, either A or a three-way tie results.

The attempted resolutions of such problems are varied and include proposing refinements of Nash equilibria, more explicitly modeling communication and coordination processes, and isolating those types of games for which such problems cannot arise. We will examine aspects of the first two responses in subsequent chapters, and later in this chapter we will discuss a class of situations—two-person zero sum games—which are of special interest because Nash equilibrium strategies for them possess properties that disallow the regresses of thought our example illustrates. Nevertheless, non-uniqueness and the problem of how people coordinate in a non-cooperative game to arrive at a particular equilibrium—indeed, to

	b_1	b_2
a_1	4,0	2,5
a_2	1,4	3,2

Figure 3.2

ensure that they arrive at any equilibrium—is one that will concern us throughout this volume.

We turn now to the issue of existence, which can be a problem. For example, the simple 2×2 strategic form in Figure 3.2, which we used in chapter 1 to introduce the "he-thinks-that-I-think" regress, does not have a Nash equilibrium—at least in terms of the four possible pairs of strategies. In contemplating such a situation, however, suppose person 2 (column chooser) reasons that since the "he-thinks" regress cannot be resolved, he or she might as well toss a coin in choosing a strategy. But before doing so, suppose he or she reasons further and realizes that common knowledge allows person 1 (row chooser) to anticipate this maneuver, in which case 1 would then conclude that he or she maximizes expected utility by choosing a_1, that 2 should respond to a_1 by choosing b_2, and so on. In other words, tentatively deciding to toss a coin fails to resolve 2's dilemma because it fails to terminate the he-thinks regress.

Despite the fact that tossing a coin fails to resolve matters, notice the conceptual innovation introduced by this idea of choosing a strategy randomly. To this point we have focused on choices that specify the selection of one strategy or another with certainty. However, such choices are merely special cases of a more general type of strategy—called a mixed strategy. First,

> if s is a strategy for a player that specifies a specific action at each of that player's information sets, then s is a **pure strategy**.

Thus, aside from the random moves of nature, a determinate outcome eventually prevails if all players choose pure strategies. To this point all the strategies that we have considered have been pure. A mixed strategy, on the other hand, is defined as follows:

> If the set of strategies available to a player is $S = \{s_1, s_2, . . ., s_m\}$, then a **mixed strategy** for that player is a lottery over S, $\mathbf{p} = (p_1, p_2, . . ., p_m)$. The player is said to choose the strategy $\mathbf{p}$ if he uses this lottery to determine which pure strategy he will implement in the actual play of the game.

A mixed strategy, then, chooses a particular pure strategy by some random device. And although the toss of a fair coin does not terminate the "he-thinks" regress in our example, we want to ask whether it is possible that some other device (lottery) terminates the regress. That is, is it possible that there exists a **mixed strategy equilibrium** in which each person chooses a pure strategy in accordance with some lottery in such a way that if these lotteries are common knowledge, no one has any incentive to use a different lottery?

That the answer to this question is "Yes" is an important result in game theory. To see this in the context of our example, consider the following reasoning: Persons 1 and 2 begin with the supposition that 1 will choose a_1 with probability p and a_2 with probability $1-p$, and that 2 will choose b_1 with probability q and b_2 with probability $1-q$. For these probabilities to terminate the "he-thinks" regress notice that, from 1's perspective, the choice between a_1 and a_2 is effectively a choice between two lotteries defined by the probabilities with which 2 chooses b_1 and b_2 (the chance q of 4 and the chance $1-q$ of 2 versus the chance q of 1 and the chance $1-q$ of 3). However, if 1 uses the lottery $(p,1-p)$ to choose between a_1 and a_2 and if there is some chance of choosing a_1 as well as a_2 (if $0 < p < 1$), then the lotteries offered by a_1 and a_2 should yield the same expected utility. Otherwise, if $u_1(a_1)$ does not equal $u_1(a_2)$, then person 1 can improve his expected payoff by switching from $(p, 1-p)$ to choosing with certainty the strategy that yields the greater expected return—$(p,1-p)$ can not be an equilibrium strategy. That is, the expected payoff from using $(p, 1-p)$ is $pu_1(a_1) + (1-p)u_1(a_2)$, and unless $u_1(a_1) = u_1(a_2)$, this expected return is increased by increasing or decreasing p. Thus, in our example we must have

$$4q + 2(1-q) = 1q + 3(1-q),$$

which implies $q = 1/4$. And if 2 has no incentive to shift from $(q, 1-q)$, where $0 < q < 1$, it must be the case that

$$0p + 4(1-p) = 5p + 2(1-p),$$

which implies $p = 2/7$. Hence, we have established that the pair of lotteries $((2/7,5/7), (1/4,3/4))$ constitute a Nash equilibrium.

Example: Recall our example from section 2.4 of a chairman who prefers to have ties broken in an agenda by lottery rather than be empowered to break ties. This fact seems paradoxical, but only if we ignore the interdependent nature of choice and

	A	B
A	.5,.5	.9,.1
B	.9,.1	.6,.4

Figure 3.3

the fact that others will respond in their own self-interest to any alteration in someone's voting power. To see a similar "paradox" in the context of mixed strategies, suppose two candidates, 1 and 2, must decide whether to allocate the final few days of the campaign in either state A or B, since the polls tell them that these two states are pivotal. Suppose the candidates' respective probabilities of winning the election are as shown in Figure 3.3.

The mixed strategy equilibrium is for both candidates to campaign in A with probability 3/7 and in B with probability 4/7. Now suppose that prior to implementing these strategies, a new poll reveals that if candidate 1 (row chooser) alone goes to state B, his probability of winning is merely .7 (not .9, as originally thought). It would seem then that this reassessment should cause 1 to increase the likelihood of visiting A. However, the equilibrium strategy for 1 now is to go to A with probability 1/5 and to increase the likelihood of visiting B from 4/7 to 4/5. So the inference that a decrease in the value of visiting state B should lead to a lower likelihood of visiting B is erroneous, because it neglects the fact that 2 will also adjust to this change.

Aside from establishing a seemingly paradoxical result, mixed strategies are important because they offer a mathematical solution to games without pure strategy Nash equilibria. Nevertheless, their introduction raises a new set of questions. First, do mixed strategies resolve the issue of existence? The answer to this question is provided by **von Neumann and Morgenstern's Minmax Theorem**:[1]

---

[1]Requiring a finite number of pure strategies is important (although not for all games). For a game without an equilibrium, consider this example: Choose an integer, and whoever chooses the largest integer wins. Since there is no integer which is greater than all others, there is no equilibrium. Or, for another example, suppose two people must each choose a number in the interval [0,1]. If they choose the same number, they tie. Whoever chooses the largest number wins, but with this exception: if one person chooses 1 and the other chooses a lower number, the second person wins.

*Every strategic form game in which all persons must choose from fi-
nite sets of pure strategies has at least one Nash equilibrium in either
pure or mixed strategies*

A second question is: Why should a person use a mixed strategy
when, as our analysis of Figure 3.2 (as well as Figure 3.3) establishes,
any lottery over the pure strategies yields the same expected payoff
provided that the opponent chooses in accordance with his equilibrium strategy? The answer is provided in the last clause of the question. If person 2 switches to b_1 or b_2 with certainty, or to any lottery
other than $(1/4,3/4)$, and if, as we have assumed, 1 can "get into 2's
head," then 1 can take advantage of 2's decision, which in this case
at least, reduces 2's expected payoff. Thus not only does 2 have no
positive incentive to switch from $(1/4,3/4)$, switching may be dangerous.

3.3 Significance of Mixed Strategies and Domination

Despite this seemingly straightforward answer, the value of the
concept of a mixed strategy depends on the care we exercise in modeling a situation. If the strategic form accurately reflects the strategic environment, then mixed strategies are merely a mechanism
for choosing a pure strategy in such a way that opponents cannot
take advantage of their knowledge. On the other hand, if our strategic form is but a crude approximation to reality, then the notion
of mixed strategies may make little or no sense.

To see what we mean by this in such a way that we can begin
constructing a useful model of mass two-candidate elections, let us
consider a simple spatial election model in which voters evaluate
two candidates strictly on the basis of their espoused positions on a
single issue. Following the development of these ideas offered in section 1.4, suppose we can represent the alternative positions on this
issue by a segment of the real line (e.g., the interval $[0,1]$), and suppose that each voter, with a most preferred position on this issue,
votes for the candidate who adopts a position closest to his or her
ideal. That is, suppose each voter's utility function over the issue is
single-peaked, as illustrated in Figure 3.4a for the case of three voters. The candidates' strategies, then, are positions in the $[0,1]$ interval and we can let their payoffs be $+1$, 0, and -1, depending on whether
they win, tie, or lose the election.

With respect to the game between candidates, it is not difficult to
see that in this initial representation of an election, there is a unique
pure strategy Nash equilibrium in which both candidates choose the

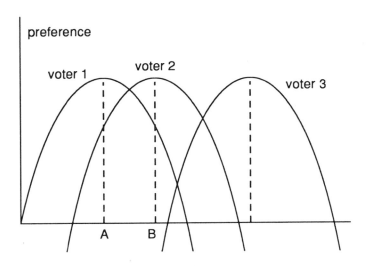

Figure 3.4a One-Issue Spatial Election

electorate's median preference (voter 2's ideal). If both candidates choose the median, the election is a tie since all voters are indifferent. Suppose now that candidate B remains at the median and that A shifts to the left to point A. Clearly, voters 2 and 3 prefer B to A, and thus A looses the election. Since the same argument applies if a candidate unilaterally shifts from the median to the right, voter 2's ideal preference is an equilibrium platform for both candidates. Of course, what we have just done is shown that the median preference here is a Condorcet winner.

The importance of this example is that there is nothing special about three versus *n* (odd) voters, provided that all preferences are single-peaked. From the definition of a median, at least half of the electorate most prefers it or positions to the right, so if one candidate is at the median and the other is to the left of the median, the candidate at the median wins. Since this argument is symmetric with respect to positions to the right of the median, and since the election is a tie if both candidates adopt the median, the median is the unique equilibrium platform in a two-candidate election. We have, then, the following result about one form of majority rule:

> ***The Median Voter Theorem****: In two-candidate elections that concern a single issue, if both candidates know the distribution of citizen preferences on the issue, if each candidate's strategy consists of a position on the issue, if citizens know the candidates' strategies, if all citizens have single-peaked preferences on the issue, and if no constraints are*

placed on the candidates' strategies with respect to the issue, then both candidates will converge to the electorate's median preference—the median, which is a Condorcet winner, is a Nash equilibrium to the corresponding election game.

The Median Voter Theorem is important because it reveals the strong centralizing tendency of simple two-candidate plurality-rule elections. It tells us, for example, that people who complain about the fact that political parties in the United States often fail to offer the electorate meaningful choices on important issues misconstrue the purpose of elections. That purpose is not necessarily to provide meaningful choices; rather, it is to select public policy in accordance with majority rule principles and to assure the rejection of radical candidates. Thus, those who prefer such outcomes must give good reasons for rejecting the median preference as a reasonable policy outcome.

Of course, we should not take the substantive implications of this theorem too far, because it treats a highly abstract circumstance that is unlikely to correspond to any election with which we are familiar. One route to understanding politics, however, consists of taking such simple models and generalizing their assumptions. To begin this process, let us consider two assumptions, namely that only two candidates compete and that the election concerns a single issue.

With respect to the number of candidates, we can see directly that there is no pure strategy equilibrium with three candidates. If three candidates have not identically converged to the same point, then the left- and rightmost candidates should move toward the center candidate, since this increases their vote. But this movement eventually makes it profitable for the candidate at the center to "jump" to the right or left of one of the candidates, thereby placing one of them in the "squeezed" position. But then this new center candidate has an incentive to jump, and so on. Thus, there is no pure strategy equilibrium. On the other hand, if we suppose that there are two candidates who worry merely about the threat of a third candidate, then the situation changes. If voters continue to vote for the candidate closest to their ideal, and if preferences are distributed unimodally, then, as we show more formally in the next chapter, an equilibrium exists in which the candidates preclude the possibility of a profitable entry by positioning themselves on opposite sides of the median. So if the third candidate enters only if he or she can win, he or she does not enter, which begins to reveal the logic behind the hypothesis that a simple plurality-rule election system fosters a two-party system.

The assumption of a single issue is also critical to the Median Voter

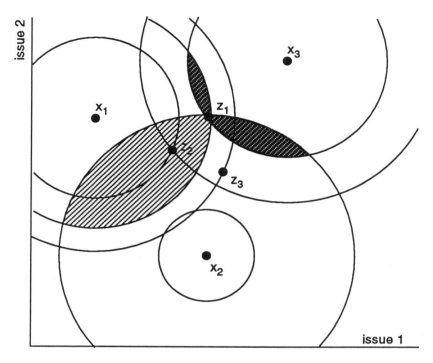

Figure 3.4b A Two-Issue Spatial Election

Theorem. Recall our discussion in section 2.4, where we offered a necessary and sufficient condition for the existence of a Condorcet winner that led to the conclusion that such winners are rare in a spatial context if there are two or more issues. To see this fact first-hand, consider an election with the same structure as before, except suppose that there are two issues and three voters.

Example: Consider the three-voter election scenario portrayed in Figure 3.4b, which concerns two issues and in which the voter's ideal points are denoted by x_1, x_2, and x_3. Since we will assume as before that the voters vote for the candidate closest to their ideal, we have drawn some circles around these ideals so we can better judge the distance of other points from them. Notice now that, contrary to the necessary and sufficient condition that we offer in section 2.4, it is impossible to pair voters in this example in such a way that the line connecting the two paired ideal points passes through the third ideal. Thus, there is no Condorcet winner—every alternative policy can be defeated by at least one other policy. In particular, consider the position z_1 and notice that all points in the three shaded regions are closer to two of the voters ideal points. Thus, the point z_2 defeats z_1 in a majority vote because it is closer to 1 and 2's ideal than is z_1, so z_1 cannot be an equilibrium, since both candidates would have an incentive to shift unilaterally to z_2. But then z_3 defeats z_2 in a majority vote as well, and thus z_2 cannot be an equilibrium. Finally, to complete the cycle, notice that z_1 defeats z_3. Thus there is no pure strategy equilibrium to a simple two-candidate election with these preferences for voters.

Example: To see that this problem of disequilibrium with pure strategies is not merely a consequence of a conceptualization of election issues that occasions circular indifference curves, suppose instead that the election concerns only the redistribution of wealth and that the candidates' strategies are proposals to distribute some fixed amount, W, of wealth among the electorate. If we assume again that there are three voters, then we can represent the issue space—all possible three-way divisions of W—as a triangle (1) where vertex i represents the outcome "voter i gets W and the remaining two voters get nothing," (2) where the midpoint of the opposite side of the triange represents "voter i gets nothing and the remaining two voters evenly divide W," and (3) where i's indifference curves are drawn as straight lines parallel to the side of the triangle opposite vertex i such that i's utility declines as we move away from this vertex. The reader should try drawing this figure (mathematicians refer to it as a baricentric coordinate system) to become convinced of two things: Regardless of the point we choose, the sum of the payoffs to all three voters is W, and any point in or on the triangle can be defeated in a majority vote by any number of other points. For example, if candidates must propose alternative divisions of $90, and if one candidate proposes ($45,$45,$0), the second can win with ($0,$50,$40), which is in turn defeated by ($45,$0,$45), which is defeated by ($60,$30,$0), and so on. Thus, short of implementing a mixed strategy, the candidates could cycle, endlessly proposing alternative distributions.

Having thus concluded that two-candidate multi-issue elections and elections that concern wealth redistribution do not give rise to games with pure strategy Nash equilibria, we might then be tempted to turn to the concept of a mixed strategy in order to make predictions about candidate platforms. However, even if we ignored the technical matter that the number of pure strategies is not finite in our examples, it is nevertheless difficult to imagine two candidates spinning spinners, tossing coins, or rolling dice at the beginning of their campaigns in order to select a platform or proposed distribution. And although candidates may have incentives to formulate ambiguous strategies, such ambiguity and mixed strategies are not one and the same thing. With ambiguity, the candidate appears before the electorate as a lottery, whereas with a mixed strategy, the candidate merely uses a lottery to select some pure strategy before the vote.[2]

The particular reason we are reluctant to assert that mixed strategies make sense in our election models is that election campaigns are dynamic events in which candidates can alter tactics as events unfold. This fact did not bother us in unidimensional elections, because if a Condorcet winning platform exists, then candidates (or their parties in the nomination process) will be drawn to such a platform, regardless of the details of a campaign's dynamics. But if no such winner exists to attract the candidates, then these dynamics, as well as the maneuvering that occurs between parties between campaigns, appear more critical and the simple static view of the Median Voter Theorem seems out of place.

Of course, any complete analysis should not assume that dynamics are irrelevant—we should establish this assumption. In addition, we should also ascertain whether a static analysis can assist us even though we believe that the details of the process ultimately determine outcomes. To this end it is useful to introduce the notion of domination: Briefly,

> *The strategy x'* **dominates** *another, x", if x' does at least as well as x" in all contingencies (against all possible strategies by other decision makers), and if it sometimes does better.*[3]

For example, in a simple one-vote agenda, voting for one's preferred

---

[2]In fact, admitting ambiguity as a strategy only makes matters worse from the point of view of finding an equilibrium. If we conceptualize the strategy of appearing ambiguous as a probability density function over the policy space, then a candidate's strategy is characterized by the parameters necessary to represent that function. And since even the simplest such function requires at least two parameters (e.g., a mean and variance in the case of the normal density), ambiguity necessarily renders the election multidimensional.

[3]Usually, game theorists distinguish between two forms of domination: x' strongly dominates x'' if x' is always better than x'', whereas x' only **weakly dominates x''** if x' is never worse than x''. Generally, we will want to eliminate even weakly dominated strategies, and indeed, doing so often eliminates Nash equilibria which are unreasonable predictions. For example, if all persons have the same preference over some set of alternatives, it is nevertheless the case that everybody voting for their

alternative dominates a contrary vote. If one's vote is not decisive, then it does not matter what choice is made; but in the event that one's vote is decisive, then it is always best to vote for the preferred alternative (assuming, as before, that one's vote does not count negatively).

With respect now to election models, it is fortunately the case that the sort of election scenarios that Figure 3.4b illustrates, spatial elections, have strategies that dominate others. For example, if candidates are concerned solely with whether or not they win the election, then for two-candidate elections, platforms located far from all ideal points are dominated by ones that are closer to those points. And since it seems unreasonable to suppose that anyone would choose a dominated strategy, it similarly seems unreasonable to suppose that a candidate, regardless of the election campaign's dynamics, would choose such a strategy either. Similarly, for our example of a purely redistributive election, allocating all resources to one or just a few voters clearly is dominated by strategies that allocate resources to a larger number.

Of course, neither type of multi-issue election yields a strategy that dominates all others (since those examples have no Condorcet winner), and thus, the elimination of strategies that are dominated will not present the candidates with unique choices. Nevertheless, our argument, if formalized, establishes something of substantive significance. With respect to our spatial conceptualization, candidates will not choose platforms far from the "main body" of voter preferences—indeed, they will not choose platforms far from the median preference on each issue (assuming, of course, that the relevant assumptions of the Median Voter Theorem about perceptions and candidate mobility are satisfied, as well as the assumption that voter preferences correspond to simple distance from some ideal in the issue space). And if the election concerns the redistribution of wealth, the only undominated strategies are those that allocate something to a minimal majority of the electorate. Thus, despite the fact that our representation of an election is too abstract to allow us to assert the relevance of mixed strategies, the simple idea of dominance offers a useful prediction as to the general outlines of strategy.

We emphasize that we are not constrained to use this notion only in election models. Pruning voting trees illustrates the application

---

last choice is, under majority rule, a Nash equilibrium—no one has any incentive to shift unilaterally to some other strategy since doing so cannot change the outcome. Voting for one's last choice, however, is weakly dominated, and, thus, such equilibria are eliminated if weakly dominated strategies are eliminated.

of domination, because a strategy that specifies voting for something other than the alternative one prefers at the final nodes of any binary voting tree is dominated by a strategy that specifies voting the other way. The elimination of dominated strategies, moreover, can simplify an analysis considerably. In chapter 1 we note that the strategic form of the game in Figure 1.3 is a 3×54 table. However, since person 2's second decision is made after learning 1's decision, 2 has unambiguous choices at each of his last six decision nodes, and we can suppose he makes the optimal choice for himself at each of these decision nodes. Indeed, instead of supposing that each of the six branches emanating from 1's information set leads to three alternatives for 2, we can prune the form in Figure 1.3 and suppose instead that each of these six branches leads to a determinate outcome—the outcome 2 will choose, given 2's earlier decision and 1's subsequent choice. This pruning, then, reduces a 3x54 cell strategic form to one having only three rows and two columns (one for each of 2's initial decisions).

Eliminating dominated strategies is a process we can repeat as many times as possible. Working backward up an extensive form illustrates this process—pruning a bottom node and replacing it with its strategic equivalent is equivalent to eliminating dominated strategies. And when we then prune the new bottom node, we are eliminating those strategies that are now dominated in the reduced game. Thus, whenever we confront a game in strategic form, the first thing to be done is to check whether it has dominated strategies. If any player has such a strategy, then, after its elimination, we should check to see if other players now have dominated strategies.

Example: Consider the two-person strategic form in Figure 3.5a, and notice that person 2 (column chooser) does not have a dominated strategy. However, 1 has such a strategy, a_2 (which is dominated by a_1). After eliminating a_2 to get the form in Figure 3.5b, b_2 is now dominated by b_1. Eliminating b_2 to get the form in Figure 3.5c, a_3 and b_3 are dominated by a_4 and b_4, respectively. But now, as Figure 3.5d shows after the elimination of a_3 and b_3, the strategy a_4 dominates a_1, so b_1 subsequently dominates b_4, leaving us with a unique Nash equilibrium and a unique prediction about choices.

The argument that legitimizes this sequential elimination of dominated strategies appeals once again to the assumption of common knowledge. If, in our example, person 2 knows that a_2 is dominated, then both 1 and 2 know that this strategy can be ignored, and both

	b_1	b_2	b_3	b_4
a_1	3,3	2,2	4,3	3,4
a_2	2,0	1,3	0,2	2,0
a_3	3,4	4,2	2,2	0,3
a_4	4,3	2,1	3,1	4,2

Figure   3.5a

	b_1	b_2	b_3	b_4
a_1	3,3	2,2	4,3	3,4
a_3	3,4	4,2	2,2	0,3
a_4	4,3	2,1	3,1	4,2

Figure 3.5b

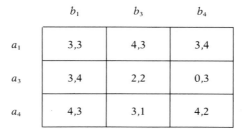

	b_1	b_3	b_4
a_1	3,3	4,3	3,4
a_3	3,4	2,2	0,3
a_4	4,3	3,1	4,2

Figure   3.5c

	b_1	b_4
a_1	3,3	3,4
a_4	4,3	4,2

Figure 3.5d

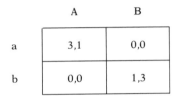

	A	B
a	3,1	0,0
b	0,0	1,3

Figure 3.6

persons can focus on the strategic form in Figure 3.5b. And this same argument, repeated, eventually eliminates all but (a_4, b_1).

3.4 A Note of Caution

Before proceeding, we want to offer a note of caution about the application of domination to reduce a game. Consider the following example:

Example: Consider the 2×2 game in Figure 3.6, with payoffs in dollars. This game has two pure strategy Nash equilibria, (a,A) and (b,B), and a mixed strategy equilibrium. But since the equilibrium strategies are not interchangeable, there is no guarantee that noncooperative play results in any equilibrium outcome. However, prior to playing this game, suppose player 1 (row chooser) can choose between throwing (T) or not throwing (NT) away a dollar and that player 2 observes this decision prior to choosing his strategy for the game.

Our instinct now is to assume that, since 1's decision is made before the play of the game and since it only affects 1's welfare, we can ignore it. Modeling the full situation, though, notice that player 1 has four strategies—(T,a), (T,b), (NT,a), and (NT,b) and player 2 has four strategies—(A,A), (A,B), (B,A), and (B,B)—which specify 2's choice, contingent on 1's prior selection of T or NT, respectively. (For example, (A,B) reads "if 1 chooses T, then choose A; but if 1 chooses NT, then choose B".) Figure 3.7 shows this extended situation's strategic form.

Consider what happens when the (weakly) dominated strategies are equentially eliminated:

1. Delete (T,b) because it is dominated by (NT,a).
2. With (T,b) deleted, eliminate (B,A) and (B,B) because they are dominated by (A,A) and (A,B) respectively.

	A,A	A,B	B,A	B,B
T,a	2,1	2,1	-1,0	-1,0
T,b	-1,0	-1,0	0,3	0,3
NT,a	3,1	0,0	3,1	0,0
NT,b	0,0	1,3	0,0	1,3

Figure   3.7

3. With (T,b), (B,A), and (B,B) eliminated, (T,a) then dominates (NT,b).
4. With (T,b), (B,A), (B,B), and (NT,b) eliminated, (A,A) dominates (A,B).
5. With all of 2's strategies but (A,A) eliminated, (NT,a) dominates (T,a), which yields the unique prediction (3,1).

That 1's ability to throw away money affects our prediction seems paradoxical, especially since 1 does not choose T in the equilibrium arrived at by sequential elimination. However, the relevance of a seemingly irrelevant choice can be rationalized thus: Player 2 can reason that if 1 were to choose T, then it must be that 1 intends to play a, since only the outcome generated by (a,A), (2,1) is preferred to the worst outcome that prevails if 1 chooses NT. And since 2 can assume that 1 can anticipate this reasoning, 2 must believe that 1 can anticipate 2's choice of the best response to a, A, in the event that 1 chooses T. So 2 concludes that it is common knowledge that T leads to the outcome (2,1). But if 1 chooses NT instead, it must be that 1 intends to get a higher payoff. Since only the choice pair (a,A) yields 1 a more preferred outcome than (2,1), the choice of NT must mean that 1 plans to choose a. Thus, 2 should choose A.

If we accept this reasoning, then we must also conclude that we are likely to overlook the potential relevance of seemingly irrelevant choices in other contexts—especially those in which coordination is required to achieve some equilibrium outcome. This example warns us, then, that our predictions need not always be robust against subtle differences in our representation of a situation. And although game theory does not tell us what model is correct, at the very least it makes us aware of the possibility that our conclusions about political processes may be sensitive to the ways in which we portray those processes.

There is, however, an alternative interpretation of our analysis that directs our attention away from modeling problems to solution theory itself. Recall that after (T,b) is eliminated, we eliminate (B,A) and (B,B) because (A,A) and (A,B) are superior in the event that 1 chooses (T,a). But later we conclude that 1 will not choose (T,a), which appears to negate our original reason for eliminating (B,A) and (B,B). And it is this type of contradiction that can arise with sequential elimination of weakly dominated strategies. This is not to say that such sequential elimination ought to be avoided, or even that it is incorrect in the present example. Rather, we are merely suggesting that it, as well as any other solution hypothesis, ought to be applied carefully, with an eye to possible problems and conceptual traps.

3.5 Finding Equilibrium Strategies

Returning to the concept of a mixed strategy equilibrium, it is one thing to assert the existence of such an equilibrium, but it is quite another thing to assert that they can be readily computed or that people act in accordance with them. One issue that persists with respect to equilibria, regardless of type, concerns the hypothesis that they necessarily provide reasonable predictions about choice. We have already seen, for example, how non-uniqueness occasions problems, which is an issue that will become more problematical as we proceed to more complicated scenarios. However, now is as good a time as any to pause, reflect on what we have discussed thus far, and see in particular whether we can avoid such problems for any special class of situations.

Let us begin with a simple scheme for calculating mixed strategy equilibria. Our first step in approaching any strategic form game of more than trivial complexity should be to eliminate all dominated strategies, iterating the process as many times as is possible (being careful to avoid the type of problems described in the previous section). If we are lucky and are left with a 2×2 game, then we can solve for the mixed strategy equilibrium by repeating the steps we took to analyze the game in Figure 3.1. Specifically, after writing the expressions for the expected values of a_1 and a_2 in terms of q (2's mixed strategy), we solve for q by equating these two values. Similarly, we solve for 1's mixed strategy by equating the expected values of b_1 and b_2. But suppose we are left with an $m \times 2$ game, where $m > 2$. Fortunately, the same principles apply as before. Letting the

	b_1	b_2
a_1	14,3	2,5
a_2	11,10	9,6
a_3	5,2	11,8
a_4	2,1	13,4

Figure   3.8a

player with two strategies, 2, use the mixture $(q,1-q)$, letting $u_1(a_i)$ denote the expected value to player 1 of strategy a_i—$qu_1(a_i,b_1)$ + $(1-q)u_1(a_i,b_2)$—and letting $(p_1,p_2,.\ .\ .,p_m)$ be 1's mixed equilibrium strategy, then if p_i and p_j are both greater than zero, it must be the case that $u_1(a_i) = u_1(a_j)$. And if $p_k = 0$, then it must be the case that $u_1(a_k) < u_1(a_i)$. Of course, if $0 < q < 1$, it must also be the case that $u_2(b_1) = u_2(b_2)$.

Example: Consider the 4×2 game in Figure 3.8a. Assuming that person 2 abides by the mixed strategy $(q, 1-q)$, and writing the expressions for $u_1(a_1)$ through $u_1(a_4)$, we get

$$u_1(a_1) = 12q + 2, \qquad u_1(a_2) = 2q + 9,$$
$$u_1(a_3) = 11 - 6q, \qquad u_1(a_4) = 13 - 11q.$$

Plotting $u_1(a_i)$ against q (see Figure 3.8b) shows that there are several instances in which two of these values are equal, but 1's expected payoff is greatest when $u_1(a_1)$ equals $u_1(a_2)$. This fact implies that there is an equilibrium mixed strategy for 1 that involves only a_1 and a_2, which reduces the situation to a 2×2 game that we can solve as before—the solution being $((2/3,1/3,0,0),(7/10,3/10))$. There is, however, a second solution when the lines for a_2 and a_4 intersect, so equilibria are not unique. But the remaining intersections cannot be equilibria since if 2 chooses the corresponding value of q, we can increase 1's payoff by shifting to a pure strategy—one that corresponds to a line that lies above the intersection.

Solving larger games, including those with more than two decision makers, is more complicated. We may have to guess about which

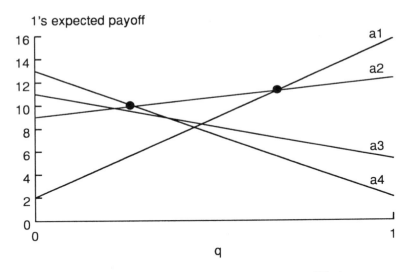

Figure 3.8b Finding the Mixed Strategy Equilibrium

strategies have nonzero probabilities associated with them, and the equations we must solve will involve many more probabilities. But without minimizing the computation complexity involved, the procedures for solving larger games are essentially refinements and generalizations of the method we have just illustrated—they make use of the fact that any two strategies, say a and a', with nonzero probability associated with them must yield equal expected returns against the opponents' strategies. And if a'' is any strategy with zero probability assigned to it, then its expected return against the opponent cannot be greater than what a and a' yield. Some games can be solved, moreover, using various tricks. For instance, suppose a two-person game is symmetric in the following way:

> ***Symmetric two-person game****: A two-person game in strategic form is symmetric if both persons have identical feasible strategy sets, and if, when they switch strategies, they switch payoffs.*

Our previous examples of two-candidate elections illustrate symmetric games, because we did not suppose that either candidate held any advantage over the other and because both candidates could choose from an identical set of strategies.

Suppose then that the players in a two-person game are indistinguishable in the way implied by symmetry. In this instance, if (a^*,b^*) is an equilibrium, then (b^*,a^*) must be an equilibrium as well, because the labeling of one player as 1 and the other as 2 is arbitrary.

	b_1	b_2	b_3
a_1	1,-1		$x,-x$
a_2			
a_3	$y,-y$		$z,-z$

Figure 3.9

This fact can frequently be used to facilitate a game's analysis, but if we assume also that the game is constant sum, we can prove something stronger. Briefly,

> **Constant-sum game**: *A game is constant sum if the sum of the payoffs across players is a constant, regardless of the strategies chosen by the players. A game is* **zero sum** *if this constant is zero.*

If candidates maximize plurality, then the corresponding election game is zero sum since the sum of pluralities is necessarily zero. Alternatively, if candidates maximize their probabilities of winning, then the game is constant sum since probabilities must sum to a constant, 1. Of course, any constant sum game is equivalent to a zero sum game, because we can always subtract this constant from one player's utility function without affecting the information that this function conveys about a person's ordinal preferences or attitudes toward risk.

The reason we isolate zero- and constant-sum games from the rest is that their two-person counterparts (but not *n*-person games, $n >$ 2) have special properties that make them especially interesting and amenable to analysis. Consider the game in Figure 3.9, in which only the payoff in the (a_1,b_1) cell is specified. Suppose we are also told that both (a_1,b_1) and (a_3,b_3) are equilibrium strategy pairs. What we want to show now is that (a_1,b_3) and (a_3,b_1) are equilibria as well and that neither of the players cares which equilibrium prevails.

We begin by observing that since (a_1,b_1) is an equilibrium, it must be true that

$$1 > y \text{ and } -1 > -x.$$

And since (a_3,b_3) is an equilibrium, we must have

$$z > x \text{ and } -z > -y.$$

Eliminating minus signs and putting all inequalities together yields

$$1 > y > z > x > 1,$$

which is satisfied only if the entries in all four corner cells are
(1,-1). This fact, in turn, implies that all four corner cells are equilibria. For example, since (a_1,b_1) is an equilibrium, player 1 (row
chooser) has no positive incentive to switch unilaterally to a_2 from
a_1 if 2 chooses b_1. But then it must be the case that 1 would not
switch from a_3 to a_2 either. Repetition of this argument proves our
assertion.

That (a_1,b_1) and (a_3,b_3) being equilibria implies that (a_1,b_3) and (a_3,b_1)
are equilibria as well is a property we call **interchangeability**, and
if people are indifferent as to which equilibrium ultimately prevails,
we say that the equilibria are **equivalent**. That all equilibria for two-
person constant sum games satisfy these two properties tells us that

> *Coordination problems cannot arise in two-person constant sum games.
> If each player chooses a strategy that is involved in some equilibrium,
> then the players necessarily arrive at an equilibrium. Moreover, they
> have no preference as to which equilibrium ultimately prevails.*

And putting this fact together with what we already know about
symmetric two-person games, we can conclude that for any two-person constant sum game,

> *if (a^*,b^*) is an equilibrium, then symmetry implies that (b^*,a^*) is an
> equilibrium and, invoking interchangeability, that (a^*,a^*) and (b^*,b^*)
> are equilibria as well. Symmetry, however, also requires that both per-
> sons receive the same payoff at (a^*,a^*), so if the game is zero sum,
> then each must receive an expected payoff of zero in equilibrium. Hence,
> equivalence implies that both persons in a symmetric two-person zero
> sum game must receive an expected payoff of zero from any Nash equi-
> librium.*

Thus, if the candidates in a two-candidate election have wholly
symmetric opportunities, then regardless of what we assume about
the electorate or procedures, if Nash equilibria exist, there is one
such equilibrium in which the two candidates adopt identical strategies. Moreover, regardless of which equilibrium prevails, the expected outcome is a tie. This fact may appear obvious, and it may
hardly qualify as one that would be debated extensively by those
who are concerned primarily with the substantive domain of politics. Nevertheless, it is comforting to know we can set this fact aside
as an established rule about an ideal form of two-candidate, democratic elections.

We offer this discussion of symmetric two-person zero-sum games
not merely because they model an interesting class of situations (those
in which two persons are locked in a wholly conflictual situation),

but also to show the kinds of abstract conclusions our approach sometimes allows. Our conclusion about equilibria in two-candidate elections makes some severe assumptions that are not necessarily satisfied in reality (notably, the assumption that citizens do not begin the campaign with inherent biases toward one candidate or the other, as well as the assumption that the candidates are afforded equal access to all strategies, which almost certainly is violated if one candidate is an incumbent). Nevertheless, once we accept those assumptions as a starting point for modeling elections, we reach a conclusion that allows considerable freedom in accommodating other aspects of an election.

3.6 Zero Sum and Maxmin

Two person zero-sum games have an additional property that, although it does not necessarily rationalize mixed strategy equilibria, gives us confidence that a pure strategy equilibrium prevails whenever such an equilibrium exists. Suppose each person evaluates his or her strategy on the basis of the worst outcome that can prevail if that strategy is chosen. That is, suppose each person reasons as follows: "Regardless of what I decide to do, my opponent can anticipate my thoughts and select a best response strategy, which, owing to the zero sum character of the situation, does me the greatest harm. Thus, I should choose a strategy that maximizes my minimum payoff." We would not want to try to extend this reasoning to other types of games, especially if there are mutual gains to be realized from coordination. But it is useful to know that

> *If a two-person zero sum game has a pure strategy equilibrium, and if both persons choose strategies that maximize their minimum payoff (a* **maxmin** *strategy), an equilibrium is realized.*

The proof of this proposition proceeds as follows: If (a^*, b^*) is an equilibrium that yields the utility outcome $(c, -c)$, then c is the minimum payoff that player 1 should associate with a^*—if there was some payoff lower than c associated with a^*, the corresponding outcome must give 2 more than $-c$, in which case player 2 would unilaterally switch from the presumed equilibrium strategy of b^* in order to receive that payoff. Similarly, since a^* is an equilibrium strategy for 1, it must be that unilaterally moving cannot raise 1's payoff and may even decrease it. Hence, the minimum payoff 1 associates with any other strategy cannot exceed c. So a^* is player 1's maxmin strategy, and a parallel argument establishes the same thing for player 2.

We might question whether such pessimism is warranted in all circumstances—even zero sum ones. But again we must keep in mind our assumption that all aspects of the game are common knowledge and that any uncertainties or inabilities should already be incorporated into the game's structure. Of course, it is not always practical to model every feature of a situation and we may choose to modify our interpretations from time to time in order to incorporate those features of reality that we have excluded. Nevertheless, if we believe that a zero sum game models a situation with "sufficient" accuracy, choosing maxmin strategies seems only reasonable.

3.7 Multiple Equilibria and Coordination

As we noted earlier, one problem that plagues game theory is that many situations give rise to multiple equilibria that cannot be excluded on the basis of game-theoretic arguments. Imagine a situation in which each of two people must choose the number 0, 1, 2, or 3. If the numbers chosen sum to 3, each player earns ten dollars; otherwise each player loses five dollars. This game, then, has four pure strategy equilibria—(0,3), (1,2), (2,1), and (3,0). But, a priori, there does not seem to be any reason to suppose that one equilibria will be more likely to prevail than another. Indeed, because some coordination is required to ensure an equilibrium, there is no guarantee that an equilibrium will ultimately prevail.

Now, however, suppose we modify the situation so that both persons must choose numbers between 0 and 10, and suppose that both persons receive a positive payoff only if their numbers sum to 10. In this instance, players might regard the number 5 as having special significance because of its centrality. Moreover, if each player believes that the other is likely to choose 5, then 5 is an optimal response that becomes, in effect, a self-fulfilling prophesy. Thus, the players can implicitly coordinate to achieve an equilibrium owing to a consideration exogenous to the analysis—a particular strategy that serves as a focal point for each person's deliberations.

The implicit coordination that focal point strategies allow can derive from other sources. Consider this possibility:

Example: Nations 1 and 2 must each choose between being intransigent (I) or flexible (F) for some upcoming tariff negotiation. If both choose I, no agreement is possible and no benefits accrue to either side. If both choose F, the benefits from open trade are distributed evenly between the two sides; and if one chooses I while the other chooses F, then an agreement is reached

	I	F
I	0,0	4,2
F	2,4	3,3

Figure 3.10

in which the intransigent side gets the lion's share of benefits. Thus, the game describing the choice of bargaining strategy is as described in Figure 3.10.

This game has three Nash equilibria: the pure strategy pairs (I,F) and (F,I) that yield the outcomes (4,2) and (2,4), respectively, and the mixed pair (p = (1/3,2/3), q = (1/3,2/3)) that yields both players an expected payoff of 2 2/3. The difficulty here, of course, is that because the equilibrium strategies are not interchangeable (although the game is two-person, it is not constant sum), there is no guarantee that an equilibrium will prevail, so the outcome (0,0) is a very real possibility. Suppose it is common knowledge, however, that the religious precepts of country A's team require an inflexible commitment to national pride on rainy or cloudy days but that it attaches supreme importance to harmonious relations on sunny days. Both teams, then, can rely on the weather to coordinate their choices. Notice also that acting in accordance with the implications of A's religion is self-enforcing, because neither side has any incentive to deviate unilaterally from choosing (F,I) on sunny days and (I,F) on rainy or cloudy ones. Indeed, owing to the coordination that a fixation on the weather allows, such religious precepts become self-ful-filling prophesies—good things happen (equilibria are realized) when decision makers abide by them, and bad things happen (outcomes such as (0,0) prevail) when they do not.

This example shows that seemingly extraneous events can determine final outcomes if the players use those events to coordinate strategies. Thus, anything from sun spots to nonbinding pregame communications might provide a basis for the coordination necessary to ensure an equilibrium outcome. We also see that a society that believes in bizarre causal relations might nevertheless be able to provide statistically conclusive evidence that their beliefs ought to be taken seriously.

In this context it is interesting to examine the role of international organizations as mechanisms for avoiding conflict. It is often asserted, of course, that organizations such as the United Nations can perform a function beyond that of providing lucrative salaries, luxurious apartments, and the right to violate traffic regulations at will in New York City to otherwise unemployable bureaucrats. The interesting issue is how such a function is performed when these organizations cannot enforce any agreements reached under their auspices. However, if we modify the scenario in which the game in Figure 3.10 is played, we can explicitly see the role of third-party mediation in ensuring mutually beneficial outcomes:

Example: Referring to Figure 3.10 again, suppose a mediator is hired but is paid a fee only if A and B successfully avoid the outcome (0,0). Assuming, however, that neither A nor B is willing to relinquish its sovereignty, the mediator knows that anything it recommends is not binding and can be unilaterally ignored by either party. Seeking to ensure receiving the fee, suppose the mediator randomly recommends (I,F), (F,I), and (F,F), each with a one-third probability, but also suppose the mediator only tells each player what that player should do. The players, of course, are free to ignore this advice, but if each believes that the other will abide by it and if each is aware of the mediator's motivations (i.e., each knows that the mediator seeks to secure an equilibrium outcome), then abiding by the mediator's advice is a Nash equilibrium in which each realizes an expected payoff of three. For example, if A is told to choose I, then A believes B has been advised to choose F, in which case A should abide by the advice and choose I; on the other hand, if A is told to choose F, then A will believe there is a fifty-fifty chance of (F,I) versus (F,F) prevailing if he abides by the advice—which corresponds to an expected payoff of 2.5—whereas defecting to I in the face of this belief yields an expected payoff of two. Thus, as before, abiding by the advice is a best response. Since an identical argument holds for the other player, abiding by the advice is a Nash equilibrium.

3.8 Relation of Subgame Perfect Equilibria to Nash Equilibria

The two principal ideas we have introduced in this chapter are subgame perfect equilibria and Nash equilibria. But game theory would hardly qualify as a "theory" if these two ideas were not related in a coherent way. And in fact, we can interpret subgame per-

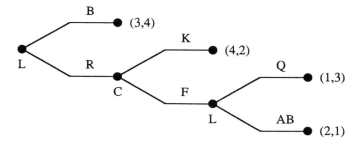

Figure 3.11a

	F	K
x_1	3,4	3,4
x_2	2,1	4,2
x_3	1,3	4,2

Figure   3.11b

fect equilibria as a refinement of Nash equilibria because of two facts. First,

Every subgame perfect equilibrium must be a Nash equilibrium,

because a subgame perfect equilibrium is but a conjunction of best responses that are best responses within all subgames. And second,

Not every Nash equilibrium is subgame perfect.

Example: Consider again the game in Figure 1.13a, which we redraw in Figure 3.11a after inserting some utility numbers. Notice from Figure 3.11b that in its strategic form, (x_1,K) as well as (x_3,F) are Nash equilibria. However, from Figure 3.11a we see that only the equilibrium (x_3,F) is subgame perfect: L chooses AB at the bottom node, so C chooses K at the next node, in which case L chooses R at the top node.

Subgame perfection can also be used to eliminate Nash equilibria that common sense tells us are unreasonable and unlikely to prevail. Consider again our pay raise example from section 1.5, and recall that in section 2.2 we conclude that legislator A should vote against the raise, while B and C vote for it. On the other hand, if we look at Figure 1.11—the strategic form representation of this situation—we see that there are a great many Nash equilibrium outcomes. Specifically, we count forty five cells that correspond to Nash equilibria and which account for outcomes as diverse as all three legislators voting against the raise, any two voting for the raise, and all three voting for the raise.

> **Example**: Consider any of the agendas that we have described in this and the previous chapter, but rather than analyze the corresponding voting trees by backward reduction, suppose everyone uses the strategy "at every decision node that pairs two alternatives, vote for the alternative standing highest in the alphabet." As long as there are three or more voters, this strategy nevertheless describes a Nash equilibrium (although not a strong one). If everyone abides by it, no individual defection changes any vote outcome, in which case no one has a positive incentive to defect. Clearly, though, such silly strategies are not subgame perfect. Similarly, if everyone holds identically the same preference in an agenda, but if everyone consistently votes for their least preferred alternative as the agenda unfolds, including on the last ballot, then for the same reason, this strategy describes a Nash equilibrium in which the least preferred alternative prevails.

Certainly, subgame perfection provides a considerable refinement in these instances.

> **Example**: Lest we conclude that we can abandon the notion of Nash equilibrium altogether in favor of subgame perfection, consider the extensive form in Figure 3.12a, which has three subgames, as denoted by the dashed boxes, and the corresponding strategic form in Figure 3.12b. Notice first that the strategic form has three Nash equilibria, denoted by "*," although the two equilibria associated with the (30,10) payoff entries are clearly redundant. However, if we look only at the strategic form, then we fail to appreciate that person 1 should never choose a_2, and, therefore, that the (25,20) cell is not subgame perfect. Specifically, the extensive form shows that person 1 must first choose between two simultaneous move games. The first game yields the Nash equilibrium outcome (30,10), whereas the second game yields the Nash equilibrium outcome (25,20). Hence, person 1 ought to choose a_1 in order to secure the more preferred equilibrium, so only (30,10) is a subgame perfect. Thus, although the

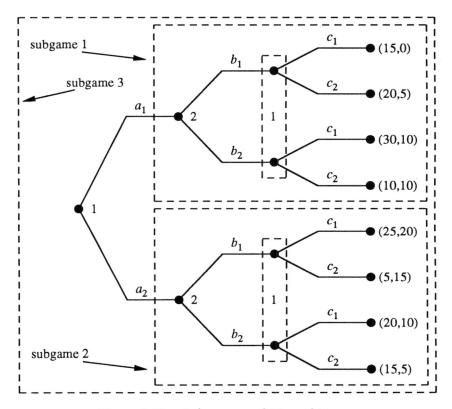

Figure 3.12a   Subgames and Normal Forms

notion of subgame perfection helps us refine our predictions, we still require the notion of a Nash equilibrium to predict the consequences of choosing a_1 as against a_2.

3.9 A Problem for Future Consideration

To this point we have discussed extensive and strategic forms as though their analysis were unexceptional. Consider, however, the scenario in Figure 3.13, which models a game called the Centipede Game because of the appearance of its extensive form. Suppose each person must formulate a strategy based on the premise that the players will not be allowed to communicate or coordinate their choices in any way. Thus, player 1 has the first move and can choose to take $40 or he can pass the decision on to player 2, who receives $10 if 1 takes the $40. Player 2's choice is between taking $80 (in which

	always b_1	always b_2	$a_1 \Rightarrow b_1$ $a_2 \Rightarrow b_2$	$a_1 \Rightarrow b_2$ $a_2 \Rightarrow b_1$
a_1 then c_1	15,0	30,10*	15,0	30,10*
a_1 then c_2	20,5	10,10	20,5	10,10
a_2 then c_1	25,20*	20,10	20,10	25,20
a_2 then c_2	5,15	15,5	15,5	5,15

Figure 3.12b Strategic Form of Figure 3.12a

case 1 gets $20) or passing the decision back to 1. Player 1 chooses between taking $160 (and 2 gets $40), or once again he can pass the decision on to 2. Player 2 chooses between taking $320 (in which case 1 gets $80) or he can pass, in which case player 1 gets $640 and 2 gets $160.

This situation has a unique subgame perfect equilibrium in which 1 takes the first offer of forty dollars. That is, the subgame perfect equilibrium strategy for both players is "Never pass the decision on to the other person." We suspect, nevertheless, that most people, if asked to play this game, will "take the chance" and postpone the initial offer. (Notice, moreover, that we could easily extend this game with additional moves so the "lost opportunity" of taking the first offer is quite great.) This conjecture may be unwarranted in general, but aside from the skepticism (and uneasiness) of game theorists about this solution, we do in fact have some experimental evidence to reject this subgame perfect equilibrium. The issue before us, then, is to identify the implicit or explicit assumptions that this example forces us to reconsider.

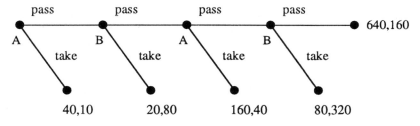

Figure 3.13 Centipede Game

One way to see the problem is to examine more carefully our analysis of the last decision nodes of players 1 and 2. In deriving the subgame perfect equilibrium, 2's last node begins a subgame, and our approach thus far is to suppose that whenever 2 is at such a node, 2 chooses his dominant strategy, which is to take the offer of $320. Working backward up the extensive form, this result leads 1 to the conclusion that, should he find himself at his next-to-last decision node, then he should accept the offer of $160, because passing the decision on to 1 will yield B a payoff of $80. Similarly, player 2 should choose at his first opportunity to take $80, rather than allow 1 to take $160, leaving 2 with $40. Finally, player 1 should initially choose $40 rather than allow 2 to take 80, leaving 1 with $20.

After analyzing the game in this way, though, 2 might pause and say to himself, "The only way I can reach my first decision node is if 1 makes an irrational initial choice. But if 1 is capable of irrationality at his first node, why should I assume that he is not capable of the same thing later. Moreover, player 1 is confronted with the same dilemma, since he must conclude that in order to reach his second decision node, I must have acted irrationally at my first opportunity to act. In any event, I cannot determine what rationality means in this context." Put differently, accepting as legitimate the implications of working backward up this extensive form appears to necessitate rejection of the rationality hypothesis, and, in particular, rejection of the supposition that the rationality of both players is common knowledge!

Such scenarios cause great consternation among game theorists, and in response, a number of solutions have been proposed. One solution (we postpone consideration of others until later chapters) is called **perfection** or **trembling hand perfection**. Briefly (and somewhat imperfectly),

> *An equilibrium is perfect if it is immune to the possibility that players, with some small probability, commit errors.*

In our example, for instance, suppose player 1 analyzes the game at his last node as follows: "Although taking $320 is 2's dominant final choice, there is some small probability (say *e*) that 2 will act irrationally or in accordance with a preference I have not anticipated, and will choose to let me have $640 instead. This possibility makes sense, moreover, since it is only an accumulation of such errors that explains how I might arrive at this decision node in the first place." Of course, once both players admit the possibility of error, they must then make expected utility calculations, and their ultimate decisions will depend on the magnitude of the error probabilities they assume are possible. At this time we cannot guess at those probabilities, but the notion of perfection requires that the presumed equilibrium remain an equilibrium for arbitrarily small probabilities of error.

Example: To first illustrate this idea in a more political context, suppose three voters all prefer alternative X over Y. Under majority rule, nevertheless, all three voting for Y is a Nash equilibrium since no person can unilaterally benefit by changing his or her vote. (Notice, though, that this is not an equilibrium that survives if we eliminate dominated strategies.) In evaluating this equilibrium, however, suppose each person acts on the supposition that each of the other voters has some small probability, e, of voting for X. Then the expected utility of continuing to vote for Y is

$$(1-e)^2 u(Y) + 2e(1-e)u(Y) + e^2 u(X)$$

and the expected utility of unilaterally shifting one's vote to X is

$$(1-e)^2 u(Y) + 2e(1-e)u(X) + e^2 u(X).$$

Since $u(X) > u(Y)$, the second expression is greater than the first, and so regardless of e's magnitude, our voter should switch to X—voting for Y is not perfect. A parallel argument, on the other hand, establishes that voting for X is perfect.

Thus, the idea of perfection eliminates the "silly" equilibrium in which everyone votes for the least preferred alternative.

To see the implications of this argument for our Centipede Game example with respect to the equilibrium we identify by working backward up the extensive form, let e be the probability 2 makes an error at his first decision node, and suppose player 1 is contemplating switching from "take $40" to "pass the decision on to 2, and if 2 passes on the decision, take $160." This alternative strategy yields an expected dollar payoff of $20(1-e) + 160e$, so if e is sufficiently great, passing on the decision makes sense. Nevertheless, only the strategy of accepting $40 initially corresponds to a perfect equilibrium since, if e is small enough, 40 exceeds $20(1-e) + 160e$.

Thus, although the notion of perfection eliminates some equilibria that are clearly bogus, it does not resolve all problems. We must still explain an action in our example that we believe is likely to be observed—a failure to accept the initial $10 offer. One way out of this dilemma, of course, is to suppose that people believe that the e's are quite large. However, this supposition opens new research topics, including the analysis of how people's beliefs about error might change as a game proceeds. We postpone consideration of such possibilities until chapter 5, though, and turn our attention in the next chapter to some games of special interest to political science. That chapter ends, then, with a somewhat tantalizing, but incomplete, hypothesis as how people might come to cooperate in our example so as to realize payoffs greater than $40 and $10.

Suggestions for Further Reading

The spatial elections model introduced in section 2.8 provides one of the most important ways of representing political preferences. It, as well as the Median Voter Theorem, can be attributed to Duncan Black, *The Theory of Committees and Elections*, Cambridge: Cambridge University Press, 1958. However, the seminal volume applying this perspective to elections is Anthony Downs, *An Economic Theory of Democracy*, New York: Harper and Row, 1957. A good general survey is given by James Enelow and Melvin Hinich, *The Spatial Theory of Voting*, New York: Cambridge University Press, 1984, and an edited volume by these same two authors, *Advances in the Spatial Theory of Voting*, New York: Cambridge University Press, 1989, will introduce the reader to current research efforts. With respect to the possibility of cycles in multidimensional models of elections, recall that the key result is provided in the essay by Charles Plott cited in the previous chapter. Although there are a number of subsequent elaborations, the fact that cycles can extend everywhere throughout the policy space was established by Richard D. McKelvey, "Intransitivities in Multidimensional Voting Models and Some Implications for Agenda Control," *Journal of Economic Theory*, 12 (1976): 472–82. The mathematically advanced reader should also consult R.D. McKelvey, "Covering, Dominance, and the Institution Free Properties of Social Choice," *American Journal of Political Science*, for a discussion of the limits that the concept of domination place on probable candidate platforms in spatial elections. These and other results in spatial theory are reviewed and interpreted in William H. Riker, *Liberalism Against Populism*, San Francisco: W.H. Freeman, 1983. In particular, Riker argues that the instability of majority rule that spatial analysis reveals ought to discourage "political engineers" from designing political systems that correspond to populist or direct democracy formats. For a clearly presented contrary view, however, see Jules Coleman and John Ferejohn, "Democracy and Social Choice," *Ethics*, 97 (1986): 6–25.

The Centipede Game that we discuss in section 3.13 was first presented in Robert Rosenthal, "Games of Perfect Information, Predatory Pricing, and the Chain Store Paradox," *Journal of Economic Theory*, 25 (1982): 92–100. This essay represents but a small piece of the research that seeks to refine equilibrium concepts beyond the ideas of Nash and subgame perfection. Such research, however, is best left to the advanced reader.

Exercises

1. A (row chooser) and B (column chooser) must play the following 2×2 game:

8,−8	4,−4
2,−2	6,−6

Beforehand B can pay four dollars to a third person to learn A's decision.

   a. Draw the full extensive form assuming that A does not know whether or not B purchased the information.

   b. Portray the corresponding strategic form.

   c. Solve the game for equilibrium strategies.

   d. Repeat part a assuming A moves first, at which time B can then pay A four dollars to learn A's choice.

2. Games A–C are all zero-sum. (Payoffs are to row chooser.) What is the expected value of game A for row chooser?

40	play game B
play game B	play game C

Game A

10	40
60	30

Game B

40	30
30	60
40	20

Game C

3. Find all the Nash equilibria for the following five 2-person, zero-sum strategic form games (all payoffs are to row chooser):

1	1	4	4
5	5	3	3

2	−2	3	−3	4	−4
2	−2	2	2	1	−1
1	−1	0	0	3	−3

5	−5	6	−6
7	−7	4	−4

100	100	2,000	20
20	2,000	1,000	1,000

0	2	0	1
1	0	−1	1

4. Does the following zero sum strategic form game possess a pure strategy equilibrium (games within cells are played if that cell is realized as a result of players' initial strategies)?

	b_1		b_2		b_3
a_1	10		1	3	6
			4	2	
a_2	7	10	10	20	6
	6	5	5	10	
a_3	8		5		5

5. The Median Voter Theorem states that if an election concerns one issue, the median preference of the electorate is an equilibrium in the sense that it cannot be beaten in a majority vote and that in two-candidate contests, both candidates should adopt the median preference as their platform. We also know that there is no such equilibrium with three candidates if those candidates choose their platforms simultaneously. However, is there a pure strategy equilibrium with four candidates? To simplify your argument, assume that the voter ideal points are spread out uniformly across the election issue, and assume either an even or odd number of voters, whichever facilitates your analysis.

6. Going into the home stretch of a research and development project, you are six months ahead of the competition. To bring the project to completion requires finishing the development stage, and you have two strategies: Risky and Safe. Safe take two years but is guaranteed to work. Risky takes only a year, but there is a fifty percent chance it will get you nowhere, in which case you will have to return to the safe strategy and take an additional two years. In six month your competitor (who cannot observe your decision) will confront an identical choice between Safe and Risky strategies with the same properties as your alternatives, and they too must switch to Safe if their Risky choice fails. Only the first to complete is awarded the patent, and due to limited resources it is not possible to pursue both strategies simultaneously.

   a. Which strategy should you pursue to maximize your chance of winning?

b.   Do you want to keep your move hidden?

7.   Draw the extensive form corresponding to the following description and solve for equilibrium strategies: "There are two dark boxes. Player 1 hides a pearl in one of them: then player 2, not knowing which box contains the pearl, peeks into one of them. If the pearl is in box 1 and she looks there, she sees it with a one-half probability. If it is in box 2 and she looks there, she sees it with a one-half probability. If she looks into the wrong box, she sees nothing (and is not even told that the box is empty)." The payoff is five to player 2 and minus five to 1 if 2 finds the pearl; otherwise there is no payment.

8.   Consider the following scenario: With one opportunity to bet remaining in the game show, player A has $7,200, player B has $5,000, and player C has $3,601. Assume that there is no benefit to being second versus third, and that the player with the most money wins that amount of money in cash. Each player must decide whether to bet All or Nothing. Prior to betting (which they must do simultaneously), nature tosses a fair coin to determine which "state of the world" will pertain: in State 1 persons A and B win their bets, but C loses; in State 2 persons A and B lose their bets, but C wins. Assume that if a player bets "all" and wins, his wealth is doubled. If he loses, his wealth is zero. If a player bets nothing, his wealth does not change. The player with the most money at the end of the game wins. Draw this situation's extensive form and show what each player does in equilibrium.

9.   "Cat" and "mouse" each start at opposite corners of the simple maze shown below. It takes five seconds for both animals to traverse one segment, but the passages are sufficiently narrow that neither animal can turn about in the maze. If the cat eats the mouse, its payoff is +1 and the mouses's is −1; otherwise these payoffs are reversed. After twenty seconds, the mouse, if available, will be rescued from the maze.

    a.   Letting a strategy be a complete plan as to which way to turn (left, right, straight ahead) at each juncture in the maze, does this game possess an equilibrium in pure strategies, assuming that neither the cat nor the mouse can observe the other as it traverses the maze (until of course, it is "too late")?

    b.   Does your answer change if the mouse is rescued only after thirty seconds?

c. Does your answer to part (a) change if both the cat and the mouse can observe what the other does after each 5-second interval? If so, how and why?

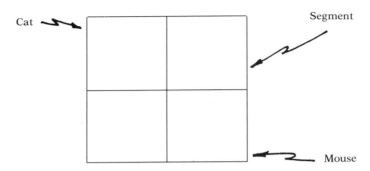

10. Prior to playing a game, a fair coin is tossed to determine which of the following two games will actually be played:

9, 5	1, −3		3, 0	9, −2
3, 7	4, 6		9, 9	3, 8

If neither player observes the outcome of the coin toss, how much would 1 (the row chooser) pay to learn the outcome of the toss (assume that all payoffs game are in terms of dollars and that utility and money are equivalent) and for what information cost is 2 indifferent between learning and not learning the outcome of the coin toss?

11. You are a member of a committee that must decide between A and B. As things stand now B defeats A, but you hate B, so you've introduced alternative, C, which will be put to a vote against B; then the winner will be pitted against A. You are hoping that C will beat B, but lose to A. The outcome, though, depends on your argument for C and the argument of your opponent. The social ordering will be determined by those arguments. Your preferences are A > C > B, and your opponent's preferences are B > C > A. You (row chooser) and your opponent (column chooser) each have two alternative arguments, and they yield the following social preference orders under majority rule:

	Argument 1	Argument 2
Argument 1	B > C > A (transitive)	C > A > B > C (a cycle)
Argument 2	C > B > A > C (a cycle)	C > B > A (transitive)

If you must each choose an argument without knowing your opponent's choice, and if everyone is sophisticated, what outcome prevails?

12. Let two political candidates each have two strategies as indicated in the table below, and let the probability that candidate 1 receives specific pluralities from the four possible joint strategy choices also be as indicated. If the objective of both candidates is to maximize their probability of winning the election, what, if any, is the equilibrium to this game? How does this equilibrium change if both candidates seek to maximize their expected plurality?

$p(0) = 5/8$ $p(400) = 1/8$ $p(800) = 2/8$	$p(8) = 1/2$ $p(0) = 1/8$ $p(-80) = 3/8$
$p(-400) = 1/2$ $p(400) = 1/2$	$p(0) = 3/4$ $p(-75) = 1/8$ $p(-125) = 1/8$

13. Referring to our discussion of Figure 3.10 and mediation, show that if both players are fully informed about the mediator's advice—about the advice given to the other player—then the mediator's role as a coordinator of strategy vanishes.

14. Consider the following *false* "theorem," and find both a zero sum and a non-zero-sum counterexample: "If a two-player game has no pure strategy equilibrium, it has a unique mixed strategy equilibrium."

15. Players 1 and 2, acting simultaneously, must each first choose whether to play L or R. If they both play L, they then play game

A below (all payoffs are in dollars); otherwise, the toss of a fair coin determines whether game B or C is played. (The outcome of the toss is revealed immediately.) Prior to their initial choice, though, player 1 (row chooser) can offer 2 any amount of money for the right to make 2's choice of R or L. Determine what amount, if any, player 1 ought to offer 2 as well as the value of the scenario to players 1 and 2.

0,4	0,2
4,2	1,1

A

1,3	2,1
4,3	3,2

B

1,4	6,1
5,1	0,4

C

16. Recall the game from elementary school called "one, twice, three, shoot." One of the players chooses "even" and the other player gets "odd." On the count of three, each of the two players simultaneously casts out either one or two fingers. If the total number of fingers is even, then the "even" player wins, while if the sum is odd, then the "odd" player wins. Suppose the payoff is one for the winner and minus one for the loser.

   a. Show the extensive and strategic forms for this game.

   b. Show that this game has no pure strategy equilibria.

   c. Prove that "acting randomly" is the only equilibrium.

   d. Suppose the rules of the game are changed so that at the count of three a person can hesitate. If both hesitate, each receives a payoff of 2, whereas if only one hesitates, that player loses 1 and the opponent gets 0. What is the outcome now?

17. Consider the following two games:

10, 4	4, 0
8, 2	8, 6

14, 14	4, 16
10, 2	0, 20

   a. If a coin is flipped to determine which game will be played, what is the Nash equilibrium of the situation in which neither player knows the outcome of the coin flip and the players choose their strategies simultaneously?

b. Model part (a) in extensive form.

c. If, in part (a), one of the players can pay the coin flipper, who is not one of the game players, to reveal the outcome of the coin toss to both players before they choose their strategies, which player (row or column) would be willing to pay more for this information?

d. Suppose that instead of a coin toss and simultaneous moves, one of the players is allowed to choose the game to be played, and that after revealing that choice to the other player, the players chose their strategies in sequence, first column chooser, then row chooser. Find the Nash equilibria for the following four games that this scenario allows.

i. Row chooses the game and goes first.

ii. Row chooses the game and column goes first.

iii. Column chooses the game and row goes first.

iv. Column chooses the game and goes first.

18. In a two player game the following pairs of actions lead to the following outcomes:

(Player 1 Action, Player 2 Action) → *(1's Utility, 2's Utility)*

(L,L)	*(3,6)*
(R,R)	*(1,5)*
(C,C)	*(6,8)*
(L,R)	*(9,6)*
(R,L)	*(9,9)*
(L,C)	*(6,1)*
(C,L)	*(2,2)*
(R,C)	*(4,4)*
(C,R)	*(4,3)*

a. What is the outcome of this game if 1 goes first and 2 observes 1's action and then chooses his own action?

b. What is the outcome if 2 goes first and 1 observes 2's action and then chooses her own action?

c. What is the outcome if each player has to choose an action before he or she knows the other player's action?

    d. A third player enters the game. If the third player chooses L he gets the average of the payoff to players 1 and 2 for any given outcome. If the third player chooses R, he gets a payoff equal to whichever of player 1's payoff or player 2's payoff is higher. What is the outcome of the game where 1 goes first, 2 observes 1's action and chooses, and then 3 observes 1 and 2's actions and chooses.

    e. What is the outcome of the three player game if all players must choose their actions at the same time?

19. Persons 1, 2, and 3 each have a budget of B dollars, which must be allocated between goods x and y at unit prices (i.e., p_x, $p_y = 1$). Person i's utility is $u_i = x^{a_i}y$, where $a_1 > a_2 > a_3$. There are the following ways of making final decisions about how much of x and y each person will consume:

    a. People independently make decisions in the open market,

    b. With the government expropriating all wealth, two candidates for "dictator" each announce an election platform that corresponds to an identical (and feasible) commodity bundle for each person; the three persons then vote for one candidate or the other, and the victorious candidate implements his or her platform,

    c. A "dictator" is selected thus: person 1 vetoes one person from this set, and person 2 vetoes one of the remaining two persons. The survivor, using the government's budget, then selects a representative feasible commodity bundle that each person must consume.

        i. Describe each person's preferences over his or her budget constraint,

      ii. Describe the outcomes achieved under each method,

    iii. What effect if any would an expansion of the problem to three commodities have on the analysis?

4

Some Special Political Games

We have not yet developed all of the tools required to model every political process that might interest us. For example, we cannot treat situations in which people have private information about their preferences or about their capabilities, we cannot model situations in which games can repeat themselves, and we cannot yet deal with the important processes of cooperative action and coalition formation. However, so that we do not become immersed too quickly in abstract reasoning, this chapter focuses on some applications of the ideas presented in the previous chapters.

1. This chapter begins by returning to two-candidate elections in order to start the process of incorporating some additional complexity into the basic spatial model described briefly in chapters 2 and 3. Specifically, we consider how nonvoting, the electoral college, and the threat of entry by third party candidates affect our conclusions about the existence and nature of an equilibrium as embodied thus far in the Median Voter Theorem.

2. We then examine an institutional design problem—finding a mechanism that induces people to reveal truthfully their preferences over alternative policy proposals. Although we focus on a specific example, the general problem of designing political and economic institutions is profoundly important, because it moves our discipline from its dreamy "ivory tower" to a practical realm. Game theory's contribution is that instead of offering proposals on the basis of wishful thinking and vague propositions, it forces us to think about how people interact strategically when their actions are constrained by specific rules.

3. Then we show how game-theoretic reasoning can cast light on two potentially paradoxical issues—whether political parties are necessarily advantaged by increasing their representation in a legislative body, and whether is it better to commit oneself before others in voting or whether it is better to remain uncommitted in the hope of later being pivotal for one outcome or another. From these examples one might conclude that simple operationalizations of the concept of "power" equate with the mere accumulation of some resource (e.g., money, votes, military capability). This is misleading, because these examples fail to consider how others might respond to this accumulation.

4. We survey the applications of an especially important game— the Prisoners' Dilemma—which allows us to identify the common theoretical principles that are required to understand such seemingly diverse matters as classical justifications for the state, arms races, and the inefficiencies of markets and of governments. Finally, we turn to the concepts of evolutionary stable strategies, which, although not fully developed in the literature, may in the future supply us with an understanding of such topics as the emergence of altruism and the maintenance of legislative norms.

4.1 Two-Candidate Elections and the Electoral College

Perhaps no class of strategic environments lies more at the heart of democratic processes than that of two-candidate elections, and from the Median Voter Theorem we have already seen how using the ideas of dominant strategies and Nash equilibria provides some understanding of the policy biases inherent in such elections. To illustrate the additional insights that can be gained with modest effort, in this section we extend our analysis to consider the electoral college in presidential elections.

Most state and local elections in the United States use a simple winner-take-all, plurality rule format, but presidential elections are different. Rather than elect a president directly, a presidential candidate's vote in a particular state counts for nothing unless that candidate secures a positive plurality there. And even if the candidate's margin in a state is a single vote, that candidate wins all of that state's electoral vote (equal to the number of representatives from that state in the U.S. House, plus two). The winning candidate, in turn, must win a majority of electoral votes. A variety of issues arise, then, with respect to this somewhat peculiar election system. These issues include (1) the possibility that someone can win the presidency with a negative popular vote plurality, (2) the extent to which the electoral college, as compared to a national direct popular vote, discourages third parties, (3) the advantage given to small versus large states, and (4) potential policy biases.

We cannot address all of these issues, but we can begin to see some of the electoral college's influences by first considering the more general form of the redistributive election, which we discussed in section 3.3 in a three-voter context.

Example: Suppose two candidates, A and B, compete over how some fixed amount of money, X, is to be distributed among n voters, where a_i is the amount candidate A proposes to give to voter i and b_i is the amount candidate B proposes for that same voter. If we require that the sum of the a_i's and of the b_i's equal X (thereby ignoring the macroeconomic effects of tax policy), if voters vote for the candidate who promises them the greatest amount of money (thereby precluding altruism), and if the candidates' only goal is to win the election, then we have in effect described a simple two-person zero-sum game, and the question is whether such a game has a Nash equilibrium.

To see that this game does not have an equilibrium in pure strategies and that it is a game incumbent candidates prefer to avoid playing, suppose that n is odd, and, without loss of generality, suppose that the sum of the allocations A proposes for voters 1 through $(n-1)/2$ equals $K > 0$. That is, let

$$a_1 + a_2 + \ldots + a_{(n-1)/2} = K > 0.$$

Then, regardless of the remaining details of A's platform, candidate B can secure the support of a minimal majority and defeat A by merely setting b_1 through $b_{(n-1)/2}$ equal to 0 and by proposing that voters $(n+1)/2$ through n be awarded

$$a_i + 2K/(n+1).$$

That is, B awards voters $(n+1)/2$ through n the same as candidate A plus an equal share of whatever A proposed for voters 1 through $(n-1)/2$. Clearly, voters $(n+1)/2$ through n prefer candidate B's promise, and since these voters constitute a majority, we see that every strategy is defeated by some other allocation.

And since the game is otherwise a symmetric contest between the two candidates, it follows from our discussion of symmetric zero-sum games that no such pure strategy can be a Nash equilibrium.

This example points to at least one disadvantage shared by incumbent candidates with respect to securing reelection and it illuminates the reasons why they prefer to downplay tax reform issues in an election year. No matter what position an incumbent advocates, a challenger can find a strategy that a majority prefers over the incumbent's position.

This example has other interpretations. For instance, it illustrates a problem for presidential candidates in deciding how to allocate campaign resources such as time and money under the electoral college. Suppose that all a candidate must do to win in a state is allocate more resources to the state than the opponent. Because the electoral college has evolved into a winner-take-all contest within each state (the candidate with the most votes in a state receives all of that state's electoral votes), states are the same as the voters in our example (except that they are not equally weighted). Hence, if the candidates begin with an equal supply of resources (e.g., time), then, regardless of whatever allocations are planned, at least one candidate will prefer a different strategy.

Now consider the issue of whether we can say anything about the policy biases of this particular feature of presidential elections. In this context we note that one of the favorite forms of testimony before congressional committees evaluating reform of the electoral college envolves examining previous votes to show what would have happened had a different electoral rule been in effect. However, although its use of "numbers and hard facts" may give this exercise a certain measure of respectability, it cannot be justified on theoretical grounds, because it supposes that voters will vote the same and that candidates will campaign the same, regardless of procedure.

To see, then, how we might address the issue of ascertaining the policy biases of the electoral college when we assume candidates adjust their strategies to the procedural context of the election, suppose two candidates must compete on a single policy dimension on which all voters have well defined (single-peaked) preferences. The Median Voter Theorem tells us, of course, that if the election were held by direct vote, without the intervention of the electoral college, both candidates should converge to the electorate's median preference. But in addition if we apply this result to individual states, we

see that there is an equilibrium policy position within each state—
if preferences are single-peaked overall, then they are single-peaked
among any subset of citizens. However, the formal proof of the Median Voter Theorem can be extended to imply something stronger.

> *If preferences are single-peaked, then, not only does the median pref-*
> *erence stand highest on the social preference order under majority rule*
> *(because it is the Condorcet winner), but the order is wholly transi-*
> *tive—if x and y are two alternatives to the same side of the median,*
> *and if x is closer to the median than is y, then x defeats y; and if z is*
> *any other alternative such that y defeats z, then x defeats z.*

Thus, at least in those instances in which a single dominant issue
occupies the stage, we can be anthropomorphic in our thinking and
we can speak of a state as a voter with an ideal point at the median
ideal point of the voters in that state, with a utility function that
declines monotonically as we move away from the median in either
direction, and with a voting weight equal to its vote in the electoral
college.

Using this argument to analyze the potential policy biases of the
electoral college, consider the following simple example:

Example: Suppose there are three states with 7, 5, and 3 voters
and three alternative policy platforms. Figure 4.1 gives a possible preference distribution in these states and shows that, although more than half of the voters most prefer policy 1, which
is thereby the equilibrium platform in a two-candidate direct
vote election, policy 2 is the median preference in states 2 and
3. So, regardless of whether electoral votes are awarded to states
on the basis of their population, or whether each state receives
two extra electoral votes, the electoral votes of states 2 and 3
are sufficient to ensure that policy 2 is the equilibrium platform
under the electoral college.

Our example shows, then, that the electoral college can occasion a
policy distortion whenever there is a strong asymmetry in the distribution of preferences within states. Of course, without some appropriate data about preferences, we cannot say whether this distortion has been significant historically or whether it is significant
today. But we can now see how the Median Voter Theorem gives us
a handle on exploring this issue further. In particular, it shows us
how we might approach the debate over whether the electoral college or a direct vote favors urban versus rural voters, blacks versus
whites, industrial workers versus agricultural workers, and so forth.

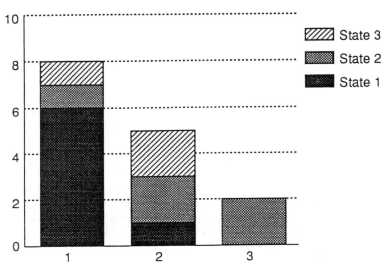

Figure 4.1: Policy Bias With the Electorial College

4.2 Turnout and Responsible Political Parties

The Median Voter Theorem tells us that under some fairly severe assumptions, majority rule elections exhibit a strong force on the two major parties that move the election platforms of those two parties toward the "center" of the electorate's preference distribution. However, believing that candidates or their parties would be "responsible," and believing that being responsible necessitates providing "meaningful" choices for voters, many commentators on American politics bemoan the empirical manifestations of "convergence to the median." Typically, these same commentators lament the low voter turnout rates that characterize U.S. elections (as compared to the turnout rates of other democracies). Some persons blame these rates on the indistinguishability of the candidates while others blame the indistinguishability on these rates—implying that, whatever the relationship, these is something amiss in America's democracy. Let us explore the issue of whether low turnout levels and candidates who fail to be distinct are symptomatic of "something wrong" with the way majority rule functions.

Suppose, in particular, that not only are citizens willing to abstain from voting, but (in accordance with the equation specifying expected utility of voting versus abstaining that we derived in chapter 1) that their frequency of voting is a function of the utility difference they perceive between the nominees of the two major parties. Thus, let us formulate a model in which citizens punish candidates (by staying home on election day) for failing to provide a distinct choice. In particular, assume that if the two candidates converge identically to the median, then, regardless of policy preference, each citizen's probability of voting is some small number $0 < p_o << 1$. Assume further that the feasible policy space that serves as the candidates' alternative election strategies is represented by the interval $[0,1]$ and that each person's utility for the policy x is given by the function

$$u_i(x) = 1 - |(x_i - x)|$$

where x_i denotes the citizen's ideal position on the issue and where $|.|$ denotes absolute value. Thus, utility declines linearly as we move away in either direction from a person's ideal. Finally, to model abstention, suppose person i's probability of voting is given by the function

$$p_i(A,B) = p_o + a|u_i(x_A) - u_i(x_B)|,$$

where a is some number which ensures that $p_i(A,B)$ doesn't exceed 1, and A and B are the positions adopted in the election by candidates A and B respectively. Thus, in accordance with the idea that voters ought to punish candidates for appearing similar and that they should reward a preferred candidate for offering a choice that is distinct from the opponent, the probability of voting increases as the utility difference between the candidates increases. With respect to specific probabilities of voting as a function of a voter's ideal,

1. A voter whose ideal lies precisely midway between x_A and x_B is indifferent between the candidates' policy positions. Thus, such a voter votes with the minimum probability, p_o.

2. Assuming, without loss of generality, that $x_A < x_B$, a voter to the left of x_A votes with probability

$$p_o + a|u_i(x_A) - u_i(x_B)| = $$
$$p_o + a|1 + (x_i - x_A) - 1 - (x_i - x_B)| = $$
$$p_o + a|x_A - x_B|,$$

which is a constant since this probability does not depend

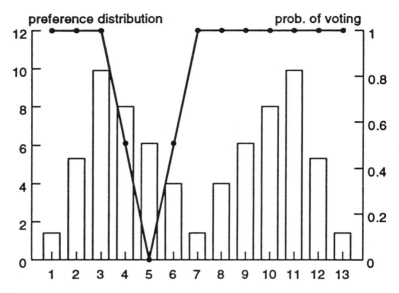

Figure 4.2: Equilibrium With Abstentions

on x_i. Similarly, everyone with ideal points to the right of x_B vote with the same constant probability.

3. As we move from x_A to $(x_A+x_B)/2$, the probability of voting declines from $p_o + a|x_A - x_B|$ to p_o, and as we move from $(x_A+x_B)/2$ to x_B, it increases from p_o to $p_o + a|x_A - x_B|$.

The dark line in Figure 4.2 illustrates this function for $p_o = 0$.

Now consider the remaining part of Figure 4.2, which shows a symmetric and bimodal distribution of preferences for an electorate of sixty seven voters. We've located candidate B at the median preference, policy 7, and candidate A at one of the two modes of the distribution, policy 3. Notice first that, because the probability of voting is a constant (0) through the electorate if A and B both choose the median, such convergence implies a tie. Candidate A's shift from the median increases turnout, but the question is whether this shift A produces any gain for A. To see that the answer is "No," notice that by moving to 3, A increases the probability of voting of all voters at and to the right of the median to 1, and these voters prefer B. In addition, B gets additional expected votes from voters with ideal points at 6, and thereby is the expected victor. In fact, this move by A yields B an expected vote of 36 and yields A an expected vote of

21; so A's expected plurality declines from zero to -12 if he shifts from the median to 3.

Of course, our model is especially simple, and a more realistic one should consider more general utility functions in multidimensional issue spaces, as well as more general relationships between utility and probabilities of voting. Nevertheless, the implications of this example are clear. First, a low turnout rate does not indicate necessarily that there is something amiss in democracy. Indeed, it may indicate that democratic institutions are working as intended and that low turnout is the result of there not being rigidities in the system precluding one party or the other from nominating an effective candidate. High turnout, on the other hand, might indicate that extremist activists in one party or the other have gained control of that party's nomination processes and secured the nomination of a candidate that cannot win and that is removed from the mainstream of public opinion. Second, our example establishes that the failure of the two parties to nominate candidates who offer distinct choices may be merely the logical consequence of majority rule electoral institutions. Thus, those who bemoan this fact must propose different institutions and must offer good arguments why median policies, in the abstract, are inferior to policies that lie nearer one extreme or the other.

4.3 Elections With More Than Two Candidates

The preceding discussion assumes that there are only two candidates or parties. This assumption makes our analysis especially simple for two reasons: (1) We can rely on the specialized results about two-person zero-sum games as well as about symmetric versions of those games; and (2) citizens are presented with a relatively simple task of abstaining or voting for the candidate they most prefer. Once we admit the possibility of more than two candidates, however, a number of new questions arise:

1. If parties or candidates are free to enter an election, what is the equilibrium number of parties?

2. If parties or candidates are free to enter an otherwise two-party system, what strategies will the two established parties adopt in anticipation of new entrants or in the attempt to forestall entry?

3. If the number of candidates exceeds two, what spatial positions are in equilibrium?

4. If voters must choose among more than two candidates, how
    can we accommodate the fact that some voters may choose
    to vote for their second-ranked candidate whenever their
    most-preferred candidate has little chance of winning?

Of course, each of these questions is related to the others. Any
completely general analysis must answer the fourth question, for example, before it can satisfactorily answer the first or the second. And
at this point we must admit that we do not have general answers to
all of these questions. Instead, we can answer certain questions by
assuming answers to the others. The vast opportunities for research
are made even more apparent, moreover, if we realize that winner-
take-all plurality rule is but one voting procedure out of a vast array
of possibilities. Other possibilities include elections in which several
candidates can be elected simultaneously from the same constituency. Even this system has multiple variants that include allowing
voters a single vote that they can cast for one candidate versus allowing them to vote for more than one candidate. And in the event
that elections are merely a preliminary step to the selection of a
chief executive in the context of a parliamentary system of government, voters must be concerned as well with how their selection of
candidates affects the process of coalition formation in parliament.

We cannot begin to address the vast array of theoretical issues
that arise when we contemplate the variety of electoral institutions.
Nor can we survey the research, however limited, that already exists
about such matters. Instead, let us focus in a simple way on the second question that we list above—the strategies that two established
candidates take in anticipation of the entry of a third candidate.

Example: Assume that an election concerns a single issue that
can be represented by the line segment $[0,1]$, that all voters vote
sincerely for the candidate closest to their ideal, and that voter
ideal points are distributed uniformly on the interval $[0,1]$. If
we suppose now that candidates 1 and 2 must simultaneously
choose their spatial positions, c_1 and c_2, respectively, before candidate 3 chooses a position, then what we want to show is that
$c_1 = .25$ and $c_2 = .75$ is an equilibrium, and that candidate 3
sets his strategy, c_3, at $.50$—that is, the 3-tuple $(.25,.75,.50)$ is
an equilibrium. To prove this we first establish two simple
facts about our model. The first fact comes from the assumption
that voters vote on the basis of which candidate is closest to
their ideal, so if x is to the left of y, then all voters to the left of
$(x+y)/2$—the midpoint between x and y—prefer x to y whereas
all voters to the right of $(x+y)/2$ prefer y to x. The second fact

comes from the assumption that voter ideal points are distributed uniformly over the interval [0,1]. Thus, if only those voters in the interval $[x,y]$ most prefer candidate i, then candidate i's share of the vote is $y-x$, because, with a uniform distribution, this difference measures the share of the electorate with ideal points in the interval $[x,y]$.

Proceeding now by backward reduction, we look first at candidate 3's responses to the various strategies of candidates 1 and 2. A simple paper-and-pencil exercise reveals that at the presumed equilibrium, candidate 3 receives one quarter of the vote and that its vote share remains constant if it moves to the left or right, provided that it stays between .25 and .75. If, on the other hand, it moves to the left of candidate 1 or to the right of candidate 2, then its vote share must be less than one quarter. Hence, given that 1 and 2 choose .25 and .75, respectively, candidate 3 has no positive incentive to choose any position other than .50.

Now consider the possibility that candidate 1 chooses a position closer to the center, such as .3. Without the threat of candidate 3, such a move increases 1's share of the vote. But now candidate 1 should anticipate that 3's best response is to forgo positions between $c_1 = .3$ and $c_2 = .75$ and to choose instead a position slightly to 1's left, which gives candidate 3 approximately 30% of the vote. Candidate 1, then, gets the votes of all voters whose ideal points lie between .30 and the midpoint between c_1 and c_2—$(.30 + .75)/2 = .525$. Hence, 1's share of the vote, after 3's response, is .525 -.30 = .225, which is less than what 1 gets if he had simply stayed at the original equilibrium strategy of .25.

An equivalent argument establishes that candidate 2 will not want to move away from .75 toward the median; and a similar argument shows that neither candidate 1 nor candidate 2 has any incentive to adopt a position further from the median preference than .25 and .75, respectively. Thus, the strategy pair (.25,.75) is an equilibrium, which tells us why two candidates, fearing the entry of a third competitor, choose not to converge to the electorate's median preference.

From the assumption that preferences are uniformly distributed, it is straightforward to calculate that a third candidate cannot secure more than 25% of the vote, regardless of what point in the interval [0,1] it chooses as its platform. This fact raises the question of why a third candidate would enter in the first place. However, we should keep in mind that it is the threat of entry rather than its realization that causes divergence from the median. We can easily imagine an electoral dynamic, then, in which candidates 1 and 2 try to differentiate themselves by setting their platforms away from the median at the early stages of a campaign; but as the threat of a third candidate entry fades, both candidates should then try to shift their positions toward the median.

Before jumping to empirical applications, however, we should accommodate the possibility that some voters will not vote sincerely for a third candidate if that candidate has no chance of success. And, indeed, we can begin to discern in such examples a theoretical basis for Duverger's hypothesis that simple plurality rule fosters competition between two as against three or more, parties—although our model is far too simple to allow us to validate that hypothesis.

4.4 The Single Transferable Vote

With the exception of our brief discussion of the electoral college, to this point we have been concerned largely with simple majority or plurality-rule systems. However, one of the important potential contributions of game theory is the analysis of alternative voting procedures. Admittedly, few alternative election systems have been analyzed to date with any great care, and we suspect that such analyses will be a fruitful area of future research. Here, however, we will illustrate some of the basic principles of game theory by considering a rather complex election procedure—Hare voting, which is also called the single transferable vote procedure.

Example: Hare voting, named after its inventor in 1850, Sir Thomas Hare, seeks to ensure proportional representation when a committee of m members must be selected from $n > m$ candidates within a single constituency. Its potential advantage, then, is that it is an alternative to securing proportionality by manipulating district boundaries in a single-member district system, which commonly results in rancorous debates and lengthy court cases. In its simple form, then, this procedure operates as follows:

1. Each voter, $j = 1, 2, \ldots, v$, begins with a voting weight, w_j, equal to 1.

2. Each voter casts a ballot that ranks the n candidates from first to last. (We could assume that voters submit partial lists,

but this possibility complicates the analysis since it greatly expands voter strategies.)

3. Letting

$$W_i = \sum_{j=1}^{v} \delta_j w_j$$

where $\delta_j = 1$ if voter j's ballot currently ranks candidate i first, and equals 0 otherwise, then candidate i is elected if

$$W_i \geq q = It\left[\frac{v}{m+1}\right] + 1$$

where "It" represents "integer portion of."

4. There are now two possibilities:

    a. The requirement that $W_i \geq q$ fails to hold for any candidate. First, strike from all ballots the names of those candidates who receive no first-place votes. Then delete from the ballots the names of those candidates who receive the fewest first-place votes. In the event of ties, use a fair lottery to eliminate candidates. (If the number of candidates surviving at any stage in this process equals the number of seats to be filled, then those candidates are elected.) Return to step 3.

    b. The requirement that $W_i > q$ holds for at least one candidate. Elect all candidates for whom $W_i > q$, and delete their names from all ballots.

5. If candidate i is elected, then, after deleting i from all ballots, set

$$w_j = (W_i - q)/K$$

for voters who had i ranked first on their ballots at the time if i's deletion where K is the number of ballots that rank i first. Return to step 3 unless all committee positions are
filled.

Example: To illustrate this procedure in an especially simple situation, suppose nine voters, who must choose two candidates from the set {*a,b,c*}, submit the following ballots ranking these candidates:

a	a	a	a	a	b	b	c	c
b	b	c	c	c	a	c	a	b
c	c	b	b	b	c	a	b	a

The quota *q*, in this instance, is 4, which candidate *a* satisfies. Thus, *a* is elected, and is deleted from all ballots. But notice that *a* actually receives 5 votes—one more than the quota. So in this example, the first five voters—those who ranked *a* first and who can be thought of as having used four fifths of their vote to elect *a*—are each reassigned the voting weight $w_a = (5 - 4)/5 = 1/5$. At this point, the vote for *b* totals 12/5 whereas the vote for *c* totals 13/5. Since neither of the remaining two candidates meets the quota, candidate *b*, with the lowest vote total, is eliminated and *c* joins *a* on the committee.

Suppose now that one or more of these voters contemplates voting strategically—that is, let us ask whether sincere voting is a Nash equilibrium

> **Example (continued)**: Consider whether a voter holding the preference "*a* preferred to *b* preferred to *c*" secures any advantage by ranking *b* above *a*. If one such voter does so, then candidate *a*'s vote equals the quota but *a* has no excess votes to transfer to *b* or to *c* after being elected. After *a* is elected and eliminated from all ballots, candidate *b* has three first-place votes while *c* has but two. Candidate *c*, then, is eliminated and *b* is elected. Thus, insincerity in the form of ranking *b* above *a* is rewarded.

Of course, we cannot conclude from this discussion that the final outcome will be {*a,b*} since we have not shown that an insincere ballot by a single voter is an equilibrium.[1]

> **Example**: The previous example is uninteresting in one sense—the Condorcet winner, *a*, is elected regardless of whether any individual defects from sincerity. Generally, we prefer that Con-

---

[1]Whether the described defection yields an equilibrium depends on attitudes towards risk. Let a voter who holds the preference "*a* preferred to *c* preferred to *b*" contemplate responding to the first defection by ranking *c* above *a*. Now all candidates have three first-place votes, so one of them must be eliminated by chance. Thus, this voter's action depends on whether {*a,b*} is preferred to an equiprobable lottery over {*a,b*}, {*a,c*}, and {*b,c*}.

dorcet winners be selected if they exist, but there is no guarantee that Hare voting elects such a candidate. To see this, suppose 38, 37, and 24 voters, respectively, hold each of the following
three preference orders over five candidates:

a	b	c
e	d	d
d	e	e
b	c	a
c	a	b

If three candidates are to be selected, $q = 25$ and the final outcome is $\{a,b,e\}$—a and b are elected with 13 and 12 excess votes,
respectively, which gives 13 votes to e, 12 to d, and 24 to c. Since
no candidate meets the quota, the candidate with the fewest votes,
d, is eliminated, electing e with 25 first-place votes. But d is a
Condorcet winner and since it is never the case that any individual is pivotal, no one has an incentive to defect from sincerity
by casting a insincere ballot.

This example, however, is reminiscent of those voting situations
in which "bogus" equilibria exist whenever no individual voter is
pivotal that can only be eliminated by the notions of subgame perfection, perfection, or elimination by weak domination. Thus, ascertaining whether sincere voting is a reasonable equilibrium in this
example and learning whether the Condorcet winner is unlikely to
be elected requires the application of these ideas. Instead, though,
let us consider another example that shows that Condorcet winners
need not be elected in equilibrium even when individual voters are
pivotal.

Example: Suppose 25, 25, 25, 8, 8, and 8 voters, respectively,
hold the following six preference orders over four candidates:

a	b	c	d	d	d
d	d	d	a	b	c
b	c	a	b	c	a
c	a	b	c	a	b

If three candidates are to be elected, then $q = 25$, and the sincere
voting outcome is $\{a,b,c\}$ even though d is a Condorcet winner.
Notice now that if a voter such as one that holds the first preference ranks d first, the outcome is $\{d,b,c\}$. But under any reasonable assumption as to how preferences over sets of candi-

dates relate to preferences over individual candidates, $\{d,b,c\}$ is the voter's least preferred possibility. Thus, this voter (and by similar reasoning, all others), has no incentive to shift unilaterally to an insincere ballot.

After admitting that Condorcet winners need not be selected by Hare voting, there is one final possibility that we might consider— namely, that insincere voting, whenever it does occur, renders the selection of a Condorcet winner more likely. However, as our final example shows, insincere voting can actually lead away from the selection of such a winner.

Example: Ignoring the preferences in parentheses for the moment, suppose 18, 17, 32, and 32 voters respectively hold the following four preference orders:

a	a	(c)	c	b
b	c	(a)	b	a
c	b	(b)	a	c

If everyone votes sincerely, a is elected because its vote, 35, exceeds the quota of 34—at which point b is elected because its share of a's excess vote exceeds c's share, thereby breaking the tie between b and c in favor of b. So the Condorcet winner, b, is elected in a sincere ballot. Now consider the incentives to be strategic. In particular, suppose a voter of the second type casts a ballot that corresponds to the preference in parenthesis. As before, a is elected, but now c's vote exceeds b's so b is eliminated on the second round. The reader can confirm, moreover, that this single insincere ballot is an equilibrium.

Aside from the questions about Hare voting that they reveal, our examples show that no voting procedure can be understood completely until we explore fully the incentives of voters to act strategically. But this fact raises a new question, namely whether any voting procedure is immune to the possibility that voters will choose to act strategically. That is, is there any procedure that is guaranteed to elicit "honest" preferences from voters. This is the issue to which we turn next.

4.5 Manipulation and Incentive Compatibility

Of all the political institutions studied by using the tools this volume reviews, elections receive the closest scrutiny. Let us, however,

leave elections to consider a different problem. Recall that our discussion of agendas shows that revealed preferences do not always
correspond to sincere preferences—to the preferences people actually hold over outcomes. Of course, the possibility that one might
have an incentive to misrepresent one's true preferences should not
come as any great surprise. Nevertheless, the misrepresentation we
see in simple agenda voting, and the fact that the details of an
agenda—the order in which the motions are brought to the floor for
a vote—can profoundly affect final outcomes, signals the importance of this subject. Indeed, such examples reveal an important
avenue of research—studying how political institutions affect people's incentives to reveal one type of preference as against another.
After all, democracies place great store in public opinion, and it would
help to know how to gauge that opinion in the context of our political institutions.

Research into learning how one agenda leads to one outcome
whereas another agenda leads to a different outcome and learning
the incentives to vote strategically in agendas constitute a small part
of a more general enterprise—**institutional design**—the design of social institutions that guide actions so that once people are free to
act within the constraints set by those institutions, outcomes of one
sort but not of another prevail. On a grand scale, of course, the Framers of the U.S. Constitution understood that institutional design
was an important component of political theory. They also understood the nature of the problem in immediate practical terms. For
example, in his notes on the Constitutional Convention, Madison offers this summary of Benjamin Franklin's views on the method of
selecting judges:[2]

> Doctor Franklin observed, that the two modes of choosing the
> Judges had been mentioned, to wit, by the Legislature, and by
> the Executive. He wished such other modes to be suggested as
> might occur to other gentlemen; it being a point of great mo-
> ment. He would mention one which he had understood was
> practised in Scotland. He then, in a brief and entertaining man-
> ner, related a Scotch mode, in which the nomination proceeded
> from the lawyers, who always selected the ablest of the profes-
> sion, in order to get rid of him, and share his practice among
> themselves. It was here, he said, the interest of the electors to
> make the best choice, which should always be made the case if
> possible.

---

[2]James Madison, *Journal of the Federal Convention.* E.H. Scott, ed. Chicago: Scott,
Foresman and Co., pp. 108–9, 1989.

The particular problem of institutional design confronting the Framers in this instance was ensuring that those who selected judges would, acting in their own self-interest, select able judges. Put differently, they sought an institution that was **incentive compatible** in the sense that equilibrium behavior would yield able judges.

In more contemporary terms, the problem of institutional design and incentive compatibility confronts legislators when empowering an executive agency to act. Will the interests of decision makers within the agency lead them to act so as to achieve the outcomes Congress desires, and how can Congress design an agency and mechanisms for monitoring agency performance so as to shape those interests in a particular way? What bureaucratic structure should regulate federal-state interactions? What are the advantages and disadvantages of a parliamentary system of government?

Such a list of questions could be extended for pages, but for a simple yet illuminating example of the opportunities for invention in this area, as well as for the application of game-theoretic reasoning, consider the incentive effects of tax systems. We know, of course, that the provisions of a tax system have profound social consequences. The heavy investment of U.S. consumers in housing, for example, is, to a considerable extent, a consequence of the fact that mortgage interest and property taxes are deductions from federal income taxes. Tax structure, however, can not only shape preferences. It can also distort their expression. For example, suppose a social planner is interested in determining whether some costly public works project (such as increased expenditures on education or highways) is in "the public interest." Realizing the difficulty in defining this interest, suppose the planner settles on a simple scheme: People will be asked how much they value the expenditure in dollars, and if the total reported value exceeds the project's cost, then it will be deemed worthwhile.

The difficulty with this approach is that those who anticipate paying little in taxes, in order to influence the outcome in favor of the project, have an incentive to overstate their evaluations whereas this value will be understated by those who sincerely believe that the project's cost to them exceeds its benefits. This problem is commonly manifested, for example, in the public utterances regarding the grand benefits to be associated with some local public works project (e.g., domed stadiums, mass transit systems) by local businesses and elected officials when the funds for that project come from the federal government and therefore are paid for by taxpayers outside of the political district in question. The particular problem here

voter	Project A			Project B		
	benefit	tax cost	net value	benefit	tax cost	net value
1	60	40	20	65	50	15
2	40	40	0	30	50	−20
3	25	40	−15	25	50	−25
4	75	40	35	140	50	90
5	90	40	50	90	50	40
sum	290	200	90	350	250	100

Table 4.1: Evaluations for Two Projects

is that the tax structure is not designed to elicit honest preference statements.

The specification of a system that elicits such preferences is an example of the more general problem of institutional design, and to illustrate some possibilities, consider the following scenario:

Example: Suppose five people, 1, 2, 3, 4, and 5, must choose between two projects, A and B, and suppose that the respective benefits and costs of these projects are as shown in Table 4.1. With respect to these preferences, notice that in a majority vote, project A defeats project B four to one, whereas project B produces the greater net benefit. The greater efficiency of B, then, might lead these voters to hope that their elected representatives and government planners will ignore the majority preference and choose B. But suppose that the information Table 4.1 summarizes is not common knowledge. Thus, if asked to state their valuations, persons 1, 2, 3, and 5 have an incentive to overstate the value to them of A, whereas 4 has an incentive to overstate the value of B. Rather than abide by the results of a simple poll of voters in this example, suppose as an alternative we implement the following tax system:

	Summed net valuations		
Excluded voter	A	B	Incremental tax
1	70	85	0
2	90	120	0
3	105	125	0
4	55	10	45
5	40	60	0

Table 4.2: Computation of Incremental Tax

1. Each person reports a net valuation for each project.
2. The reported net valuations are summed, and the project with the highest sum is chosen.
3. Each voter's evaluations are deleted and replaced, one at a time, to ascertain if that person's report materially affects the group's decision.
4. In the event that a report affects the decision—if a different project would have been chosen had that person been absent from the poll—then that person pays an incremental tax equal to the difference in valuations between the two projects without that person's preferences being taken into account.

With respect to our example, if everyone tells the truth, the numbers in Table 4.2 summarize the total valuations for the two projects after we exclude one voter's report. Notice that only voter 4 is decisive for project B, so in the event of sincere revelation of preferences, only voter 4 pays an incremental tax, which in this case equals forty five dollars.

We can question the relevance of Table 4.2 since it is based on facts that are by assumption unknown, but the remarkable feature of the tax scheme just outlined is that telling the truth is not only an equilibrium strategy but is dominant as well.

Example (continued): To see that telling the truth is a dominant strategy in general under the proposed tax scheme, suppose that, excluding the voter in question, the summed valuations for A and B are u_A and u_B (which may or may not be based on sincere preferences), suppose that $u_A > u_B$ (so A is chosen if the voter in question is ignored), and suppose that the voter's actual net utilities from A and B are u^*_A and u^*_B. What we want to establish is that telling the truth is dominant regardless of the valuations that others report. An appeal to symmetry then establishes that the proposed tax scheme is **dominance solvable**, and that truth-telling corresponds to the unique Nash equilibrium.

Briefly, we have two possible contingencies: Telling the truth renders the person in question decisive; and telling the truth does not render that person decisive. With respect to the first possibility, if telling the truth changes the outcome, the truth costs our voter $u_A - u_B$ in additional taxes. However, since the truth is decisive, it must be the case that when we add this voter's valuations, B is chosen. Hence,

$$u_A + u^*_A < u_B + u^*_B.$$

But this inequality implies that

$$u_A - u_B < u^*_B - u^*_A,$$

which is to say that the tax, $u_A - u_B$, is less than the difference in value between the projects, so our voter prefers to pay the tax rather than have the less preferred project chosen.

Now suppose that telling the truth does not render the voter decisive, in which case

$$u_A + u^*_A > u_B + u^*_B,$$

and telling the truth entails no additional tax. But if our voter misleadingly inflates the reported value of B so as to reverse this inequality in order to secure the more preferred project, then the voter must pay a tax of $u_A - u_B$, which exceeds $u^*_B - u^*_A$. Hence, the incremental tax exceeds whatever benefit the voter associates with project B as against project A.

We can imagine applying such a scheme to a variety of decisions, such as when university faculty must choose between candidates for some vacancy. Although debating the issue may make people more cognizant of the advantages and disadvantages of alternative candidates, rather than decide by using a majority vote, faculty could be asked how much they are willing to pay for each candidate. There are, nevertheless, some practical difficulties. First, although we have shown that telling the truth is a dominant strategy, we have not shown what might happen if people collude to form coalitions, which is a possibility that we do not consider until later.

Second, there is the issue of what to do with the incremental taxes that are collected. Unfortunately, we cannot redistribute the money among the participants without destroying the incentives for truth-telling we have established. In particular, if people know that part of their incremental tax will be returned to them, then they may have incentives to "shade" the truth a bit in favor of preferred projects or candidates. To maintain incentives, then, the money must be destroyed. Destroying money, though, is not Pareto efficient and we might hope that the amount burned is less than the gains associated with choosing the correct project or candidate.[3] Alternatively, we might try to design a mechanism with different properties. Indeed, several tax schemes have been proposed that eliminate this type of inefficiency. Unfortunately, they require abandoning the possibility that truth-telling is dominant and settling instead on establishing that truth-telling is merely a Nash equilibrium. The disadvantage here, of course, is that in practice we may require several iterations before responses converge to an equilibrium.

Third, there is the possibility of "income effects" —the possibility that some people would be unable to pay their incremental taxes, and thus they would be forced to understate their preferences or to not participate in the decision at all.

There is a fourth problem with this scheme that is more evident if we suppose that more than two projects are under consideration. Specifically, by representing the value of each project in terms of dollars, and by letting people be compensated for the selection of one project as against another by some transfer of money, we have assumed that utility and money are equivalent and that a person's utility for money does not change as a function of the project selected. Indeed, this assumption permits us to circumvent the consequences of a profoundly important theorem about social decision processes. That theorem, known as **Gibbard and Satterthwaite's Manipulability Result**, states that

---

[3]An outcome is Pareto efficient (or Pareto optimal) if there is no other feasible outcome that makes someone better off without diminishing the utility of anyone else.

> *If social processes concern more than two alternatives and if they sat-*
> *isfy all of Arrow's axioms except the requirement of transitive social*
> *orders (including the axiom that all preferences over the alternatives*
> *are feasible, which is invalidated by the assumption that utility and*
> *money are equivalent—the assumption that we can write $u(x) = ax +$*
> *b for any person's utility for the amount of money x, where a and b*
> *are constants), then we cannot preclude the possibility that, regardless*
> *of what others do, one or more persons will have a strategic incentive*
> *to disguise their true preferences.*

In particular, we cannot preclude the possibility that for any social decision process, preferences will be configured in such a way that "telling the truth" is not a Nash equilibrium—indeed, that there will be no equilibrium, truthful or otherwise.

We have, of course, already seen the incentives for strategic maneuver in committee agendas and thus we are able to identify those circumstances in which the votes of legislators on bills and amendments may not correspond to their sincere preferences. Gibbard and Satterthwaite's result tells us that for any agenda with more than two alternatives and two voters, there exists at least one set of preferences such that one or more voters will strategically cast a ballot that does not correspond to their sincere preference. We can also conclude that under plurality voting, if there are three or more candidates, then there are voter preferences such that some subset of the electorate will vote for their second choice.

To illustrate matters in a different context, suppose Congress is designing a bill and that we can represent the relevant alternative policies as positions on a line. Suppose the status quo is the point 0, suppose the president, who must sign the bill, prefers the position $P > 0$, and that the majority of the legislature prefers policies greater than P. Assuming that everyone prefers policies as close as possible to their ideal, the question is whether members of the legislature will reveal their preferences sincerely. Suppose the median preference within the legislature is $L_m > P$. If the median prevails under majority rule as the bill's provision and if L_m is closer to P than is 0, the status quo, the president will, of course, sign the bill. In this event, the decisive median legislator has no incentive to report anything other than his sincere preference. On the other hand, suppose L_m is further from P than P is to 0, in which case, if L_m prevails in the legislature, the president will veto the measure in favor of the status quo since 0 is closer to the president's ideal than is L_m. In this event, then, at least a majority of the legislature (all those with preferences at and to the right of L_m) have an incentive to report a bill closer to P than is L_m in order to avoid the veto.

This outcome in the legislature is little more than the implicit bargaining that frequently occurs between executive and legislative branches. Our example also hints at the incentives a president possesses for trying to convince the public and the legislature beforehand that he prefers policies closer to the status quo than is in fact the case. Hence, although our scenario is simple, it nevertheless reveals how strategic maneuver is an inherent part of politics.

This result is important in the study of politics, then, because it reveals that strategy is a pervasive feature of our subject and that we can never be certain (barring some strong assumptions about preference) that revealed preferences are sincere. Our only hope for understanding the relation between preferences and choice, then, is to model social processes carefully so as to learn the incentives for strategic maneuver.

4.6 The Paradox of Power

Earlier, in section 2.3, we offer an example in which the chairman of a committee prefers having the power to break ties delegated to a fair lottery rather than having the power to break ties himself. The rationale for this conclusion is that if the power to break ties is common knowledge, other participants may have incentives to avoid those circumstances in which the chair has the opportunity to exercise that power. We are thereby led to question those studies that implicitly fail to accommodate the possibility that the sources of political power at times follow a complex, convoluted logic—that more resources of any sort do not necessarily imply greater power. The implication we must draw from such examples is that for those who wish to understand politics and who believe that the concept of power, however defined or operationalized, is somehow central to politics, it is important to realize that the mere accumulation of "things" that seem to denote power may actually diminish a person's ability to control outcomes, or to realize more preferred outcomes.

To see that the paradoxical possibility our example uncovers is not limited to voting in agendas, consider this proposition: any increase in the number of seats that a party controls is advantageous to the party, and therefore a measure of a party's "power" is the seats it controls. We should, of course, refine this proposition to exclude possibilities in which one party gains control of additional seats while some other party secures control of a majority, because it is obvious in this circumstance that the gain is offset by what has happened elsewhere. Instead, then, let us consider situations in which one party gains seats at the expense of one or more other parties in such a way that no other party gains seats.

Example: Suppose that the distribution of seats in a 100-member, three-party parliamentary assembly is (32,33,35) and that this distribution changes to (35,32,33). The question, then, is whether party 1 prefers a change in which it gains seats at the expense of the other two parties.

To answer this question we must first specify the voting rules within the Parliament, so suppose all decisions are made by a plurality vote. This means that, in a three-party Parliament, any two parties can dictate the outcome, but if the parties vote differently, the largest party predominates. Suppose in addition that the parliament is considering three alternatives, A, B, and C, and that preferences are those occasioning the usual illustration of the Condorcet Paradox:

Party 1:	*A*	*B*	*C*
Party 2:	*C*	*A*	*B*
Party 3:	*B*	*C*	*A*

Consider now a secret ballot in which each party has three strategies: vote for A, for B, or for C. If seats are distributed (35,32,33), then the game's strategic form is as shown in Figure 4.3a. (For example, if party 3 chooses A, if 2 chooses B, and if party 1 (row chooser) chooses C, then C prevails because party 1 has more votes than either 3 or 2; however, if party 3 and 2 both vote for A, then A prevails regardless of what party 1 chooses.) Notice that for party 1 (row chooser), voting for A dominates voting for B or C, voting for A is dominated by voting for B or C for party 3, and that voting for B is dominated by voting for A or C for party 2. Eliminating these dominated choices, then, reduces the situation to the "game" in Figure 4.3b. But this reduction implies that voting for C is a dominant choice for parties 2 and 3. Hence, alternative C prevails as the final outcome. Thus, the "strongest" party realizes its least preferred alternative, and the "weakest" party successfully secures its ideal preference.

Clearly, then, party 1 in our example should prefer a reversal of roles, with some other party (notably, party 3) controlling a plurality of seats. Quite directly, then, our example demonstrates that "power" is not a simple variable measured by the accumulation of some commodity—in this instance, parliamentary seats. Instead, our example shows that the empirical determinants and measures of

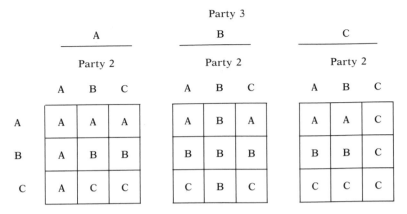

Figure 4.3a

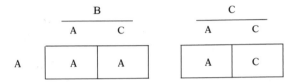

Figure 4.3b

power—conceptualized as the ability to secure favorable outcomes—can be defined only in the context of the strategic environment of those who wish to exercise it.

4.7 The Prisoners' Dilemma

Example: In Puccini's opera *Tosca*, the chief of police (Scarpia) condemns Tosca's lover (Cavaradossi) to death but offers to save him in exchange for Tosca's favors. Tosca consents. The problem as posed, offers Tosca two alternatives: keep the bargain, or double cross Scarpia by stabbing him when he comes to her. Similarly, Scarpia must decide whether to issue blank or live ammunition to the firing squad that Cavaradossi will face. If the bargain is kept, Tosca's satisfaction in getting her lover back will be marred by her surrender to Scarpia, and Scarpia's satisfaction is diminished by having to reprieve his rival. If Tosca double-crosses Scarpia and gets away with it, she wins most and he loses most; and vice versa. If both double-cross, both lose but

	keep bargain	double-cross
keep bargain	−10,−10	−20,20
double-cross	20,−20	−15,−15

Figure   4.4

not so much as each would have lost had he or she alone kept the bargain.

We are interested in showing that this scenario illustrates a particular game that has been the focus of an extraordinary amount of theoretical, substantive, and experimental scrutiny—the Prisoners' Dilemma. To see the structure of this game more explicitly, we must assign some specific payoff numbers to the four possible outcomes. Choosing some arbitrary numbers that nevertheless seem reasonable and consistent with preferences, letting Tosca be the row chooser and Scarpia be the column chooser, we get the game illustrated in Figure 4.4. Notice in particular that we have assigned payoffs in such a way that both players have a dominant strategy—to double-cross the other. However, if both double-cross, then an outcome prevails (−15,−15) that they unanimously prefer to avoid in favor of some other outcome—in this instance, both Tosca and Scarpia prefer to keep their original bargain.

Interest in games like the one that Figure 4.4 illustrates arises because we can use them to formulate a justification for establishing the coercive institutions of governments and because we can also use them to understand the flaws of collective action inherent in those institutions. The Prisoners' Dilemma also illuminates our understanding of such diverse processes as interest group politics, the imperatives of arms races, the sources of market failure, and even voting itself. Repeated play versions of the dilemma, moreover, are used to model the explicit cooperation of vote trading in legislatures, as well as the agreements characterizing interstate relations in anarchic international systems. Exploring the many nuances and forms of this dilemma, then, illustrates the variety of insights game-theoretic reasoning can provide.

Although its name comes from a scenario in which two prisoners who must decide whether or not to confess to a crime they have jointly committed, we can portray the dilemma in a more substantively relevant form:

	don't install (don't cooperate)	install (cooperate)
don't install (don't cooperate)	0,0	$7,−$3
install (cooperate)	−$3,$7	$4,$4

Figure 4.5

Example: Suppose two people must decide whether or not to install pollution control devices on their cars. Each device costs $10. Suppose further that the clean air each device produces is worth $7 to each person (that is, both persons benefit from the installation of each device), and that the benefit from two devices is $14 per person. Assuming that the benefit to both persons of the status quo is zero, Figure 4.5 shows a strategic form in which only the choices of installing (playing cooperatively) and not installing (not cooperating) are available.

The essential features of a Prisoners' Dilemma this example illustrates are, first, both persons have a dominant strategy—to not install the device—and, second, the equilibrium that prevails from the selection of these dominant choices is Pareto inefficient—both persons unanimously prefer the outcome that prevails if they had each chosen their dominated strategy.

To see that this game illustrates a real dilemma for the two participants, imagine that both persons are allowed to communicate prior to playing the game and that both agree to install devices. However, when left alone to make their actual decision, each person can reason thus: If the other person installs a device, then my best choice is to renege on the agreement. And even if I keep the agreement, what guarantee do I have that my counterpart will do the same, since, after all, his dominant choice is also to renege. In fact, if the other person reneges, I would be a fool to install the device since its marginal benefit does not exceed the cost.

For perhaps a more personally relevant example, imagine that you are soon to take a final exam, which the instructor has assured the class he will grade on a curve. Suppose that if everyone studies or if no one studies, everyone's final grade will be precisely what they earned on the midterm—although those who earned an "F" on the midterm remain optimists and believe that regardless of what others do, since it is only an accident of nature that earned them their "F," studying on the final can only help. Finally, suppose that on the last day of class, after the instructor leaves the classroom, everyone swears a blood oath not to study and to enjoy the weekend in those pursuits that preoccupy the fantasies of undergraduates. The motivation for this agreement, of course, is that if everyone studies, then grades will not change, but time will be "wasted." Now you sit in the solitude of your dormitory room, contemplating whether or not to study, knowing that your grade will drop if even one person reneges. And of course, if everyone else reneges, you would be a fool not to study. Such are the torments of youth.

Returning to more political possibilities, examples such as the one Figure 4.5 portrays illustrate one justification for the intervention of governments into markets—namely, to correct for the failure of a decentralized allocation system to take account adequately of the consequences that one person's actions have on others. In this instance, the inefficiency results from each person's failure to take account of the benefits his actions have for the other person. One function for a government, then, would be for it to alter incentives. Specifically, both persons could readily agree to entrust to some "third player" (government) the power to coerce them into making the proper choice by, say, inspecting autos and levying fines for those found without pollution control devices. If fines are set properly, everyone installs a device, no fines are collected, and a Pareto efficient outcome prevails. (At this point the reader can surely sense the abstract quality of our argument.)

We do not want the reader to believe, however, that Prisoners' Dilemmas point only to problems with markets. Consider the fact that although incumbent legislators appear to have a profound advantage over others in winning elections, public opinion polls reveal that legislatures in general and the U.S. Congress in particular are not always regarded in high esteem. Consider also the perpetual conflicts arising between the legislative and executive branches of government over such matters as tariff legislation, methods for reducing the federal debt, and spending in general. Although it is tempting to regard such conflicts as the consequence of the "clash of powerful personalities" and the divergence in the priorities of Congress and the president, the question remains as to why these priorities differ when both the president and the Congress are, in effect, elected by the same electorate and why powerful personalities necessarily clash in this context.

To see what insights the Prisoners' Dilemma might offer into these patterns, consider the following possibility:

	$k < (n-1)/2$	$k = (n-1)/2$	$k > (n-1)/2$
a_1	0	0	$-kC/n$
a_2	0	$B-(n+1)C/2n$	$B-(k+1)C/n$

Figure   4.6

Example: Suppose a legislature consists of n (odd) districts, and that voters in each district must choose between two type of representatives:

a_1: *A representative who will oppose all inefficient legislation even if such action means that the representative must oppose inefficient programs that benefit the legislator's district*

a_2: *A representative who will do whatever is required to see to it that his or her district is not "shortchanged" and who will seek whatever legislation directly benefits the district*

Suppose the legislature, operating under majority rule, kills inefficient pork (programs for districts in which the cost, C, exceeds the benefit, B) if a majority of the legislature opposes it (if a majority of districts choose a_1), but that it approves all requests if a majority of legislators submit and support such programs for their districts (if a majority of districts choose a_2). Keep in mind that if a program is passed, its benefit accrues only to a particular district, but that its cost must be borne by all n districts. Assuming that the costs of all programs submitted for consideration are equal, letting k be the number of other districts that choose a_2 and elect a legislator who will seek pork for his or her district, Figure 4.6 shows the payoffs to a particular district from each of its two choices, given the several relevant contingencies.

Notice now that a_2 dominates a_1 if the benefit B exceeds $(n+1)C/2n$—if, for large legislatures, $B > C/2$. (The critical column in Figure 4.6 is the second since if the appropriate inequality is satisfied there it is satisfied in the third column.) Of course, the same argument holds true for all districts, all districts choose a_2, and all districts realize a payoff of $B - C$, which can be negative (and probably is in the case of pork). Thus, although voters might prefer electing representatives who are especially adept at securing special benefits for their districts (such as incum-

	Payoff from Bill's Passage					
Legislator	A	B	C	D	E	F
1	3	3	2	−4	−4	2
2	2	−4	−4	2	3	3
3	−4	2	3	3	2	−4

Table 4.3

bents who hold positions of seniority within Congress), if the overall performance of the legislature is judged by the general performance of the economy (to which $B - C$ contributes), then we can explain the seemingly paradoxical fact of incumbent electoral advantage and low esteem of Congress as an institution. Also, as a source of conflict between executive and legislative branches, presidents and presidential candidates are presumably free to choose any cell in Figure 4.6 as the policy of their administration or as an election platform, and thus they should resist policies leading to cells such as $B - C$.

Although this Prisoners' Dilemma might benefit incumbents because they are viewed as being better equipped to deliver goodies to their districts such as military bases, defense contracts, domed stadiums, urban transit subsidies, and the like, there is a dilemma of vote trading that can plague a legislature.

Example: Suppose legislators 1, 2, and 3 are contemplating the disposition of bills A, B, C, D, E, and F, where each of their payoffs from a bill's passage is as shown in Table 4.3 (a bill's defeat pays 0, and let payoffs be additive across bills). Notice that if the legislators vote their preferences, all bills pass and each legislator earns +2. Legislator 1, however, might notice that his loss from having D pass exceeds his gain from having C pass, whereas exactly the opposite is true for legislator 2. Thus, we might anticipate that 1 and 2 will trade votes on these bills, with 1 voting against C and 2 reciprocating by voting against D in order to defeat both measures. Having consummated this trade, 1 sees a similar opportunity with legislator 3 with respect to bills E and F, whereas 2 sees just such an opportunity with 3 on bills A and B. If all trades are made, though, no bills pass,

Legislator 3

	trade		refrain	

	Legislator 2		Legislator 2	
	trade	refrain	trade	refrain
trade	0,0,0	4,−4,4	4,4,−4	2,2,2
refrain	−4,4,4	2,2,2	2,2,2	2,2,2

Figure 4.7

and each legislator's payoff, 0, is less than what he or she gets if no trading had occurred.

Given the inefficiency of unrestrained vote trading, suppose each legislator considers refraining from such activity, hoping that others will do the same. This possibility yields the game in Figure 4.7, where "trade" means exhibiting a willingness to trade with anyone else who shows the same willingness, "refrain" means being unwilling to trade with anyone, and where profitable trades require the agreement of two legislators. As this figure shows, trading is a dominant strategy, so the outcome (0,0,0) seems unavoidable (barring, of course, coalitional deals to deliberately exclude one legislator from making any deals).

Prisoners' Dilemmas also cause problems for other types of political decision makers. It is, of course, commonplace to view the role of special interests—especially "monied special interests" —as something sinister in campaigns. We are, after all, accustomed to the view that such interests scurry about the political landscape, buying influence and policy to the detriment of everyone else. However, consider this problem:

Example: Two interest groups with diametrically opposite preferences must decide whether or not to contribute to their preferred candidate. The election of a preferred candidate is worth $500 to a group, the election of the challenger is worth −$500, a campaign contribution costs $400, and the candidate with the greatest "war chest" wins. (If both receive equal contributions, the outcome is a tie, which is broken by a coin toss.) Figure 4.8 portrays this situation's strategic form and reveals that the in-

	contribute	don't contribute
contribute	−400,−400	100,−500
don't contribute	−500,100	0,0

Figure   4.8

terest groups are trapped in a Prisoners' Dilemma. So rather than view these groups as "buying" favorable outcomes, we can view them more sympathetically as being expropriated from by the candidates.

For a somewhat more fanciful example that perhaps helps us explain the logic of some government regulations (especially those that fix prices in otherwise competitive industries) consider the following situation, which we offer in the form of an exercise:

Example: The buggy-whip industry is in trouble: There are far too many producers of buggy whips (exactly two), so the price for such items has declined to $6 each, while inflation has driven costs of manufacturing to $4/whip. At a $6 price tag, 400 whips/month/firm can be sold. Such a profit margin is unacceptable, so the firms have met and agreed to form a cartel to fix prices at $8/whip, in which case 250 whips/firm will be sold. But if either firm cheats on this agreement and charges $6, it will capture the entire market of 800 whips. Abiding by the time-honored political maxim, "I seen me chances and I tooks them," you are a legislator with sufficient power to force the government to regulate the price of whips "in the public interest" — no one, of course, wants "inferior" quality whips flooding the market, especially those made in some distant Asian country. What is the upper limit on the campaign contribution you can demand of the two members of the whip industry?

To answer the question this problem poses, Figure 4.9 portrays the strategic form confronting the firms. If both firms charge a market price of $6, each earns $800 (400 whips sold at a profit of $2/whip) whereas if both charge $8, each earns $1,000 (250 whips sold at a profit of $4/whip). A defecting firm earns $1,600 and the other earns nothing. For an enterprising legislator, then, there is an opportunity

	charge $6.00	charge $8.00
charge $6.00	$800,$800	$1,600,$0
charge $8.00	$0,$1,600	$1000,$1,000

Figure 4.9

	increase arms	decrease arms
increase arms	25,25	200,−100
decrease arms	−100,200	100,100

Figure 4.10

to "earn" $600 from each firm as gratitude for government enforcement of a whip cartel.

Our final example of the application of the Prisoners' Dilemma to politics concerns strategic arms races.

Example: Suppose that each of two national leaders can either increase spending on armaments or decrease spending. If both choose the same strategy, the security of both is unchanged and worth, say, 100. Suppose further that the cost of any increase in armaments is 75. However, if one country disarms unilaterally, suppose it is overcome by its adversary, which gains 275, which is an outcome that is worth −100 to the vanquished leader. The strategic form of this situation is portrayed in Figure 4.10, which reveals that both persons have increasing arms spending as their dominant choice.

The imperatives of the Prisoners' Dilemma in this case suggest that if asked, "Are the United States and the Soviet Union more likely to reach an arms agreement (1) if they more earnestly and honestly approach arms negotiations, (2) if negotiators learn to trust what the other side says, or (3) if domestic political-economic considerations render the costs of pursuing arms buildups unacceptable?" we must answer that it is only the last possibility that can lead to a resolution of matters. What is important to appreciate about Prisoners' Dilemmas is that we cannot resolve them with simple communication and coordination devices. Regardless of whatever agreements are reached beforehand, once the participants in the dilemma are left alone, the choice of a dominant strategies seems inevitable.

However, there appears throughout the interpretative literature the seemingly reasonable hypothesis that such dilemmas are more problematic in situations that concern a great many people than in situations that concern a few or only two. An industry dominated by a few firms might be able to enforce a cartelized price even though defecting to a lower price is myopically dominant. On the other hand, an industry with a great many firms or an industry in which the entry of new firms is relatively easy (the household moving industry, for example, or barbershops and taxis) have greater difficulty enforcing agreements among themselves, and thus, *ceteris paribus*, it is in these more competitive and larger industries that we should see the greatest demand for legal price fixing in the form of government rate regulation. The logic underlying such hypotheses is that with but a few players, defection to the dominant strategy is readily observed so that sanctions of different sorts can be implemented. However, if there are a great many people involved, each can reason that his or her defection will cause little harm to others and that as a consequence, the defection might go unnoticed and unpunished.

To see this in an especially salient context, recall our example of studying for an exam graded on a curve, which we noted corresponded to a Prisoners' Dilemma. Agreements among students not to study might be effective if the class is small since any marked improvement in individual grades would change the curve and would be immediately apparent to everyone, in which case a defection might make it difficult to maintain social relationships. However, if the class is large, singular improvements in grades can go unnoticed or can be attributed to chance. The particular difficulty is that because a defection from the cooperative arrangement is apparent in a small group, such groups are generally better equipped to apply post-play sanctions on recalcitrant players without implementing explicit mechanisms for detecting defections. But if detection is more difficult, the group may have to make use of a more formal device, such as a pre-exam party in which attendance is taken. Thus, informal social norms may be sufficient in small groups, whereas larger groups may have to invent detection and enforcement mechanisms—which, of course, makes the task for larger groups much like the one that confronts people who seek to resolve large-scale dilemmas with governmental mechanisms.

To see more explicitly the role that detection and enforcement can play in resolving Prisoners' Dilemmas, consider again the arms race

	increase arms	decrease arms
increase arms	25,25	200−175p, −100+125p
decrease arms	−100+125p, 200−175p	100,100

Figure 4.11: Arms Race with Possible Detection of Defections

example in Figure 4.10. Now, however, suppose that if either player defects from an agreement to decrease arms, that defection is detected with probability p by the opponent, who, before final payoffs are realized, can then adjust his strategy to increase arms as well. Hence, if 1 initially chooses to increase and 2 chooses to decrease, the outcome (200,−100) prevails only with probability $1−p$—the probability that 2 fails to detect the defection, whereas the outcome (25,25) prevails with probability p, which is the probability that 2 detects the defection and makes the appropriate adjustment of increasing as well. Since this argument is symmetric for a unilateral defection by 2, Figure 4.11 portrays the corresponding strategic form game:

It now follows that (decrease, decrease) is also an equilibrium strategy pair if the probability of detection, p, exceeds 4/7. This does not mean that this second equilibrium will necessarily prevail, but it does offer some reason for supposing that the two countries can coordinate to resolve the dilemma in favor of a mutually preferred outcome.

4.8 The Repeated Prisoners' Dilemma

The preceding examples illustrate how a simple 2×2 game can lead to the consideration of important substantive issues. In fact, the dilemma is more central to politics than our examples suggest. Consider, for example, the question of the process whereby interests in a democratic society impact on public policy. One possibility is that those interests impact through the electoral process—that candidates, sensing an opportunity to secure votes, respond accordingly. However, consider the possibility that, in a society in which members of the legislature are elected in single-member districts, a particular political interest is geographically spread too thin to constitute a significant part of any constituency. Such citizens, then, have an incentive to organize for political action, but if their interest requires the provision of a service that, once supplied to one person, cannot be withheld from anyone else (e.g., clean air as in our example from Figure 3.5), then these citizens confront a Prisoners' Dilemma. Specifically, if some organization forms to lobby for governmental provision of this good, each person thus benefitted has an incentive to avoid the costs of supporting the lobbying effort. Thus, the Prisoners' Dilemma tells us that we cannot assume, *a priori*, that every interest in society will organize effectively to secure or defend its position.

Understanding how groups overcome such dilemmas is, of course, a major component of political theory and leads immediately to speculation about the role of leadership, about the incentives for politicians themselves to entrepreneur collective action, and about the potential role of preexisting institutions. However, before we consider such possibilities, we should first confront the fact that unlike in the real world, in our examples each game occurs in complete isolation. For example, abiding by agreements in legislative vote trading scenarios may confront legislators with a dilemma, but it certainly is not a dilemma in which legislators hope to participate only once. Thus, we should consider the possibility that the expectation of repetition alters people's incentives to choose one strategy over another. Tariff negotiations among countries also form a dilemma because each country that is party to the negotiation prefers to defect unilaterally from any agreement. As with vote trading, however, countries must deal with each other on a continual basis, so a defection in one instance has implications for subsequent action and negotiations. Similarly, arms races also concern the ability of participants to not only detect a defection to a dominant choice, but to respond to that defection, followed presumably by a renewed arms race dilemma.

This discussion suggests that it is not a prudent research strategy to treat many of our examples as we have—as strategic situations isolated from the flow of events over time—and that any complete analysis should examine the context of that game and the larger extensive form in which it is imbedded.

Of course, the Prisoners' Dilemma, like any game, can be part of nearly any scenario. But our discussion of vote trading suggests that a useful place to begin is to view vote trading as a repetition of the same game among legislators. Hence, one scenario that is especially interesting has the Prisoners' Dilemma being replayed by the same participants.

Before we try to write down an extensive or a strategic form for a repeated game, however, we must decide whether it is repeated a finite and known number or times or whether it is repeated an unknown or infinite number of times. This choice is critical, because if a game is repeated a finite number of times so that the terminal nodes of the corresponding extensive form are apparent and well defined, we can analyze that form by backward reduction. However, if a game such as the Prisoners' Dilemma is repeated an indefinite number of times (or, equivalently, if the terminal point is uncertain), then there is no point at which we can begin the backward reduction process. Indeed, if only one branch leads to a repetition, then backward reduction cannot be attempted and we must use other analytic tools to make predictions.

Interest in the repeated Prisoners' Dilemma does not arise, however, because it reveals interesting analytic problems. Rather, we can attribute that interest to the fact that people, whether observed in the experimental laboratory or in everyday activity, seem able to use the fact of repetition to "solve" this dilemma—to avoid mutually disadvantageous outcomes. Legislators do not wholly succumb to granting every constituency a benefit so as to wholly bankrupt the state (although the evidence is mounting that this is not always the case); the trading relations of states do not necessarily evolve into an anarchy in which each state imposes the highest tariff barriers sought by the interests within them; people do contribute to charities even though they might each be better off by defecting to a pattern of non-contribution; and subjects in the laboratory when playing the Prisoners' Dilemma frequently choose to cooperate.

This last observation—from the experimental laboratory—suggests that repetition of the dilemma is an important variable in understanding the patterns of cooperation that do emerge. This observation gains theoretical sustenance, in turn, from the idea that if a person defects to a dominant strategy in an early play of the dilemma, others can sanction that person in successive plays by refusing to cooperate. If, for example, a legislator defects from a vote-trading agreement, then legislators can refuse to trade with that person subsequently, and if a firm defects from the cartel price, then others can threaten to defect as well, in which case the gains from unilateral defection are lost. Robert Axelrod offers the example of trench warfare in World War I as an example of repetition resolving the dilemma.[4] Both German and French troops, facing each other from their trenches, doubtlessly had survival as a primary objective, and when ordered to shell the opposing side, the dominant strategy

[4]*The Evolution of Cooperation*, New York, Basic Books, 1984.

in a single play of the "game" was to kill as many of the enemy as possible. But in its repeated version, a form of cooperation emerged in which mortars would be aimed imperfectly. If the French or Germans aimed well, the other side would respond in kind, and if either aimed poorly, this action was reciprocated. As a consequence, the commands of both sides confronted the problem of two armies who refused to kill each other with efficiency. In short, repetition allows more complicated strategies than simply "cooperate" or "defect" — it allows players to signal a willingness to cooperate and it allows player to punish each other if either defects from cooperation.

The difficulty, however, with the idea that mere repetition solves the dilemma for participants is that it is illogical in the case of a finitely repeated dilemma. Suppose, in particular, that a dilemma is to be played some finite number of times between two persons and that the number of repetitions (as well as all other aspects of the situation) are common knowledge. Both persons know that defection is dominant (subgame perfect) in the last play of the game— by assumption, nothing follows this last play and so the last subgame corresponds to a single play of the dilemma. But this means that it is futile to cooperate on the next to the last trial in the hopes of inducing cooperation on the last. Thus, both persons should defect on the next to the last play as well. The continuation of this argument establishes that the only subgame perfect equilibrium to the finitely repeated Prisoners' Dilemma is defection at every opportunity.

This situation changes importantly, however, if we suppose that the dilemma can be replayed an indefinite number of times. The first thing that changes, as we have already noted, is that we can no longer use backward reduction. But the second thing that changes is that the number of strategies available to people becomes infinite (e.g., cooperate on every round; cooperate on every ith round; cooperate until the other person defects, in which case defect for j rounds; and so on). This multiplicity of strategies, in turn, opens the door to the existence of a plethora of Nash equilibria and to a reemergence of the problem of coordination to achieve any particular equilibrium.

Before we can adequately address this issue, however, we must consider a third thing that changes when we allow indefinite repetition. In particular, although we might assume that people merely accumulate payoffs in the finitely repeated dilemma, we cannot make this same assumption in the infinitely repeated case since, if all payoffs are positive, payoffs accumulated ad infinitum imply that every strategy yields the same total—infinity. Moreover, such an assumption makes little behavioral sense, because it is only reasonable to suppose that people weight payoffs received early more than they weight payoffs that will be realized only in the distant future. This fact means that we should suppose that people discount future payoffs and evaluate strategies by the present value of the payoffs they realize.[5]

To represent this assumption formally, suppose that $u_{it}(x_1,x_2)$ is person i's utility in period t when 1 uses the strategy x_1 and 2 uses the strategy x_2. Then using the same formula we use to calculate present values in accounting, i's discounted payoff from x_1 across periods $t = 1, 2, \ldots$ and so on, is

$$u_i(x_1,x_2) = u_{i1}(x_1,x_2) + ru_{i2}(x_1,x_2) + \ldots + r^{t-1}u_{it}(x_1,x_2) + \ldots$$

where r is the rate with which person i discounts payoffs. Admittedly, such an expression is formidable if the utility number in each term is different from the rest, but if all terms are the same, then we can use the following mathematical identity (which applies so long as $0 \leq r \leq 1$) to simplify the analysis:

$$1 + r + r^2 + r^3 + \ldots + r^n + \ldots = 1/(1-r).$$

To see now how we use this identity, suppose, for a numerical example, that the dilemma portrayed in Figure 4.5 is repeated, and that both persons choose to cooperate (install) all the time, regardless of what the other does. In this event, both persons receive an infinite but discounted stream of four-dollar payoffs. Thus, the discounted present value of (install always,install always) is $4/(1-r)$. On the other hand, if both persons defect to their dominant choice, then their payoff is an infinite repetition of zeros, or merely zero.

Which strategies are in equilibrium in this repeated game depends on the strategies (out of the infinity of possibilities) that we allow the two players to consider. However, since we are merely interested in illustrating the fact that repetition alone can induce cooperation as a Nash equilibrium, consider these four strategies: (c_1) cooperate always; (c_2) defect always; (c_3) cooperate as long as the other person cooperates, but defect forever when the other person defects for the first time; and (c_4) play tit for tat. Recall that strategy c_4 requires

---

[5]Equivalently, we can suppose that even if people do not discount, there is always some probability, p, that the next play will be the last (an assumption which almost certainly is better suited to the example of trench warfare cited earlier). Some simple algebra shows that this assumption leads to the same analysis we are about to undertake.

	c_1	c_2	c_3	c_4
c_1	$4/(1-r)$	$-3/(1-r)$	$4/(1-r)$	$4/(1-r)$
c_2	$7/(1-r)$	0	7	7
c_3	$4/(1-r)$	$-3/(1-r)$	$4/(1-r)$	$4/(1-r)$
c_4	$4/(1-r)$	-3	$4/(1-r)$	$4/(1-r)$

Figure 4.12: The Infinitely Repeated Prisoners' Dilemma

that a person cooperate on the first trial, and then on trial t it has that person matching what the other person chose on trial $t-1$. Of course, two tit-for-tatters or a tit-for-tatter and someone choosing c_1 or c_3 never defect and thereby they both realize the payoff of $4/(1-r)$ from their strategies. On the other hand, a tit-for-tatter playing against a person who chooses c_2 gets a payoff of -3 in the first round, and zero thereafter, whereas the opponent receives $+7$ in the first round and 0 thereafter. These calculations, then, allow us to describe the strategic form of the game by using these repeated strategies, and Figure 4.12 gives this form for the four identified strategies (entering only row-chooser's payoffs since the situation is symmetric for column chooser).

The argument that repetition can induce cooperation is made, now, by observing that (c_4,c_4) is a Nash equilibrium provided that $4/(1-r) \geq 7$, or equivalently, that $r \geq 3/7$—so cooperation is an equilibrium if neither person discounts the future too greatly.

It is important to emphasize at this point that we have merely established that repetition **can** induce cooperation; we have not shown that repetition necessarily leads to cooperation. The reason why we cannot show this is also illustrated by our example. Notice that the strategy pair (c_2, c_2)—(defect always, defect always)—is also an equilibrium. Thus, repetition adds equilibria, but it does not rid us of the "undesirable" one. Infinite repetition, in fact, leads to new problems. Because infinite repetition allows an infinity of pure strategies, equilibria multiply to keep pace. And we now know through various **folk theorems** (named as such because it is uncertain who first proposed or established them) that

In an infinitely repeated game, any outcome that gives each player what that player can guarantee for himself if he plays the game without co-

> *ordinating with anyone else—any outcome that satisfies the security value of each player—can correspond to an equilibrium.*

As a result of such theorems, game theorists have sought to limit the strategies that they think are most likely to be considered by players. **Stationary strategies**, for example, require that a player make the same choice every time he encounters strategically equivalent information sets—information sets that encompass the same number of decision nodes such that the nodes in such sets can be matched with identical subsequent subgames. Defecting always and cooperating always are stationary, but tit for tat is not since it requires a player to condition his action on the opponent's previous decision. **Trigger strategies** have players playing cooperatively until someone defects, at which point the strategy "triggers" a permanent punishment. The strategy c_3 is a trigger strategy. Trigger strategies are a special case of **punishment strategies**, of which tit for tat is the most familiar example. Finally, game theorists have examined strategies that allow only certain degrees of complexity. All of the strategies in Figure 4.12 are simple because they do not require that a player store much information about past moves; but a strategy that says "in the event of a defection punish for five rounds" requires a player of more complexity because the player must now count periods. We will not review this research because most of it requires complex analytic structures. We merely point to its existence in order to demonstrate that game theory is not yet a closed area of inquiry.

4.9 Evolutionary Stable Strategies

The problem that the infinitely repeated Prisoners' Dilemma illustrates and that plagues many of the models that people use to understand politics is, as we have just noted, the fact that equilibria need not be unique and, as the folk theorems establish, that equilibrium outcomes can encompass a great many possibilities. Consequently, a considerable research effort has been devoted to formulating refinements of Nash's original idea (such as the ideas of subgame perfection and perfection reviewed in previous chapters), with the hope of narrowing predictions in some way. This research agenda has not been altogether successful we suspect, because many games have multiple and equally reasonable alternative equilibria. After all, the existence of different cultures, of different solutions to common problems across cultures, and even the existence of different languages suggest that we cannot do away with the possibility of multiple equilibria with some mathematical or conceptual trick.

This discussion, though, does not address the question of how people coordinate to ensure that some equilibrium ultimately prevails. It is one thing to say in the context of the repeated Prisoners' Dilemma that cooperative equilibria exist, but it is quite another thing to assert that people will somehow coordinate complex strategies so as to achieve such a outcome, although we could speculate that it is here that we find roles for socialization, education, and for a concept of leadership. However, rather than pursue these possibilities, the application of game theory to issues in population genetics suggests an especially fruitful approach.

The problem at hand is to understand why people are predisposed to choose one strategy (pattern of behavior) rather than another, when all strategies are part of some equilibrium. We can ask, for example, why certain norms persist in legislatures and why freshmen legislators, who may not share these norms, are nevertheless socialized to accept them (as against the possibility that some norm carried to the legislator by one or more freshmen becomes dominant). We could also ask why some standards of behavior but not others differentiate cultures. To address such questions, let us take a biological view and think of strategies as gene types in which a process of natural selection reenforces one strategy as against another. The classic illustration of what we mean by this is offered by a game called Hawk and Dove.

> **Example:** Suppose whenever one individual confronts another that each person must choose between being a hawk and being a dove. The strategy of being hawkish means to fight until injured or until the opponent retires; the strategy of being a dove is to strut about, but to retire whenever confronting a hawk. Supposing further that a winner in a confrontation gets V, a loser suffers a loss of D, where we interpret V and D as measuring long-term genetic fitness—the ability of a strategy to reproduce in the society. Hence, if similar opponents have equal probabilities of winning and losing, then Figure 4.13 portrays the expected payoffs of two competing animals:

Viewing this example as a single-play game, notice that (Dove, Hawk) and (Hawk, Dove) are equilibrium pairs if $D > V$, and only (Hawk, Hawk) is an equilibrium if $V > D$. Rather than interpret this figure as the strategic form of a two-person game, however, let us merely take Figure 4.13 as a table that tells us what payoffs are realized whenever two strategies encounter each other. Now suppose that all creatures in a society are genetically predisposed to choosing one strategy or the other and thus, all interactions are between pairs

	Hawk	Dove
Hawk	$(V-D)/2,(V-D)/2$	$V,0$
Dove	$0,V$	$V/2,V/2$

Figure 4.13: Hawk-Dove Payoffs

who abide by the same strategy—pure or randomized. But suppose also that on occasion (with the small probability p) "normal" strategies confront mutants (the norm held by the unsocialized freshman legislator?)—creatures who choose a different strategy. If, for example, society consists only of Doves, then the expected payoff to a Dove is

$$0p + (1-p)\frac{V}{2} = (1-p)\frac{V}{2} \qquad (4.1)$$

whereas the payoff to a mutant Hawk is

$$p\frac{V-D}{2} + (1-p)V = V - p\frac{V+D}{2}. \qquad (4.2)$$

Some simple algebra reveals that as long as V exceeds pD, the second expression is larger than the first, so on average mutants will "perform" better than nonmutants. If we now suppose that these payoffs also measure the ability of a gene to reproduce itself (i.e., genes with higher payoffs reproduce more successfully than genes with lower payoffs), mutants will proliferate at the expense of Doves.

On the other hand, if society consists of Hawks and it is Doves who are rare mutants, Hawks realize an expected payoff of

$$(1-p)\frac{V-D}{2} + pV = \frac{V-D+p(V+D)}{2} \qquad (4.3)$$

whereas the payoff to a mutant Dove is

$$(1-p)0 + \frac{pV}{2} = \frac{pV}{2}. \qquad (4.4)$$

Thus, as long as V exceeds D, mutant Doves will suffer relative to

Hawks. That is, with $V > D$, the strategy of being a Hawk is an **evolutionary stable strategy**.

To generalize this example, consider the following definition:

*s is an **evolutionary stable strategy** if, for any other strategy s',*

$$u(s,s) > u(s',s) \tag{4.5}$$

or

$$u(s,s) = u(s',s) \text{ and } u(s,s') > u(s',s'). \tag{4.6}$$

To see this definition's relation to our argument that Hawk is evolutionary stable, notice first that the expected return from using the strategy Hawk, $E(\text{Hawk})$, can be written

$$E(\text{Hawk}) = (1-p)u(\text{Hawk, Hawk}) + pu(\text{Hawk, Dove}) \tag{4.7}$$

whereas the payoff from Dove is

$$E(\text{Dove}) = (1-p)u(\text{Dove, Hawk}) + pu(\text{Dove, Dove}) \tag{4.8}$$

where the various values of u are given in Figure 4.13. If Hawk is evolutionarily stable, we require that $E(\text{Hawk}) > E(\text{Dove})$, or

$$(1-p)u(\text{Hawk, Hawk}) + pu(\text{Hawk, Dove}) > $$
$$(1-p)u(\text{Dove, Hawk}) + pu(\text{Dove, Dove}).$$

Since p is very small (a Dove is the rare mutant), this inequality is satisfied if

$$u(\text{Hawk, Hawk}) > u(\text{Dove, Hawk}),$$

which is what expression (4.5) requires. However, if equality holds here, then evolutionary stability requires that

$$u(\text{Hawk, Dove}) > u(\text{Dove, Dove}),$$

which is what expression (4.6) requires.

To illustrate matters further, let $D > V > 0$, and keep in mind that we are not interpreting Figure 4.13 as a game matrix, but merely as a table revealing the payoffs players receive when confronting someone of the same or different genetic type. Since neither (Dove,Dove) nor (Hawk, Hawk) is evolutionarily stable if $D > V > 0$, consider the possibility that the non-mutant (normal) members of the species each abide by a mixed strategy, say $(q, 1-q)$. Once again, if mutants (who use the strategy $(r, 1-r)$, $r \neq q$) arise with some probability, then (after some algebraic manipulation),

$$u(q,q) = \frac{V-q^2D}{2},$$

$$u(r,q) = \frac{rV+V-qrD-qV}{2}.$$

In accordance with expression (4.5), if we set $u(q,q) > u(r,q)$ we get

$$(q-r)(V-qD) \geq 0.$$

We do not know, however, whether q is greater than or less than r, and, indeed, if the mixed strategy $(q,1-q)$ is to be evolutionarily stable, it must be the case that neither strategies with $r > q$ or $r < q$ can gain a greater payoff. So the only circumstance in which we are assured that the preceding expression holds universally is if we set $q = V/D$ so that we get $0 = 0$. But for $(q,1-q)$ to be evolutionarily stable, expression (4.6) must hold. Thus, computing $u(q,r)$ and $u(r,r)$,

$$u(q,r) = \frac{qV+V-qrD-rV}{2},$$

$$u(r,r) = \frac{V-q^2D}{2}.$$

Expression (4.6)'s requirement that $u(q,r)$ exceed $u(r,r)$ becomes, after some algebraic manipulation,

$$(q-r)[V - rD] > 0,$$

which can be rewritten as

$$D(q-r)\left[\frac{V}{D} - r\right] 0 .$$

Substituting $q = V/D$ gives

$$D(q-r)^2 > 0,$$

which is necessarily satisfied whenever r is not equal to q, because D is assumed to be positive and since the squared term is necessarily positive.[6]

Let us now return to our original problem of the repeated Prisoners' Dilemma in order to assess what kind of solution the notion of evolutionary stability provides there. Before we do so, however, let us generalize (4.1) and (4.2) in a way demanded by the context of the analysis. Specifically, what we must keep in mind is that we are not analyzing merely the interactions of two specific individuals; instead, we are looking at how a particular strategy performs in a "population of strategies." Thus, it is possible that there are multiple simultaneous mutations occurring, and the ability of one strategy to predominate against another will depend not only on how the strategy does against a particular mutation but also on how each performs against other common "adversaries." To develop an appropriate notation that handles this possibility, let s_j ($j = 0, 1, 2, \ldots, n$) denote a particular strategy and let p_j denote the probability that any particular creature employs strategy s_j. Further, let s_0 denote the "normal" (nonmutant) strategy (which means that p_0 is very much larger than p_1, p_2, and so on), and let s_n denote the particular mutant strategy that concerns us. Then the extension and general form of expression (4.7) becomes

$$p_0 U(s_0,s_0) + p_n U(s_0,s_n) + \Sigma \, p_j U(s_0,s_j), \qquad (4.9)$$

and the extension and general form of expression (4.8) is

$$p_0 U(s_n,s_0) + p_n U(s_n,s_n) + \Sigma \, p_j U(s_n,s_j) \qquad (4.10)$$

where both summations are over all values of j except $j = 0$ and n.

The particular difficulty with the Prisoners' Dilemma, now, is that there are a great many strategies for which $U(s_0,s_0) = U(s_n,s_n)$ and $U(s_0,s_n) = U(s_n,s_n)$—Tit-for-Tat and Always Cooperate are two such examples, since neither ever defects against the other. One may hold an advantage over the other, however, because it performs better

---

[6]We need not assume that mixed strategies are actually employed by people. In the current interpretation, there is, in fact, a mathematical equivalence between populations whose members all abide by the same mixed strategy and a population which is composed of players who use pure strategies, where members of the population interact randomly, and the different pure strategies are represented in the population in proportion to the probabilities assigned by the evolutionary stable mixed strategy. What is required for this isomorphism, however, is that participants not be able to identify the strategy type of any other player.

against a third type of strategy that appears in (4.9) and (4.10) only after the summation signs. Suppose there are three strategies: Tit-for-Tat (TFT); Tit-for-Two-Tats (TF2T, which allows for being the victim of two consecutive defections before it retaliates with a defection); and Suspicious-Tit-For-Tat (STFT, which begins with a defection and plays TFT thereafter). Notice now that TF2T can invade a population in which everyone plays TFT if it performs better against STFT than does TFT—if

$$U(\text{TF2T},\text{STFT}) > U(\text{TFT},\text{STFT}).$$

To see that this inequality in fact holds, notice first that TF2T versus STFT yields the sequence of choices (Cooperate, Defect), (Cooperate, Cooperate), (Cooperate, Cooperate), . . .—or, using the same numbers used to generate Figure 4.12, the sequence of payoffs -3, 4, 4, 4, and so on. One the other hand, TFT versus STFT yields (Cooperate, Defect), (Defect, Cooperate), (Cooperate, Defect), (Defect, Cooperate), . . .—or, the payoff sequence -3, 7, -3, 7, -3, and so on. Thus, as long as the discount rate does not weight the second-round payoff of 7 too greatly at the expense of subsequent payoffs, TF2T can invade TFT (as when $r = 4/7$).

We can use the preceding argument, now, to establish that no pure strategy is evolutionary stable for the Prisoners' Dilemma in every possible environment. No pure strategy, of course, is dominant and thus no such strategy is at least as good and sometimes better than any other. Suppose X and Y are two strategies that earn the same payoff against each other as they do against themselves. Then there exists a strategy Z that is better against X than it is against Y, and there exists another strategy W that is better against Y than it is against X. Then, if X is the normal strategy and if Y and Z are possible mutants, Y can invade because of its relative advantage with respect to Z. On the other hand, if Y is the normal strategy and X and W are the mutant types, X can invade Y. What such an exercise tells us, then, is that the types of strategies likely to prevail as evolutionary stable strategies will either be mixed strategies or pure strategies that are dependent on the allowed types of "mutant" perturbations.

Let us conclude this chapter now by returning to the problem we discussed in the last section of chapter 2. Recall that the issue there concerned the possibility that people might not choose a perfect equilibrium by accepting an initial offer of $10 in a game that can yield considerably greater payoffs if the players postpone making subgame perfect dominant choices. To reexamine this problem in

	b_1	b_2
a_1	10,.50	10,.50
a_2	5,100	1000,50

Figure 4.14

the present context, consider an especially simple version of the game in which A has one decision node with two choices—a_1 (accept the $10 in which case B gets $ .50), and a_2 (pass the decision on to B)—and B has one decision node—b_1 (accept $100 in which case A gets $5), or b_2 (let A receive $1,000 in which case B gets $50). The strategic form, then, looks like the one in Figure 4.14.

Notice now that this game is much like a Prisoners' Dilemma, except that B's first strategy only weakly dominates the second. If we can imagine, then, a society in which people play this and similar games a great many times in their life, perhaps even alternating roles between A and B, then we should also be easily able to construct an analysis of this situation that parallels our analysis of the Prisoners' Dilemma and in which the strategy pair (a_2,b_2) emerges as an equilibrium from repeated play or emerges as part of an evolutionary stable strategy. If we suppose, for example, that societies that produce people who frequently choose a_2 and b_2 will be more productive than those in which people choose a_1 and b_1, and that more productive societies will flourish at the expense of less productive ones, then we can imagine a proclivity to choose a_2 and b_2 as part of society's social fabric, even perhaps as part of each person's genetic makeup.

Suggestions for Further Reading

The discussion in sections 4.1–4.4 illustrates some of the modeling of electoral processes that game theory allows, and reveals that we are not limited to analyzing only two-candidate elections under simple majority rule. Presently, however, the comparative analysis of alternative electoral systems is an area desperately in need of further development. The interested reader should begin with the series of essays by Gary Cox, "Electoral Equilibrium under Alternative Voting Institutions," *American Journal of Political Science*, 31 (1987): 82–108; "Centripetal and Centrifugal Incentives in Electoral Systems," *American Journal of Political Science*, 34 (1990): 903–35; and "Multicandidate Spatial Competition," in James Enelow and Melvin Hinich's edited volume, cited in the previous chapter. Insofar as the issue of the response of candidates to the threat of entry, see Thomas R. Palfrey, "Spatial Equilibrium with Entry," *Review of Economic Studies*, 51 (1984): 139–56. Coincidentally, on the issue of the tendency for plurality systems to yield two parties, see Thomas R. Palfrey, "A Mathematical Proof of Duverger's Law," in P.C. Ordeshook, ed., *Models of Strategic Choice in Politics*, Ann Arbor: University of Michigan Press, 1989, and Timothy J. Federson, Itai Sened, and Steven G. Wright, "Rational Voting and Candidate Entry Under Plurality Rule," *American Journal of Political Science*, 34 (1990): 1005–16. These last two essays, though, use game theoretic tools that are discussed in chapter 5. With respect to our discussion of Hare voting in section 4.4, examples of additional problems with this procedure are offered in Steven J. Brams and Peter C. Fishburn, "Some Logical Defects of the Single Transferable Vote," in Arend Lijphart and Bernard Grofman, eds., *Choosing an Electoral System*, New York, Praeger, 1984. However, the analysis of strategic voting under this and other complex procedures remains an important research frontier.

The topic of incentive compatibility is, as our quotation from Benjamin Franklin indicates, an old one, but the application of game theory is relatively new. Little of this literature, however, has made its way into political science, and it remains primarily in the "economic domain." A good introductory treatment of the tax system that we consider in Section 4.5 is offered in Allan M. Feldman, *Welfare Economics and Social Choice Theory*, Boston: Kluwer-Nijhoff, 1980. For a general discussion of the substantive problem in the context of specific case studies, see Elinor Ostrom, *Governing the Commons: The Evolution of Institutions for Collective Action*, NY: Cambridge University Press, 1990.

Ostrom's text can also serve as a good introduction to the substantive significance of the Prisoners' Dilemma, the topic of sections 4.7 and 4.8. The applications of this game as a model of various political-economic processes is, as section 4.7 indicates, substantial. However, the seminal essay on the substantive application of the Prisoners' Dilemma to politics is Mancur Olson, *The Logic of Collective Action*, Cambridge: Harvard University Press, 1968. The source of illustration of the potential inefficiency of legislative action is taken from Emerson Niou and Peter C. Ordeshook, "Universalism in Congress," *American Journal of Political Science*, 29 (1985): 246–58; our example of the dilemma of vote trading is from William H. Riker and Steven Brams, "The Paradox of Vote Trading," *American Polit-*

ical Science Review, 67 (1973): 1235–47; and the source of our example of arms races is from R. Harrison Wagner, "The Theory of Games and the Problem of International Cooperation," *American Political Science Review*, 77 (1983): 330–46. Most current theorizing, though, focuses on the topic that section 4.8 introduces—the sustainability of cooperation via repeated play of the Dilemma. The seminal text here is Michael Taylor, *Anarchy and Cooperation*, NY: Wiley and Sons, 1976, but the reader should also consult Taylor's other volume, *The Possibility of Cooperation*, Cambridge: Cambridge University Press, 1987, and Robert Axelrod, *The Evolution of Cooperation*, 1984, NY: Basic Books. Insofar as current research directions are concerned, perhaps the most interesting are: Jonathan Bendor and Dilip Mookherjee, "Institutional Structure and the Logic of Ongoing Collective Action," *American Political Science Review*, 81 (1987): 129–54, which focuses on the possibility of using a federalized (decentralized) system to facilitate monitoring defections from cooperation; William T. Bianco and Robert H. Bates, "Cooperation By Design: Leadership Structure and Collective Dilemmas," *American Political Science Review*, 84 (1990): 133–47, which considers the role of leadership in initiating and sustaining cooperation; and Randall L. Calvert, "Reciprocity among Self-Interested Actors: Uncertainty, Asymmetry, and Distribution," in the previously cited edited volume by Ordeshook, which considers the possibility of cooperation when people are asked to cooperate (in the form of granting favors) only probabilistically.

On the topic of evolutionary stable strategies, there are a great many sources which the reader might consult in this newly developing field. However, the best starting point is John Maynard Smith, *Evolution and the Theory of Games*, Cambridge, Cambridge University Press, 1982. Our discussion of the evolutionary stable properties of tit-for-tat is taken from Robert Boyd and Jeffrey P. Lerderbaum, "No Pure Strategy is Evolutionary Stable in the Prisoners' Dilemma Game," *Nature*, 327 (1987): 58–9.

Exercises

1. Suppose two presidential election candidates, who maximize their probability of winning, must decide how to allocate three days among six states. Whoever allocates the most time to a state wins that state and whoever wins the most electoral votes wins the election. The states' electoral votes are as follows: 27, 27, 24, 18, 2, and 2. Assume that all ties are broken by a coin

toss and that transportation technology renders days non-divisible.

    a. Does the corresponding two-candidate election game have a Nash equilibrium in pure strategies?

    b. Does your answer change if the three largest states have the same electoral weight?

    c. Does your answer to part (a) change if days are divisible?

    d. Does your answer to part (a) change if the candidates have four days to allocate?

    e. What allocations would you predict would be made to the smallest states under the various circumstances described above? Why?

    f. How are your answers to (a-e) changed if the candidates maximize expected electroal college vote plurality?

2. Suppose there are six voters, 1, 2, 3, 4, 5, and 6, who are all concerned with the same issue, who have most-preferred positions that are ordered the same as their labels (i.e., 1 most prefers the leftmost position and 6 the rightmost position), and who have single-peaked preferences on this issue. Also, suppose that weighted voting is used and that voter i has i votes. If two plurality-maximizing candidates are free to adopt any position on the issue as their election platform, and if all of the conditions for the Median Voter Theorem are otherwise satisfied, which voter's ideal point will they adopt as their platform?

3. In addition to choosing a policy on the real line, suppose the candidates can also try to mask their positions by presenting themselves as lotteries—as probability distributions over the feasible policy space. Suppose that two parameters—the mean and variance—characterize a candidate's strategy (such as when that strategy corresponds to a normal density function), and that voter i's utility for position x is $u_i(x) = -(x_i - x)^2$. Describe the two-candidate election equilibrium if all other provisions of the Median Voter Theorem apply.

4. Apply the Median Voter Theorem to solve the following questions, using this data:

voter	ideal pt.	candidate	promise	mother
A	1	I	3	A
B	2	II	5	B
C	3	III	7	C
D	4	IV	9	D
E	5	V	9	E
F	7			
G	9			
H	11			
J	13			

    a.   Assuming that you like to win and that only one of the other candidates listed above will compete against you, which of the above candidates would you like to be?

    b.   Suppose five voters are actually the candidates' mothers, who, if given the opportunity, vote for their children regardless of the effect on their own utilities. Except for this restriction on preferences, assume that all conditions of the Median Voter Theorem hold. Given the maternal relationships identified in the data, how would your answer change?

5. Consider a twenty five voter electorate that is distributed across five districts (A,B,C,D,E). Five voters live in each district, and each voter is identified by his or her district (e.g., each a lives in A) and his or her ideal point on the policy $X = [1,9]$. Suppose the ideal points of the voters are as follows:

$x=1$	$x=2$	$x=3$	$x=4$	$x=5$	$x=6$	$x=7$	$x=8$	$x=9$
b	b	b	a	a	a	a	a	d
e	c	c	b	b	c	c	d	d
e	c	e	d	d	e			
				e				

All voters have single-peaked preferences. The electorate chooses a policy on X by using the following procedure: First, using majority rule, voters within each district choose a legislator from two possible candidates, where these candidates compete by choosing positions on X. Second, the five legislators, who are constrained to most prefer the policy they advocated in getting elected and to offer that policy as a proposal before the full legislature, meet and must decide, by majority rule, which point on X will be the new policy.

    a.   Tell which policy will be chosen assuming that all legislators are sophisticated and choose an agenda at random from the set of possible binary agendas, and explain why.

    b.   How does your answer to (a) change if states A and D and the voters in them are eliminated?

    c.   How does your answer to (a) change if states C and E and the voters in them are eliminated?

6. Consider a nine-voter electorate in which voter i's ideal point on the issue equals i. Suppose a two-candidate election is held and that all of the assumptions needed for the median voter result hold except that candidate I must choose voter 3's ideal point as his stated policy. Candidate II has no such restriction.

    a.   Who wins the election?

    b.   Below are four possible descriptions of the outcome. Decide which of the following statements are true.
        i.   The median voter's ideal point must be the outcome.
       ii.   The median voter's ideal point cannot be the outcome, but another voter's ideal point can be the outcome.
      iii.   The median voter's ideal point cannot be the outcome and neither can any other voter's ideal point.
      iv.   Either the median voter's ideal point or another voter's ideal point can be the outcome.

7. Suppose an electorate consists of five votes with the following preferences over the three platforms that each of two candidates might choose:

voters 1 and 2:	A	B	C
voter 3:	A	C	B
voters 4 and 5:	C	B	A

Suppose each voter, after each candidate (simultaneously) chooses his or her platform, votes for his or her preferred candidate with probability p and for the opponent with probability $1-p, p > 1/2$. If a voter is indifferent, $p = 1/2$. What is the final outcome (A, B, or C) if both candidates maximize their expected plurality?

8. Consider the following twenty nine-player game, where two players (I and II) are candidates and the other players, $(1,2,. . .,27)$, are voters. Candidates will compete for office by using one of four possible campaign strategies, (A,B,C,D), to recruit voters that will vote for them. The outcome of the election will be determined by which of the two candidates has recruited the most voters. In the first stage of the game, the two candidates simultaneously choose one of the four campaign strategies. For some combinations of campaign strategy choices (BB, CC, DB), the candidates must debate. Candidates choose debate strategies simultaneously, but afterward they both learn the other's campaign strategy. Below is a table that shows the results of different combinations of campaign strategies. The cell values represent the number of voters recruited by candidate I (row chooser); 27 minus the cell value equals the number of voters recruited by candidate II (column chooser).

	A	B	C	D
A	15	3	21	7
B	9	12 | 27 / 0 | 15	5	13
C	17	19	24 | 17 / 14 | 18	23
D	11	12 | 13 / 11 | 14	27	11

After the campaign, the winner of the election is determined by majority rule. Thus, the candidate that recruits a majority of voters, wins the election.

    a.   Which candidate wins the election?

    b.   If campaign laws are changed so that strategy D cannot be chosen, which candidate wins the election?

    c.   Suppose you are hired by the candidate who expects to lose in part (a) in order to propose a series of districts and an electoral rule that ensures a different electoral outcome (after recruits are recruited). You are not restricted in the number of districts you can use, or how you can allocate candidate I and II's supporters within and across districts; however, there must be the same number of voters in each district.

9. A nine-member legislature using majority rule faces a budget which allows them to pass two of three proposed programs (A,B,C). The legislature has the following preference orders (ranked from most to least preferred):

Legislator

1	2	3	4	5	6	7,	8	9
B	A	B	A	C	C	B	A	C
C	B	A	C	A	B	A	C	B
A	C	C	B	B	A	C	B	A

You chair the legislature and are legislator 1. The voting procedure is as follows:

First, vote whether to keep or veto alternative B. If B is vetoed the voting ends and alternatives A and C are implemented. If B is kept, then vote whether to keep or veto alternative C. If C is vetoed, the voting ends and alternatives A and B are implemented. If C is kept, then vote whether to keep or veto alternative A. If A is vetoed, the voting ends and alternatives B and C are implemented. If A is kept, one member of the legislature must choose which alternative should be vetoed.

    a.   As chairman, should you choose yourself to make this veto decision or legislator 4?

    b.   Assuming that legislator 4 makes the veto decision, design an agenda of the type illustrated in which B and C are nevertheless passed.

10. In a seven-person electorate, all election outcomes depend on the candidate's positions on one policy dimension, and the ideal point of voter i on this dimension, x_i, equals i. All voter utility functions are of the form $u_i = -|W - x_i|^2$ where W is the policy position of the winning candidate and x_i is voter i's ideal point. In this electorate there are two political parties. Voters 1, 2, and 7 are in party X. Voters 4, 5, and 6 are in party Y. Voter 3 is in neither party. There are four possible candidates—X_1, X_2, Y_1, and Y_2. Party X uses majority rule to nominate X_1 or X_2. Party Y uses majority rule to nominate Y_1 or Y_2. All voters then choose among the two nominated candidates to determine W, the policy position of the winning candidate. Assume that all assumptions necessary for the Median Voter Theorem hold except in the case where they conflict with the statement of the question. Use the concept of Nash equilibrium to find the possible locations of W in the following two situations.

   a. Voters are nonstrategic when nominating a candidate.

   b. Voters are strategic when nominating a candidate.

11. Let four individuals have the following net valuations over the three alternatives, A, B, and C:

person	A	B	C
1	30	0	50
2	45	65	0
3	10	20	45
4	50	35	0

Assume that each person must report a valuation for each alternative and that the alternative chosen is the one with highest summed valuation. Assume also that taxes are collected as described in Section 4.5.

   a. How much incremental tax will be paid by each person?

   b. Suppose persons 2 and 3 can hire an agent who will coordinate their responses (reported evaluations), including lies. Should they hire such a person if the fee is not too great?

12. For what values of *x* is the following game a Prisoners' Dilemma?

x,1	3,−4
1,3	2,3

13. What is the minimum fine someone could levy such that the following game is not a Prisoners' Dilemma (payoffs are to the row chooser and column chooser faces an equivalent choice)? What minimum fine renders the game not only not a Prisoners' Dilemma but establishes the "efficient" strategy as dominant?

0	9
−1	3

14. If free competition reigns in an industry, 20 million units of that industry's products will be sold by each firm at a net profit of $1 per item. But if they collude to set a higher price, each firm will sell 15 million units at a net profit of $2 each. If one firm defects to a lower price, its sales will soar to 35 million units while every other firm will sell nothing, and the creditors will begin to circle overhead. Senator Billie Bob proposes a licensing agreement whereby each member of the industry must pay a tax of $.20/item to produce the product at the fixed price that the cartel prefers—ostensibly to insure that "destructive competition" does not "leave hard-working Americans unemployed." What is the upper limit on how much money he can extract from each firm in the form of campaign contributions to his party?

15. If the cartel price for some commodity earns each firm ten million dollatr, if each firm can earn $3 million in the competitive market, and if each firm can, by defecting from the cartel, capture the entire market, which of the following games best illustrates this situation (all numbers are in millions)?

a.

10,3	12,0
0,12	3,10

b.

10,10	20,0
0,20	3,3

c.

0,0	10,0
0,10	3,3

d.

10,10	0,20
20,0	3,3

e. None of the above

16. You direct Consolidated Smoke and you must decide whether or not to agree to meet the president of Acme Sludge so that the two of you can fix prices for your similar products, in which case your corporations each earn $220 million. Both of you recognize however that the situation is a Prisoners dilemma: at the market price, you each earn $90 million, while if only one defects from the agreement, his corporation earns $300 million and the other corporation earns "zip." Being competitive entrepreneurs with your MBA's, neither of you trusts the other to maintain any agreement reached. An additional danger is that federal antitrust investigators (with probability .4) will detect your agreement, negate the price fixing scheme, and impose a fine of $50 million each. Congressman I. M. Crass, however, proposes to offer legislation that will make the cartel legal and enforceable in a court of law, and that will provide the regulatory teeth to maintain it; but he demands some assistance in the next election, say $50 million from each firm. The problem is he wants his money up front, before the legislature votes, and he can promise only a fifty-fifty chance that the proposed legislation will pass. Assuming that you make the best decision possible in the circumstances, what are your firm's expected profits?

17. Three students, 1, 2, and 3, have enrolled in Political Theory and the instructor has announced beforehand that he will award one A, one C, and one F (no pass-fail option this quarter). Homework does not count towards the final grade and the students have earned scores of 55, 65, and 70 respectively on their midterm exam. Each student associates a payoff of 2, 1, and −1, respectively with receiving an A, C, or F, and each knows that if they study at maximum effort they will earn an 80 on the final exam, and a moderate-low effort will yield a grade of 40. Suppose that, *ceteris paribus*, each student prefers as little effort as possible, but is willing to study if doing so changes that student's grade for the better. A student's final grade is based on

his or her relative standing as determined by the sum of mid-term plus final exam grades.

    a. Assuming that all three students must decide whether or not to study without being informed about the action taken by any other student, portray the situation in strategic form, with letter grades denoting the outcomes in each cell.

    b. Is there a determinate final outcome?

    c. Suppose students 1 and 2 can observe 3's action beforehand. Does this change this decision and the final outcome?

18. Suppose voter ideal points are distributed uniformly on the interval [0,1] and that, unless otherwise noted, all conditions of the Median Voter Theorem are satisfied. Suppose three candidates, 1, 2, and 3, must choose their positions in [0,1] sequentially—first 1, then 2, then 3.

    a. Establish (without excessive formalism, even if that requires cutting a few corners) that the equilibrium matches the one outlined in the last example of section 4.3 in which candidates 1 and 2 choose their positions simultaneously.

    b. Why do you think these answers are the same?

19. Two farmers must share an irrigation system, which they use by alternating their access to it day-by-day. The farmer whose turn it is to extract water on a particular day must choose between taking the allotted share (for a benefit of 0 to himself and a cost of 0 to the other farmer) versus taking more than the allotted share (for a benefit of B to the farmer in question and a cost of C to the other farmer). However, the farmer who must otherwise sit idly by for the day can choose to inspect his opposite number's activities at a cost to himself of K. If an excessive extraction is detected, the farmer is empowered to fine the offender an amount F, which can be kept as compensation for any economic injury.

    a. Assuming that all parameter values exceed zero, and taking a myopic one day view, for what parameter values is there a pure strategy equilibrium in which the farmer inspects with certainty?

b. Assuming that there is no pure strategy equilibria, what is the mixed strategy equilibrium?

c. Suppose that one of the farmers is to be picked at random as the one to use the irrigation system, and suppose the parameters are set such that (take more than allotted share, inspect) is a pure strategy equilibrium. Can we raise the value of F so that the farmers prefer that there not be any pure strategy equilibrium over what they would expect to get from playing the game with the old parameter values?

20. Two lobbyists, 1 and 2, each seek legislation that is diametrically opposed to the legislation sought by the other. Since we cannot construe this legislation as being "in the public interest," they must decide when to contribute money to a legislator's campaign war chest. (Assume legislators "come cheap," so the size of the contribution can be ignored in the calculation of a lobbyist's payoff.) The legislator sees no reelection threat and intends to convert this war chest into a personal retirement fund. But in the science-fiction world of this problem, suppose the law frowns on all such activities and that as a consequence, neither lobbyist dares to make a second offer if his or her first one is refused. The exact nature of the legislator's behavior, however, is unknown, so both lobbyists employ the following model: If the lobbyists commit at times t_1 and t_2 $(0 < t_1, t_2 < 1)$, respectively, and if $t_i < t_j$, then the probability that the contribution leads the legislator to support i is t_i. If the legislator does not commit to supporting i at this time, he either supports the legislation sought by j with probability t_j or he supports no one with probability $1-t_j$. The possibility exists, then, that the legislator never commits and that neither lobbyist gets he wants. Assume that the payoff of no legislation to a lobbyist is equivalent to an even chance that one or the other lobbyist gets his or her way.

a. If lobbyist i $(i = 1$ or $2)$ makes the first move (by choosing $t_i < t_j$), lobbyist j learns this fact at that time and also learns the legislator's response to i's offer. Letting a strategy be the time at which to make the offer, does this situation have a pure strategy equilibrium, and if so, what is it?

b. How is the situation changed if an offer and its rejection (but not its acceptance) cannot be observed by the competing lobbyist?

21. Show that if the "normal" strategy in a society playing the Prisoners' Dilemma is TFT, and if the allowable mutants are STFT, ALLD (always defect), and TF2T, then TF2T can invade if the probability of ALLD is low compared to STFT, whereas the opposite is true if ALLD is more common.

5

Games With Incomplete Information

5.1 Incomplete Information

Thus far we have assumed that any uncertainty we choose to incorporate into our models has nature's random moves as its source. More importantly, if nature's moves are revealed to one person, we assume that they are revealed to everyone, so that there are no informational asymmetries—no one has any private information, aside, possibly, from the choices they make as the situation unfolds. More generally, though, many important political processes can be modeled only if we assume that decision makers have private information, such as the details of their own preferences or their capabilities. A great many examples and subsidiary questions come easily to mind:

> What costs are terrorists willing to incur after hijacking a plane, and how willing should a government be to make concessions or to risk sacrificing hostages?

> What are a weapon system's capabilities that might not be observable or measurable by other countries, and how does this asymmetry in information affect the willingness of countries to engage in arms control negotiations?

> How can a congressional committee monitor and regulate an executive agency when it knows that the agency will have better information about the program's performance than Congress once that program goes into effect?

> How should we approach a negotiation if we don't know an adversary's willingness to compromise or how it values time?

> When some voters are informed about a legislator's actions and others are not, what weight will the legislator give to the informed versus the uninformed members of his constituency?

> With respect to the important issue of strategic deterrence, will a

country be willing to actually implement its threat to launch a mutually costly counterattack if attacked?

These examples have one common element: One person knows something that another does not know—costs, capabilities, policy position, program performance, and so on. Thus, it appears that parts of the extensive forms that we might create to represent these situations will be unknown to different persons and, therefore, that answering these questions will require tools in addition to the ones that previous chapters offer. Indeed, we will have to augment our tools, because the asymmetric information in our examples opens the door to new and more complicated forms of "he-thinks-that-I-think" regresses and to more complicated forms of strategic interaction.

To see the nature of the problem, consider first this restatement of the "he-thinks" regress that led to the development of the idea of a Nash equilibrium for a two-person scenario:

> *I believe that you believe that the game we are playing is . . ., in which case you will conclude that . . . is an appropriate equilibrium strategy. And you believe that I believe that the game we are playing is . . ., in which case you will conclude that I will choose . . . as my strategy.*

At this point we can label the game "solved," because our beliefs, by assumption, are identical. In contrast, suppose our beliefs are not identical because we each hold some private information. Of course, each of us might reasonably be expected to begin the "play of the game" with some initial guess about what it is that we don't know and about each other's information. But since these are only guesses, we might find, as the situation unfolds, that each of us is making choices that are inconsistent with initial suppositions—instead of choosing . . ., I observe you choosing something else. At this point both of us might have reason to revise our initial guesses about the situation, but such reasoning opens the door to thoughts of the following variety:

> *If I know something that you don't know and if you are aware of your own uncertainty, then I may try to deceive you. However, based on what you know about the situation's strategic structure, you might try to infer my knowledge from what I say or do as the situation unfolds. Of course, I know you will try to make such inferences, and therefore I will choose my strategy carefully so that it is not only a best response to your actions, but also so that it leads you to believe things that induce actions on your part that are advantageous for me. However, you know that I am trying to do this, and therefore you have reason*

to interpret my actions carefully—possibly as part of an attempted deception.

To bring matters closer to home, recall those glorious years in which dating and thoughts about it led to endless periods of introspective agony. "If I tried to kiss her, would she humiliate me with rejection or would she respond in kind?" "Will he ever try to kiss me, or is he dating me merely to pass the time until he can get a date with . . .?" "How can I signal my desire for a deeper relationship?" "If I ask her out again, will she say no?" "Has he failed to ask me for a date because he's interested in someone else, or is he too shy to make the first move?" The "agony" here, of course, is that at least one person knows something that the other doesn't know—in general, in fact, each knows something that the other doesn't know—in which case neither person can be certain that they understand completely the game being played.

Such situations reveal that our current typology of games—games of perfect and imperfect information—is incomplete. To this typology, we must also add games—games of **asymmetric incomplete information**—in which characteristics of the situation are revealed only to some subset of players so that one or more them knows something about the extensive or strategic form representation of the situation that others don't know.

This chapter discusses a variety of ideas associated with such games, and we begin in the next section by reexamining a critically important assumption that allowed the derivation of the Median Voter Theorem—namely, that voters know the policy positions of the candidates and that candidates know the policy preferences of voters.

5.2 Elections With Uninformed Voters

The election models that we have considered thus far all distort reality in at least one significant way—they assume that voters are perfectly informed about the candidates' issue positions, and they suppose that candidates know the criteria voters use to evaluate them. This, of course, is a curious assumption because public opinion polls tell us that citizens often vote without even knowing the candidates' names, never mind their issue positions. However, in an age when elections in particular and democratic institutions in general appear to be in ascendancy worldwide as the preferred mechanism for choosing governments and for rendering a government legitimate, we ought to ask whether democracies can function effectively in less than perfect information environments. Was the public as easily misled as political commentators would like us to believe in, say, the 1988 U.S. presidential campaign, so that a different candidate (the one from the "miracle" state) would have prevailed if a "more informative" campaign had been run? Does the incomplete information of voters and candidates merely open the door to an insidious use of money as the primary currency of democracy? Do our informational shortcomings allow a hidden "power elite" to control the state so that it can generate policies that benefit it at the expense of everyone else?

Of course, given the small chance that a voter will be decisive in any mass election, and given the cost of information, we should not be surprised by the fact that voters are uninformed. In choosing between learning about a candidate's likely performance if elected versus learning about which lawn mower is the better buy, it is not unreasonable to suppose that learning about lawn mowers is the more efficacious investment. Indeed, those voters who are informed often appear to approach politics as a sport, and they gather information for the same reason that others memorize baseball batting averages, with persons of both type approaching their subject with the understanding that they have a nearly equivalent influence on outcomes.

But consider the hypothesis that voters can effectively use relatively costless cues in deciding for whom to vote. The party identification of a candidate has long been interpreted as such a cue. However, partisan associations are based primarily on historical events, and the particular hypothesis we want to explore here is whether citizens can learn to vote by using relatively costless information that is generated during the course of an election campaign—information such as interest-group endorsements and public opinion polls that report answers to such questions as, "If the election were held today, for whom would you vote?" The particular question we would like to ask is whether we should be disturbed by the fact that citizens, in lieu of reading every news item analyzing current events and in lieu of a thorough analysis of each candidate's record, often use seemingly irrelevant contemporaneous information on which to base their decisions about how to vote (e.g., "I voted for . . . because my brother-in-law preferred . . .," or "I preferred . . . because Sam Donaldson slanted the news in favor of the other candidate").

To approach this topic in a general way, suppose again then that an election concerns a single issue and that voter preferences over this issue look like the ones that set the stage for the Median Voter Theorem. That is, suppose that each registered voter has a well-defined ideal point on the issue and his or her utility declines as we move away from that ideal in either direction. Rather than assume, however, that all citizens know the candidates' positions on this issue, suppose the electorate consists of two types of voters: (1) those who are informed about each candidate's issue position and (2) those who are uninformed. Next, suppose that a poll is published announcing which candidate in a two-candidate election is ahead and by how much.

Informed voters, of course, should not be influenced by the poll; but consider its possible effects on uninformed voters. To see that the information in such a poll need not be irrelevant to their decision and that it can serve as a potentially useful cue, consider an uninformed voter who regards himself as preferring a position to the right of "center" on the election's salient issue and who is concerned that the "conservative" candidate fits the extremist portrait painted by liberal detractors who support the opponent. If asked to vote without any information, this citizen might simply choose randomly or abstain. However, if responses to the question "If the election were held today, . . .?" indicate that public preferences are evenly divided between the candidates, then only two hypotheses are consistent with this estimate. The first possibility, of course, is that very few people know the candidates' positions and that the polls are meaningless. Barring this possibility, however, and supposing that a "reasonable" proportion of those polled know where the candidates are, then either (1) both candidates are extremists of the opposite sort or (2) both candidates are near the median respondent.

If our uninformed voter assumes that the poll contains some true information about preferences and perceptions, then regardless of whether subcondition (1) or (2) holds, the most likely possibility is that he or she is closer to the conservative than to the liberal candidate: It cannot be simultaneously true that the poll's respondents are informed and that the liberal is a moderate and the conservative an extremist, because this circumstance would produce a poll that shows the moderate holding a significant lead. Nor can it be true for the same reason that the liberal is an extremist and the conservative is a moderate. Hence, if this citizen reasonably infers a preference for the conservative and if this or other similar people are polled in a subsequent survey—including the election itself—they should no longer choose randomly but should hold a preference for the conservative.

Now consider an electorate in which each citizen's preferences on the issue are described by simple distance from the citizen's ideal point, so voters vote for the candidate who they believe is closest to their ideal. For example, suppose the electorate is divided evenly

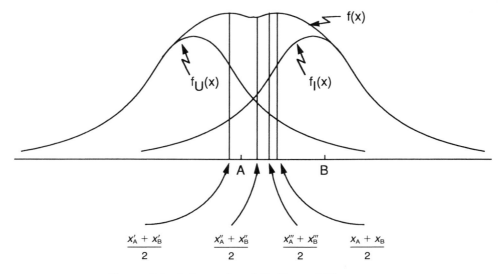

Figure 5.1 Informed and Uniformed Electorates

into uninformed and informed subparts and that the ideal point density for each subpart is as shown in Figure 5.1 (f_U and f_I, respectively, with f being the overall preference density). The upper part of this figure, which portrays the respective cumulative densities, F_U, F_I, and F, is provided so that we can more easily compute the proportion of uninformed and informed who have ideal points to the left or right of any issue position. With respect to the information available to voters, informed voters are defined as those who know the positions of the two candidates, say x_A and x_B. Uninformed voters do not know x_A and x_B but suppose that on the basis of interest-group endorsements or the candidates' party labels, they know that $x_A < x_B$. (They know that A is the "liberal," B the "conservative.")

Looking now at what happens in a sequence of public opinion polls that ask, "If the election were held today . . .?" informed voters have a clear preference. In particular, we have drawn f_I in Figure 5.1 so that 30% most prefer A and 70% most prefer B. But if the uninformed voters included in the poll are loath to admit that they are uninformed and, therefore, respond randomly, and if we assume also (for purposes of an example) that there is approximately the same number of informed and uninformed voters, then an initial poll produces the result shown in Table 5.1 under poll 1. Of course, pollsters do not know who is informed or uninformed—they merely report the aggregate (average) result, which in this instance is a forty–sixty split between A and B.

	Poll 1		Poll 2		. . .	Poll *n*	
	A	B	A	B		A	B
informed	30%	70%	30%	70%		30%	70%
uninformed	50	50	72	28		92	8
reported	40	60	51	49		61	39

Table 5.1 Poll Sequence

To this point the poll serves the interest of those who look at politics as a spectator sport. But now, in order to show how a poll might be used by an uninformed voter to make an informed decision, suppose that uninformed voters are armed with one additional piece of information—they know their preferences on the issue relative to the population. That is, suppose each uninformed voter knows what proportion of the overall electorate prefers policies to the right and to the left of his or her ideal. If an uninformed voter assumes that all others are informed, then any such voter can (inaccurately) infer from the poll whether the midpoint between the candidates is to the left or right of his or her ideal point. And this inference, in combination with the knowledge of which candidate is to the left of the other, allows a person to infer which candidate is closer to that voter's ideal. In particular, all uninformed voters with ideal points to the right of the fortieth percentile will infer that candidate B is closer to their ideal, and those to the left infer a preference for A.

Now consider what happens in a second poll. Informed voters, of course, are unaffected by the poll results because they know the candidates' positions and so they continue to divide 30–70 between A and B. But uninformed voters no longer choose randomly (although those between the 40th and 61st percentile are choosing incorrectly), and if all such voters to the left of the 40th percentile indicate a preference for A while all uninformed voters to the right of this percentile indicate a preference for B, then, as Figure 5.1 shows, uninformed voters divide 72–28. The overall poll as reported in Table 5.1 under poll 2, then, is 51% for A, 49% for B.

At this point uninformed voters with ideal points between the 40th and 51st percentiles should change their preference from B to A on the basis of a reestimate of the position of the candidates' midpoint relative to their ideal. That is, the link between polls and inferred preference introduces a dynamic to the process, and the question we should ask is whether this process ends at any particular point—is there a poll that reproduces itself and toward which this dynamic inevitably moves? Our answer to this question (ignoring some mathematical niceties) is that this process converges (poll n) to a situation in which all uninformed voters to the left of the **actual** midpoint vote for A and those to the right choose B. That is, in equilibrium, all uninformed voters act like informed ones.

To see that this result is true, notice first that if everyone somehow infers the true midpoint, then any poll will reproduce itself and therefore it cannot cause any uninformed voter to revise his or her preference. On the other hand, if the midpoint assumed by uninformed voters differs from what informed voters know, then a subsequent poll will average these beliefs and result in a new inferred midpoint that lies somewhere between reality and the old inference (where the specific average depends on the relative proportion of uninformed). A succession of such averages, then, converges to reality. Thus, we have described a situation in which voters act like simple decision makers who condition their decisions on readily available information—in this instance, on a guess, derived from the poll, as to which candidate is closer to their ideal preference. Unlike a standard decision problem, though, we have made information endogenous so that actions in one period (poll) affect information in the next, which in turn affects actions in the next period, and so on.

Turning now to the strategic problem that confronts the candidates, in deciding what policy position to adopt at the beginning of their campaign, these candidates might contemplate appealing only to the informed voters. However, if the candidates appreciate the role that polls can play, they should also appreciate that uninformed voters can eventually act like informed ones. (Indeed, we cannot preclude the possibility that the candidates will attempt to manipulate the polls to their own advantage—a possibility that is especially troublesome in those countries in which the major sources of news have party affiliations.) Thus, in anticipation of events, both candidates should plan on choosing the electorate's overall median preference, and in this way the relevance of the Median Voter Theorem can be reasserted.

Substantively, this result is important. Although we might think that the attention paid to the mass media's predictions in an election campaign is evidence that they regard politics merely as a spectator sport, the preceding model suggests that such monitoring provides a useful cue to the electorate about how to vote. We have reached this conclusion, of course, with a number of heroic assumptions, the most serious being that the election concerns a single issue and that citizens know their relative placement on the issue. Thus, if this model is to be genuinely useful, we must generalize it to accommodate more issues as well as more realistic indirect information sources for voters. In fact, this model is generalizable in the following way: Rather than supposing that uninformed voters know which candidate is to the left and which is to the right, assume, in the case of an election that concerns a single issue, that there are two identifiable subpopulations in the electorate whose preferences are polled and reported separately, and assume that uninformed voters know how preferences are distributed within each subpopulation. Uninformed voters can then use the poll results from each subpart to estimate the midpoint between the candidates as well as their left-right orientation. This approach can then be generalized to n issues by merely supposing that there are $n+1$ such subpopulations.[1]

Any complete model, of course, should also incorporate the fact that many voters use retrospective information in deciding how to vote, as they answer such questions as, "Am I better off today than I was four years ago?" Nevertheless, our discussion does expand the relevance of the Median Voter Theorem, and it shows one circumstance under which uninformed voters can learn to vote correctly and thus, one circumstance under which the candidates will maintain their incentive to converge to the median preference under less than "ideal" conditions.

5.3 A Simple Game of Incomplete Information

In order to render the analysis tractable, the preceding analysis ignores some important possibilities. Most importantly, it ignores the fact that uninformed voters can learn something else as the election campaign proceeds—namely, that the change in a poll tells each uninformed voter that there are other uninformed voters and, therefore, that the poll is an inaccurate source of information about $(x_A + x_B)/2$. In addition, we have not considered the possibility that informed voters, knowing the uninformed voters are using polls to establish a preference, might choose to deliberately misrepresent their

---

[1]Although there are technical conditions that must be placed on the distribution of preferences within subpopulations, we note that these populations need not exhaust the set of all registered voters, nor must they be disjoint. Thus, one subpopulation can consist of "friends at work," and others can be those identified in the media (e.g., "blacks," "farmers," "women over 40," and so on).

preferences so as to get uninformed voters to believe something that isn't true and thereby influence the election's outcome. Empirically, of course, we would hope that assuming that uninformed voters ignore the fact that polls change would not invalidate the general thrust of our model, and we hope also that the coordination required on the part of informed voters to influence outcomes is too great a hurdle for them to overcome. Nevertheless, any analysis that sought to explore matters to the fullest extent possible would have to allow for the possibility that both informed and uninformed voters might try to anticipate future polls in deciding what actions to take initially.

Of course, in the context of a problem in which people are unlikely to invest significant resources in strategic calculation—voting in mass elections—it is not unreasonable to regard an analysis that "explores matters to the fullest" as more a mathematical exercise than a useful model of reality. In other circumstances, however, we cannot as easily assume away this strategic complexity.

Example: A lobbyist (l) who receives twenty dollars if a particular bill passes must choose between

C: Offer a campaign contribution of fifteen dollars to a specific legislator (L) who will be pivotal on the bill's final vote for passage, conditional on the legislator (L) voting for the bill, and

~C: take the chance that the legislator will vote for the bill without the contribution

Appreciating that the magnitudes of the numbers we associate with outcomes are not designed with realism in mind, the lobbyist's payoff from each outcome is

$20   If the bill passes without a bribe having been offered

$5   If the bill passes with a bribe

$0   If the bill fails without a bribe

The problem for the lobbyist, however, is that he is uncertain about how the legislator's constituents feel about the bill, and, for purposes of a numerical example, suppose that, depending on the preferences of constituents, the legislator in question derives either $10 or −$10 from the bill's passage (and nothing if it fails). The legislator's payoffs, then, are

$25   If constituents favor the bill and if the legislator is paid by the lobbyist after voting for the bill

$10   If constituents favor the bill but no bribe rewards the legislator's vote for the bill

$5   If constituents oppose the bill but the legislator is bribed so as to vote for the bill

$0   If the legislator votes against the bill, because there is no bribe and constituents oppose the bill

−$10   If there is no bribe, constituents oppose the bill, and the legislator stupidly votes for the bill's passage

To make this example somewhat more interesting, we let the legislator have the first move in this game, which is either to ask the lobbyist for a contribution (A) or to let the lobbyist make the first approach (~A). Figure 5.2a portrays this situation's extensive form if we assume that the legislator's information about his or her constituents is no better than the lobbyist's. In this instance we give nature an initial move in which it sets constituents' preferences by setting the actual payoffs to the legislator. Thus, the legislator prefers the bill (denoted P) with probability $p(P)$, and holds the opposite preference (denoted ~P) with probability $p(\sim P) = 1 - p(\sim P)$. Notice that the top half of this figure is identical to the lower half except for the preferences the legislator associates with specific outcomes.

To this point our example merely corresponds to a simple game of incomplete information. Suppose, on the other hand, that the legislator knows something—his or her constituents' preferences and thus his or her own preferences—that the lobbyist doesn't know. It might seem that such a possibility violates our common-knowledge assumption because it disallows the lobbyist from knowing an important fact about this game. However, consider the extensive form in Figure 5.2b, which is identical to the one shown in Figure 5.2a except that it removes the information sets surrounding the legislator's decision nodes. Thus, we now have a situation in which the legislator learns nature's move and is aware of his or her own preferences before it is the legislator's turn to first act. The lobbyist, on the other hand, learns the legislator's first move but is uninformed about nature's move.

With respect now to the issue of common knowledge, notice that there is nothing to stop us from assuming that the probabilities $p(P)$ and $p(\sim P)$, as well as the information conveyed in this figure, are common knowledge. Common knowledge does not mean that one

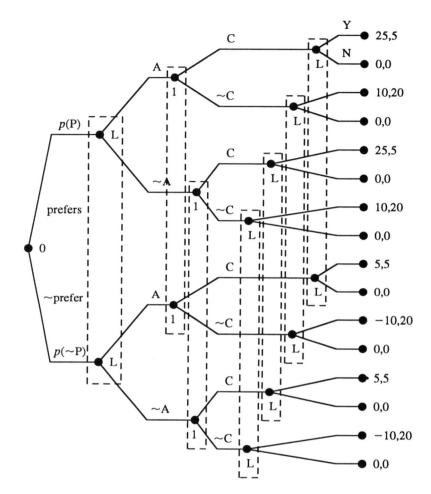

Figure 5.2a Symmetric Incomplete Information

player is precluded from knowing something that another does not
know; instead it simply requires that everyone is aware of the informational uncertainties of others, everyone is aware that everyone
else is aware, and so on. Thus, saying that the structure portrayed
in Figure 5.2b is common knowledge implies that the lobbyist believes that nature chooses between P and ~P with probabilities $p(P)$
and $p(\sim P)$, the legislator is aware of the lobbyist's beliefs, the lobbyist knows that the legislator is aware of these beliefs, . . . and so
on. Put differently, both persons are fully informed about the situ-

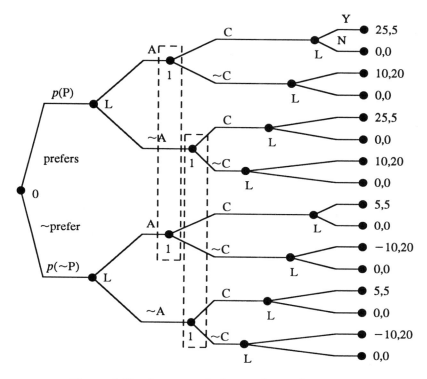

Figure 5.2b Asymmetric Incomplete Information

ation's extensive form, each is aware that the other is aware, and so forth.

Turning to this game's analysis, the lobbyist, of course, must decide whether offering the bribe is a good bet. After all, there is a chance that the legislator will vote for the bill without the "contribution." In deciding what to do and how to approach the situation, one possibility is for the lobbyist to ignore the legislator's initial move and assume simply that the probability that the legislator's constituents favor the bill equals $p(P)$. In this instance, choosing C (offering the bribe) pays five dollars whereas not offering the bribe (~C) pays $20p(P)$. This approach, however, ignores the opportunity for the lobbyist to condition the estimate of this probability on the information set reached—on whether the legislator requests a contribution. The lobbyist could try to estimate "the probability that constituents favor the bill, given that the legislator asks for a contribution," "the probability that constituents favor the bill, given that the legislator does not ask for a contribution," and so on.

At this point in our discussion, we cannot suppose that the method whereby such conditional probabilities are estimated is apparent. Indeed, it is frequently the case that this calculation can be exceedingly difficult. Nevertheless, we can indicate here the general structure of that calculation. Briefly, that calculation makes use of the strategic context of choice. Presumably, the legislator will choose a strategy that specifies whether to choose A or ~A, depending on whether nature chose P or ~P. Thus, if the legislator chooses a strategy that states, in part, "choose A if nature chooses P, but choose ~A if nature chooses ~P," and if the lobbyist knows this strategy, then, since the lobbyist observes the choice of A and ~A, he or she can then infer that nature chose $p(P) = 1$ whenever A is observed, and $p(\sim P) = 1$ whenever ~A is observed.[2] Of course, we must subsequently contend with the fact that the legislator knows that the lobbyist is making such inferences and, therefore, that the lobbyist might prefer to disguise its strategy. But these types of considerations take us ahead of ourselves to notions of equilibrium. Before we can determine what strategies will be chosen, we must first find a general method whereby persons such as our lobbyist can calculate conditional probabilities in potentially more general circumstances.

5.4 Bayes's Rule

As a first step toward analyzing the strategic complexity that private information admits, let us consider a general rule about probability that allows us to calculate conditional probabilities. However, to illustrate this rule, it is convenient to step away from strategic issues and turn our attention instead to a relatively simple one-person decision problem.

Example: A legislator must decide how to vote, believing initially that there is a .75 chance—the legislator's **prior** or initial beliefs about probability—that a majority of his constituents favor its passage. Because the bill is of such profound significance, the legislator will be reelected if and only if his vote on the bill matches the majority preference of his constituency. Thus, a pollster is hired to gauge preferences more accurately. The polls-

---

[2]Notationally, conditional probabilities are written as $p(S|e)$, where S is the outcome or state of nature in question and e is the event that is observed and upon which we condition our estimate of p. Thus, in the present context, the two probabilities being estimated are denoted $p(P|A)$ and $p(\sim P|\sim A)$, respectively.

ter, however, admits that there is only a .95 probability that the poll and the true majority preference will agree, and thus a .05 probability that the poll will indicate a majority in favor (opposed) when in fact a majority opposes (favors) the bill. To represent this situation, let

s_1 denote "a majority favors the bill"
s_2 denote "a majority oppose the bill".

Similarly, let

e_1 denote "the poll indicates that a majority favors the bill"
e_2 denote "the poll indicates that a majority opposes the bill"

In accordance with the legislator's prior probabilities,

$$p(s_1) = .75 \text{ and } p(s_2) = .25.$$

The pollster's information about the accuracy of the poll, on the other hand, can be expressed as

$$p(e_1|s_1) = p(e_2|s_2) = .95,$$
$$p(e_1|s_2) = p(e_2|s_1) = .05.$$

The legislator, however, is not concerned per se with these probabilities. Rather, when it is time to vote, he must consider the likelihood that he is at one decision node versus the other, regardless of which information sets pertains (see Figure 5.3). That is, a choice must be made, conditional on what is observed (e_1 or e_2), so that the numbers that ought to concern the legislator are the conditional **posterior** probabilities $p(s_1|e_1)$, $p(s_1|e_2)$, and so forth. For example, the probability $p(s_1|e_1)$—the probability that a majority favor the bill, given that the poll reveals that such a majority exists—corresponds to the probability, given the pollster's report, that the legislator is at the first node of the first information set.

At this point we can use a general rule about probabilities, Bayes's rule, to calculate the relevant conditional probabilities. Using some general notation, let $\{s_1, s_2, \ldots, s_n\}$ be nature's possible choices and let $\{e_1, e_2, \ldots, e_m\}$ be the events that a decision maker might observe, and upon which he will condition his guess as to the likelihood that nature makes a particular choice. Then

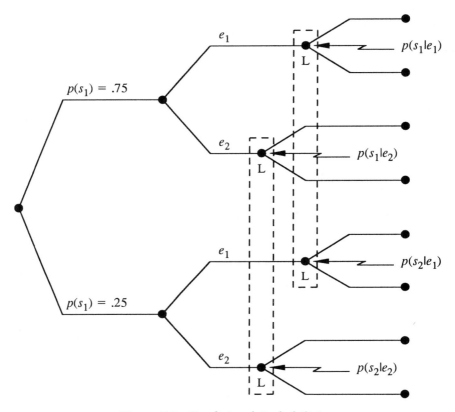

Figure 5.3 Conditional Probabilities

Bayes's Rule *is*

$$p(s_i|e_j) = \frac{p(e_j|s_i)p(s_i)}{p(e_j|s_1)p(s_1) + p(e_j|s_2)p(s_2) + \ldots + p(e_j|s_m)p(s_m)}.$$

Thus, $p(s_1|e_1)$, the probability that a majority of constituents prefer the bill, conditional on the fact that the poll indicates that the elec-torate holds this preference, is given by the equation

$$p(s_1|e_1) = \frac{p(e_1|s_1)p(s_1)}{p(e_1|s_1)p(s_1)+p(e_1|s_2)p(s_2)}$$
$$= .95 \times .75/(.95 \times .75 + .05 \times .25) = .9828.$$

probabilities:

$p(s_1)$	$p(s_2)$	$p(s_3)$	$p(s_4)$	$p(s_5)$	$p(s_6)$
A	A	B	B	C	C
B	C	A	C	A	B
C	B	C	A	B	A

Table 5.2

For another example of the application of Bayes's rule, which illustrates its use in subsequent sections, suppose you are trying to ascertain someone's preferences over three alternatives, A, B, and C. Based on your experience with similar situations, suppose the prior probabilities you associate with each of the six possible preferences orders over these alternatives are as shown in Table 5.2.

Letting e_1 correspond to "A preferred to B" and letting e_2 correspond to "A not preferred to B," clearly the preceding orders require that

$$p(e_j|s_i) = 0 \text{ if } j = 1 \text{ and } i = 3, 4, 6, \text{ or if } j = 2 \text{ and } i = 1, 2, 5,$$
$$p(e_j|s_i) = 1 \text{ if } j = 1 \text{ and } i = 1, 2, 5, \text{ or if } j = 2 \text{ and } i = 3, 4, 6.$$

Now, however, suppose you observe this person committing an act that, for whatever reason, cannot be rationalized if that person prefers A to B. So, excluding the first, second, and fifth orders as possiblities, and substituting the preceding values for $p(e_j|s_i)$, we can use Bayes's rule for computing your posterior probability on, say, the third order, $p(s_3|e_2) = $ "Problbility that s_3 prevails, given that A is not preferred to B.;; In this instance we get

$$p(s_3|e_2) = \frac{p(s_3)}{p(s_3) + p(s_4) + p(s_6)}.$$

5.5 Bayesian Equilibria

To see now how we use Bayes's rule in game theory, let us return to our legislator-lobbyist game and suppose that one or the other player is attempting to establish whether the strategy pair (a_i, b_j) is

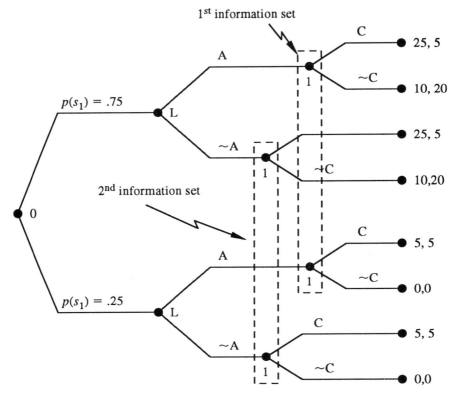

1st information set

A

C
25, 5

~C
10, 20

$p(s_1) = .75$

L

~A

25, 5

~C
10,20

2nd information set

A

C
5, 5

~C
0,0

$p(s_1) = .25$

L

~A

C
5, 5

~C
0,0

0

Figure 5.4 Initial Reduction of Figure 5.2b

an equilibrium. Keeping in mind that (a_i, b_j) is an equilibrium if and only if each strategy is a best response to the other, consider Figure 5.2b again, which, in accordance with the notion of subgame perfection, we simplify in Figure 5.4 by supposing that the legislator, L, only makes dominant choices at his second move (the game's last move). Notice that in this instance, the legislator's strategies are of the form, "If my preferences are . . ., then choose . . . but if my preferences are . . ., then choose . . . instead," whereas the lobbyist's strategies are of theform "If my opponent chooses . . . then choose . . . but if my opponent chooses . . . then choose."

The particular strategic complication confronting the lobbyist, player l, is that to evaluate his or her strategy, he or she must somehow evaluate the probability that nature has selected "prefer" (P) as against "don't prefer" (~P). We assume that $p(P)$ and $p(\sim P)$ are common knowledge, and thus known to the lobbyist, but, as we have already noted, a lobbyist who simply uses these probabilities when computing a strategy's expected value is failing to make full use of the available information. Specifically, the lobbyist observes the legislator's choice, which is itself conditioned on the legislator's preference. So, in evaluating whether the strategy b is a best response for the lobbyist to a, the lobbyist can update the estimate of the likelihood that nature has chosen one state or the other as a function of the legislator's action that is observed. And this updating, we assume, satisfies Bayes's rule.

To see how such conditional probabilities are calculated in this example and how we determine an equilibrium, suppose you are the lobbyist, and consider the pair of strategies (a,b), where

$$a = \text{"if P, choose A; but if } \sim\text{P, choose } \sim\text{A"}$$
$$b = \text{"if A, choose } \sim\text{C; but if } \sim\text{A, choose C."}$$

The first step in determining whether (a,b) is an equilibrium is to determine whether b is a best response to a, which requires first that (we calculate the expected value to l of b when L chooses a. Owing to the simplicity of our game, we can compute this expected return, denoted $E(a,b)$, quite easily by noting that, given a's specification, chooses A only if nature chooses P, which occurs with probability $.75p$—in which case, given that your strategy is b, you get 20—whereas L chooses A only if natures chooses P, which occurs with probability $.25$—in which case you get 5. Thus,[3]

$$E(a,b) = .75(20) + .25(5) = 16.25.$$

---

[3]To see that this straightforward calculation is consistent with Bayes's rule, consider the following reasoning: Suppose you find yourself at your first information set—you observe that L chooses A. Then, given that your strategy is b, you choose $\sim$C and get 20 with probability $p(P|A)$ and 0 with probability $p(\sim P|A)$. If, on the other hand, you find yourself at your second information set—if you observe L choosing A—then, given b, you choose C and get 5 with probability $p(P|\sim A)$ and 5 again with probability $p(\sim P|\sim A)$. Thus, your expected payoff from b, given that the legislator acts in accordance with the strategy a, is

$$E(a,b) = p(A)[20p(P|A) + 0p(P|A)] + p(\sim A)[5p(P|\sim A) + 5p(\sim P|\sim A)].$$

From L's strategy, however, we know that $p(A) = .75$ and $p(A) = .25$. And from Bayes's

Of course, determining whether *b* is a best response to *a* requires ncalculating the expected return to the lobbyist for each of the lobbyist's other strategies. And ascertaining whether (*a,b*) is an equilibrium requires that we determine whether *a* is a best response to *b*. However, before we determine the actual equilibrium for our example, let us first review its structure so we can generalize its analysis. Once again, the important feature of the example is that the legislator knows something about his constituency, and thus, about his preferences, which the lobbyist does not know. Although we might have constructed a more elaborate scenario by allowing the interest group to have some private information, the example's essential features are that

1. Each person is characterized by a parameter that is distributed according to a common-knowledge probability density function.

2. The value of this parameter is "chosen" by nature as the first move in the extensive form.

3. The realization of this parameter is private information. (Since the interest group has no private information, we can think of the density that characterizes its "parameter" as allowing only a single value.)

In the example, that parameter in question is the preference of the legislator's constituency and, by extension, the legislator's preference. The probability that the constituency prefers the bill, however, is common knowledge. That is, although both the legislator and the lobbyist have different information about the constituency, the legislator knows the type of information that the lobbyist possesses,the lobbyist knows that the legislator knows the extent of this information, and so forth.

We can generalize the representation of such situations now by supposing that person *i* is a particular "type," which is determined probabilistically from some set of possibilities. The notion of "type" can refer to almost anything, including even whether the player has meaningful choices and is a relevant participant in the game. Gen-

---

rule,

$$p(P|A) = \frac{p(A|P)p(P)}{p(A|P)p(P) + p(A|\sim P)p(\sim P)}$$

which equals 1 in this instance since L's strategy dictates that $p(A|P) = 0$. Similarly, $p(P|A) = 0$, $p(P|A) = 0$, and $p(P|A) = 1$, which yields $E(a,b) = .75(20) + .25(5) = 16.25$.

erally, though, we let a person's type manifest itself, as in our example, as a particular utility function. Not only does this interpretation allow us to model players who occasionally make mistakes (by maximizing the "wrong" utility function), but it also allows us to consider the possibility that a person is "irrational," by which we mean that the person acts as if he or she is maximizing some improbable or self-destructive utility function. The people who we are modeling are then characterized by a common-knowledge density function $p(t_1,t_2, \ldots ,t_n)$ that specifies the probability that person 1 is of type t_1, person 2 is of type t_2, and so forth. Finally, we suppose that after observing their own type, each person i computes the conditional density $p(t_1, \ldots ,t_{i-1},t_{i+1}, \ldots ,t_n \,|t_i)$ according to Bayes's rule. The simplest possibility, however, is that each person's type is determined independently of every other person, in which case we can characterize the population by a set of densities $\{p_1(t_1), \ldots ,p_n(t_n)$, where $p_i(t_i)$ is the common-knowledge density governing i's type. To keep our discussion of examples as simple as possible, we restrict our attention to this special case.

A *Bayesian equilibrium* to any game in strategic form is defined, now, in a straightforward way. Each person should, of course, condition their strategy on their type, because it is this type that determines preferences over outcomes. Thus, person i knows that at each of j's information sets, j's strategies will be of the form "if I am of type t'_j, then I will choose . . ., if I am of type t''_j, then I will choose. . ., and so forth." Holding everything else constant (including the choices of others if there are more than two relevant persons), the payoff i associates with particular strategies on his and j's part should be computed as follows: the utility of the outcome that follows if j is of type t'_j—the outcome that follows from my choice and the choice that j makes when he or she is of type t'_j—times the probability, $p_j(t'_j)$ that j is of this type, plus the utility of the outcome that follows if j is of type t''_j times the probability, $p_j(t''_j)$, that j is of this type, . . .and so forth. A Bayesian equilibrium is then just like a Nash equilibrium—a strategy n-tuple such that, given their types, and given the probabilities that determine types, no person has any incentive to move unilaterally to some other strategy. Similarly, a Bayesian equilibrium is subgame perfect if it is a Bayesian equilibrium for every subgame.

To complete our analysis of our legislator-lobbyist example, then, notice that L has four strategies that we can represent as follows:

a_1: *Choose A regardless of type.*

a_2: *Choose ~A regardless of type.*

	b_1	b_2	b_3	b_4
a_1	20,5	7.5,15	20,5	7.5,15
a_2	20,5	7.5,15	7.5,15	20,5
a_3	20,5	7.5,15	18.75,3.75	8.75,16.25
a_4	20,5	7.5,15	8.75,16.25	18.75,3.75

Figure 5.5   Strategic Form of Legislator-Lobbyist Game

a_3: *If t'_1, choose A; but if t''_1, choose ~A.*
a_4: *If t'_1, choose ~A; but if t''_1, choose A.*

Similarly, the lobbyist (l) has these four strategies:

b_1: *Choose C regardless.*
b_2: *Choose ~C regardless.*
b_3: *If L chooses A, then choose C; otherwise choose ~C.*
b_4: *If L chooses A, then choose ~C, otherwise choose C.*

We complete the strategic form by entering the expected payoffs into the cells of the 4×4 game matrix, where the computation of these payoffs uses the fact that $p(P) = p(t'_1) = .75$ and $p(\sim P) = p(t''_1) = .25$. For example, (a_3, b_3) yields, "the legislator chooses A and the lobbyist responds with C with probability three fourths and "the legislator chooses ~A and the lobbyist responds with ~C with probability one fourth. Thus, the expected payoff to L of (a_3, b_3) is

$$2(25)3/4 + (0)1/4 = 18.75,$$

whereas the payoff to the lobbyist is

$$(5)3/4 + (0)1/4 \ 3.75.$$

Figure 5.5 portrays the full strategic form and shows that there are two pure strategy equilibria, both involving b_2, in which L chooses a_1 or a_2. Looking back at the actions that a_1 and a_2 imply for L, we see that both equilibria in this instance are pooling equilibria—equilibria in which a person chooses the same act regardless of their

	vote	abstain
vote	$1-C_1$, $-C_2$	$1-C_1$, 0
abstain	0, $1-C_2$	1, 0

Figure 5.6   Two Voters With Incomplete Information

type or the information that nature reveals to them. Thus, in equilibrium, the interest group cannot infer anything about the legislator's type on they basis of the legislator's initial action.[4]

5.6 A Game With Two-Sided Incomplete Information

Actually, we should not be surprised to learn that the legislator's initial choice of A or ~A does not provide any useful information to the lobbyist. Because the choice of A is costless to the legislator, it never hurts to request a bribe, regardless of the attitudes of constituents. On the other hand, our example would have been more interesting if we had assumed that there is a cost associated with choosing A (corresponding, for example, to the chance that constituents learn about the request). Later we will consider such possibilities, but first we want to suppose that more than one person in a situation has private information. Fortunately, this possibility introduces no new conceptual issues.

Example: Suppose two people prefer a different candidate, and suppose, for purposes of an example, that if both vote (for their preferred candidates) or if both abstain, the candidate that voter 1 prefers wins. If C_i is person i's cost of voting, and if a person associates a payoff of 1 with his or her preferred candidate and 0 with the opponent, then Figure 5.6 describes the outcomes that prevail, given the choices of both people (row chooser = person 1, column chooser = person 2). Suppose finally that neither person knows other's cost of voting. Thus, person 1 knows C_1 but not C_2, and 2 knows C_2, but not C_1. Suppose further, however, that 1 knows that C_2 has the same chance of equaling 1/8, 2/8,

---

[4]Of course, we should determine whether there are any mixed strategy equilibria. However, in this instance, a check of possibilities reveals that any mixture over a_1–a_4 that might reasonably be an equilibrium strategy for the legislator would only induce the lobbyist to choose b_2.

and 3/8, and that 2 knows that C_1 has the same chance of equaling 4/8, 5/8, and 6/8. Thus, 'although C_1 and C_2 are random variables, person 1 faces higher average costs than does person 2.

In addition to assuming that both persons have private information, this example differs from the previous one in that neither person has any opportunity to signal anything about their private information. Thus, deception does not appear to be an issue, which might lead us to believe that we can analyze the situation in a more straightforward manner by merely substituting the expected values of C_1 and C_2 into Figure 5.6 and solving the resulting game for equilibrium mixed strategies. (There are no pure strategy equilibria.) This calculation leads to the conclusion that person 1's probability of voting is three fourths and person 2's is five eighths.

This approach, however, does not allow both persons to make full use of their information—specifically, it does not allow them to condition their decisions on the fact that each knows that the other is conditioning a decision on private information. So to see how this fact might affect our analysis, notice that this situation's extensive form, Figure 5.7, shows that each person has three information sets, and at each information set there are two choices. Thus, the number of Dstrategies is $2^3 = 8$, where a typical strategy for person 1 reads: If $C_1 = 6/8$, abstain, otherwise vote. We denote such a strategy by (a,v,v) to indicate that the person abstains if the cost of voting assumes its maximum value and that the person votes if this cost takes on a moderate or minimum value. However, four of the eight possible strategies—those that have a person voting if the cost of voting is high but abstaining if the cost is low—are easily shown to be dominated. Thus, we restrict our attention to the four strategies (v,v,v), (a,v,v), (a,a,v), and (a,a,a). Figure 5.8 (with all payoffs multiplied by seventy two) portrays the corresponding strategic form, which establishes that for the parameters of our example, ((a,v,v), (a,v,v)) is the Bayesian equilibrium. In this case, then, both voters vote with probability two thirds (that is, they each vote if either of two circumstances prevails out of the three equally likely possibilities).[5]

---

[5]To see how the payoffs in these cells are computed, consider the equilibrium cell ((a,v,v), (a,v,v)). Looking at things from person 1's perspective, if $C_1 = 6/8$, then 1 abstains and, given 2's strategy, realizes the payoffs 1, 0, and 0 depending on whether $C_2 = 3/8$, 1/4, or 1/8. Since each of these costs occurs with equal probability, when $C_1 = 6/8$, person 1 realizes an expected payoff of 1/3. Similarly, when $C_1 = 5/8$, then 1 always votes and realizes a payoff of 3/8, regardless of 2's cost and subsequent actions, whereas if $C_1 = 4/8$, then I again always votes and realizes a payoff of 1/2, regardless of 2's costs and actions. Hence, 1's overall payoff is 1/3[1/3] + 1/3[3/8] + 1/3[1/2] = 29/72.

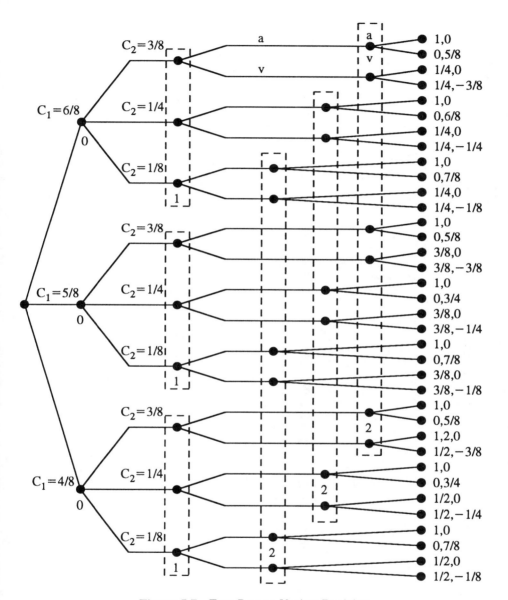

Figure 5.7 Two-Person Voting Decision

	vvv	avv	aav	aaa
vvv	27, −18	27, −9	27, −3	27, 0
avv	21, 6	29, 7	37, 5	45, 0
aav	12, 30	28, 23	44, 13	60, 0
aaa	0, 54	24, 39	48, 21	72, 0

Figure 5.8:   Strategic Form of Figure 5.7

Because in this instance the strategic form disguises the reasons why we have arrived at a different answer than the one we get if we rely simply on a strategic form calculated from simple expected values, let us consider this problem from a different perspective. Specifically, notice that each of i's strategies can be characterized by a number, C^*_i, such that i votes if the cost of voting, C_i, is less than C^*_i, and abstains otherwise. We have already seen (section 1.5) that C^*_i equals the probability that the voter is decisive times the utility difference between the candidates. That is, a citizen votes if

$$(u_1 - u_2)\text{Pr[create or break a tie]} - C > 0,$$

in which case the critical value for C that determines whether a person votes is $(u_1 - u_2)\text{Pr[create or break a tie]}$. In large electorates, though, we assume that $\text{Pr}[. . .]$ is merely a subjective estimate based on public opinion polls and the like and we ignore interactive effects. But in small electorates, $\text{Pr}[. . .]$ clearly depends on what a person thinks others will do, which is a function of what they think he will do, and so forth.

Suppose then, that we let P_i denote the probability that the citizen is decisive and let p_i be the probability that i votes. Then for our two-voter example, P_1 is a function of p_2, and P_2 is a function of p_1. The critical number C^*_1, then, equals P_1 times the utility difference between the candidates, which is 1 in our example. Thus, the citizen votes if $C_1 < C^*_1 = P_1$. The game-theoretic nature of the problem follows from the fact that, since P_1 is a function of p_2, and since p_2 is a function of C^*_2, then C^*_1 is a function of C^*_2, and vice versa— which is to say that 1's optimal strategy depends on 2's strategy (1's strategy should be a best response to 2), and 2's optimal strategy depends on 1's strategy (2's strategy should be a best response to 1). The Bayesian equilibrium identified in Figure 5.8 is merely the pair of strategies that are best responses to each other.

5.7 Agendas Reconsidered

Aside from some additional complexity in the calculation of expected payoffs, to this point, the games of incomplete and asymmetric information that we have considered do not look much different than other types of games. Without introducing any new ideas, however, what we want to show now is that rendering some information private can materially change our conclusions about things. To see this, consider voting agendas again, and recall our conclusion in chapter 2 that if an agenda includes an outcome that is a Condorcet winner, then that outcome necessarily emerges as the final outcome. Voting in Congress, however, assumes a more interesting and strategically complicated character if we suppose that not all legislators know the preferences of all other legislators. Indeed, unless we are willing to suppose that all legislative votes merely ratify and legitimize outcomes that everyone knows are foregone conclusions, agendas, especially complicated ones, almost certainly occur in an incomplete information environment. We cannot explore all ramifications of this fact, but we can address the question of whether the conclusion about the eventual emergence of Condorcet winners necessarily holds if information about preferences is private. We begin with an especially simple possibility.

Example: Consider a committee of n people who can hold one of the following three preferences, where any individual can hold preferences of type i with probability p_i, but every person knows their own type:

type 1:	A	B	C
type 2:	B	C	A
type 3:	C	A	B

in addition, assume that all voters assign a utility of 1 to their most-preferred alternative, 0 to their least-preferred alternative, and v ($0 < v < 1$) to the alternative that ranks second on their preference order. Finally, suppose that the committee uses an agenda that first sets A against B, and then the winner against C.

What we want to show is something that we suspect is not intuitive—that even if it is almost certainly true that the committee is unanimous in its preferences so that a Condorcet winner is almost certain to exist, that winner will definitely not be selected if the committee is sufficiently large.

To establish this fact we must proceed a bit differently than before since even with a 3-member committee, nature can choose any one of 27 possible committee profiles (1 of 3 profiles for the first voter, 1 of 3 for the second voter, and 1 of 3 for the third voter). Thus, even before we include the branches representing the voters' choices, our extensive form is massive. Hence, we must use some shortcuts—specifically, we must try to eliminate dominated strategies for different types of voters so as to move as quickly as possible to the identification of subgame perfect Bayesian equilibria.

We begin by noting that as in our previous analyses of agendas, regardless of the outcome on the initial ballot between A and B, everyone votes sincerely on the second ballot. Next, notice that we can identify dominant strategies for two of the voter types.

Type 2 voters: With everyone voting sincerely on the last (second) ballot, the uncertainty about preferences means that a victory for A on the first ballot yields a lottery between A and C whereas a victory for B yields a lottery between B and C. The exact nature of this lottery depends, of course, on the probabilities we assign to voters being of one type or the other. However, regardless of these probabilities, a type 2 voter prefers any lottery between B and C (his or her first and second choices) to any lottery between A and C (his or her last and second choices). From the assumption of common knowledge, then, everyone knows that type 2 voters will vote for B.

Type 3 votes: The analysis of type 3 is a bit more complicated, but once again we can show that a unique strategy is part of any equilibrium for such types. Briefly, assuming that there are n voters, there are two possibilities:

1. $(n + 1)/2$ or more other voters do not have type 3 preferences.

2. $(n + 1)/2$ or more other voters have type 3 preferences.

No voter knows with certainty which of these possibilities describes the committee, but notice that if case 2 holds, then C prevails regardless of what anyone does on the first ballot. On the other hand, if case 1 holds, then B prevails eventually if he or she wins on the first ballot, whereas either A or C can prevail if A wins on the first ballot. Since B is a type 3 voter's least-preferred alternative, voting for A on the first ballot is a dominant choice for such a type.

This discussion means that we can reduce the strategies we must consider for every voter to the following two, so that what remains is an analysis of the choices of type 1 voters over these two strategies:

s_1:   *If type 1, then vote sincerely for A.*
        If type 2, then vote for B.
        If type 3, then vote for A.

s_2:   *If type 1, then vote strategically for B.*
        If type 2, then vote for B.
        If type 3, then vote for A.

As with our previous examples, we might next try to construct a strategic form. However, given the nature of the problem, we encounter too much complexity for our liking. Specifically, if there are n voters, then the corresponding strategic form has 2^n cells that we must check as potential equilibria. At this point, however, we should keep in mind that we merely want to show that something different can occur when there is private information—namely, that a Condorcet winner does not necessarily prevail as the final outcome. Thus, we look only at two specific strategy n-tuples and forgo an analysis of those cells in the strategic form that have different voters choosing different strategies. That is, we restrict our attention to two possibilities: (1) all voters choose s_1, in which case all type 1 voters vote sincerely for A on the first ballot, and (2) all voters choose s_2, in which case all type 1 voters vote strategically for B on the first ballot.

Checking first whether the n-tuple $(s_1, s_1, \ldots, s_1)$ can be a Bayesian equilibrium, what we want to see is whether any voter has an incentive to unilaterally defect to some other strategy. Since we already know that type 2 and type 3 voters have dominant choices on the agenda's first ballot, no voter has an incentive to defect to a strategic choice when it holds either of these types of preferences. The only possible defection is from a type 1 voter who chooses to vote strategically for B.

At this point we come to the next trick in our analysis. Notice that there cannot be any **positive** incentive to defect if the voter in question is not pivotal on the first ballot. If, for example, the vast majority of voters have preferences of one particular type, then no type 1 voter can be pivotal, and, thus, no type 1 voter will have an incentive to defect unilaterally from s_1. So in ascertaining whether $(s_1, s_2, \ldots, s_1)$ is an equilibrium, we should examine whether a type 1 voter has an incentive to defect unilaterally from A to B, conditional on that voter being pivotal on the first ballot.

To see that a type 1 voter might defect in this circumstance, notice that the only situation in which a type 1 voter can be pivotal on the first ballot is if precisely $(n - 1)/2$ voters in the committee have type 2 preferences since, if everyone abides by s_1, it is only these voters who are voting for B. And in this event, a voter must evaluate the two first-ballot vote choices thus:

> *Choice 1: If the voter in question swings the outcome to B by voting for B, then that voter and the $(n - 1)/2$ type 2 voters will join on the second ballot to produce B with certainty.*

> *Choice 2: If the voter in question swings the vote to A by voting for A, then the result is a lottery between A and C. In this lottery, C prevails if there is at least one type 3 voter among those who voted for A on the first ballot and A prevails if all others who chose A have type 1 preferences. Of course, since we are holding constant the strategies of all voters but one, the $(n - 1)/2$ voters who chose A cannot be type 2 voters, and from Bayes' rule, the conditional probability that a particular one of them has type 3 preferences, given that that voter cannot have type 2 preferences, is $p_3/(p_1 + p_3)$ and the conditional probability that a particular one of them has type 1 preferences is $p_1/(p_1 + p_3)$. The probability that all of the $(n - 1)/2$ voters who chose A are of type 1, given that they are not type 2, is*

$$P(t_1|\sim t_2) = \left[\frac{p_1}{p_1 + p_3} \right]^{(n-1)/2}$$

> *and the probability that one or more of these voters has type 3 preferences is simply*

$$P(t_3|\sim t_2) = 1 - \left[\frac{p_1}{p_1 + p_3} \right]^{(n-1)/2}$$

Thus, whenever the voter in question is pivotal, choosing B yields a payoff of v, whereas choosing A yields an expected payoff of 1 times $P(t_1|\sim t_2)$ plus 0 times $P(t_3|\sim t_2) = 1 - P(t_1|\sim t_2)$, or simply $P(t_1|\sim t_2)$. Thus, this voter prefers to defect unilaterally from the strategy of always voting sincerely for A if

$$v > \left[\frac{p_1}{p_1 + p_3} \right]^{(n-1)/2}$$

Since the term in brackets is less than 1, we can make the right side of this inequality as close to 0 as we choose by increasing n. Since $v > 0$, this means that everybody choosing sincerely cannot be an equilibrium if the committee is sufficiently large.

Now let us consider the second n-tuple, $(s_2, s_2, \ldots, s_2)$ as a possible equilibrium. If a vote is decisive on the first ballot, there must be precisely $(n-1)/2$ type 3 voters since it is only voters of this type who vote for A in the conjectured equilibrium. Once again we must consider the consequences of swinging the vote to B as against A.

> *Choice 1: If our voter in question chooses B, then as before B prevails with certainty since it is only the type 3 voters who will vote for C if B wins on the first ballot.*

> *Choice 2: If the voter in question chooses A, then again a lottery results in which A prevails if all of the $(n-1)/2$ voters who originally voted for B are type 1's, and C prevails if only one of these votes has type 2 preferences since such a voter will join with the $(n-1)/2$ type 3's on the final ballot.*

Making a similar calculation as before, the conditional probability that all of the B-voters have type 1 preferences, given that they are not type 3, is

$$P(t_1 | \sim t_3) = \left[\frac{p_1}{p_1 + p_2} \right]^{(n-1)/2}$$

and the probability that one or more of them has type 2 preferences is 1 minus this probability. Thus, for the pivotal voter in question, the expected value of voting for A is 1 times $[p_1/(p_1 + p_2)]^{(n-1)/2}$, plus 0 times 1 minus this probability. The voter prefers to defect from a strategy of voting strategically for B, then, if

$$v > \left[\frac{p_1}{p_1 + p_2} \right]^{(n-1)/2}$$

As before, this inequality is satisfied if n is sufficiently great. That is, if n is sufficiently great, the situation in which all type 1 voters voting strategically for B is part of a Bayesian equilibrium.

This result establishes the profound difference between games of complete and games of incomplete information. Notice that we can make p_2 and p_3 quite small—thereby making it nearly certain that A is the unanimous or nearly unanimous preference of the committee—and still maintain a Bayesian equilibrium in which B prevails. For example, each voter has type 1 preferences with probability .99, and type 2 and type 3 preferences each with probability .005, if the committee contains 100 or more members, and if v exceeds .67, then the n-tuple $(s_2, s_2, \ldots, s_2)$ is a Bayesian equilibrium.

To see why our conclusions here differ so markedly from the ones we offer when information is complete, notice that in determining whether a particular strategy n-tuple is an equilibrium, we look only at those situations in which a person is decisive. It is only in these situations that a person might have a positive incentive to defect from one strategy to another. With incomplete information, by conditioning on such possibilities, voters are conditioning their decisions on unlikely (but feasible) events. And if people focus on these events, sincere voting becomes an undesirable strategy. When information is complete, on the other hand, such events are no longer feasible—voters know with certainty that voting sincerely is a dominant strategy—and, thus, they cannot create incentives to vote insincerely.

Despite this argument, our result might still seem counter-intuitive. We suspect ourselves that it does not apply with full force to most legislatures—that legislatures are not constantly going about passing bills that are otherwise defeated by Condorcet winners appearing simultaneously on agendas. Our reason for supposing that this is true, however, is not because we believe that there is a fundamental flaw in the preceding analysis, but because we suspect that that analysis is incomplete. Actual legislatures are characterized by considerable prevote discussion that may include straw votes among subsets of legislators, as when Republican and Democratic members meet in caucus. Prior commitments to vote one way or the other, in conjunction with nonbinding straw votes, may allow the revelation of sufficient information so as to reduce considerably the likelihood of the paradox of our example. However, before we can suppose that prevoting discussions and verbally stated commitments can materially affect our conclusions about agendas, we must consider the fact that such discussion and stated commitments can themselves be part of a person's strategy to deceive people. Thus, we must more explicitly consider the various signals that people can offer prior to acting as part of a situation's strategic character.

Another reason for speculating that our example is special is the fact that although we can be nearly certain that a Condorcet winner does exist, the probability of its existence is not one. So consider what happens if a Condorcet winner exists with certainty.

Example: Suppose voters have one of the following preferences:

type 1:	A	B	C
type 2:	B	A	C
type 3:	B	C	A
type 4:	C	B	A

That a Condorcet winner exists in this instance follows from the fact that if we order the alternatives A-B-C on a single dimension, then all preferences are single-peaked and the Median Voter Theorem applies. Of course, we do not know which alternative is the Condorcet winner since we do not know how many people of the different types actually exist in the committee.

Paralleling our previous analysis, and assuming that the agenda is A versus B, the winner against C, notice that both type 2 and type 4 voters have dominant strategies—voting sincerely for B. Holding everyone else's choices constant, let us now look at how type 1 and type 4 voters vote on the first ballot:

If a type 1 voter is pivotal, it gets A with certainty if it chooses A (since such a voter is pivotal if and only if there are precisely (n+1)/2 type 1 voters) and it cannot do better voting for B. Thus, it has no incentive to defect from a sincere strategy,

If a type 4 voter is pivotal, then both choices confront it with a lottery with a clear trade-off. If B is chosen, the voter gets its most preferred alternative, C, only if every type 4 voter constitutes a majority, whereas if it votes for A it gets C if type 3 and 4 voters are a majority. Thus, choosing between A and B involves a trade-off for a higher probability of a first choice versus accepting some probability of a last versus a middle choice.

We will not derive the exact probability relationship that guarantees sincerity, except to note that it is more easily satisfied, *ceteris paribus*, as *n* increases.[6] On the other hand, the fact that such a condition is necessary indicates that even for the case of single-peaked preferences, there is no guarantee that Condorcet winners will prevail—incomplete information is a qualitatively different situation than complete information, at least for agenda voting.

5.8 Signaling, Deception, and Deterrence

The preceding discussion suggests that to extend our analysis of agendas we should consider more complicated agendas. Unfortunately, such an extension requires a level of analysis inappropriate for this text. In particular, the feature of our examples that renders them tractable (although it might not seem so to most readers) is that they allow only two ballots. With only two opportunities to vote, voters cannot use what they might learn on the first ballot to effect how they act subsequently. Although a voter's initial beliefs about probabilities (the voter's priors) are revised after the first ballot, this information cannot lead to any changes in behavior because everyone votes sincerely on the second (final) ballot. But voting gains an added strategic dimension with three or more ballots—not only must one vote to direct outcomes toward one's preferences, but, as in our legislator-lobbyist example, voters must also be concerned with what others might infer from one's actions. That is, in games of incomplete information, the possibility exists that a person can learn something valuable as the game unfolds—players can begin to refine their estimates of the preferences of others, and if the game allows non-trivial multiple stages, then the "manipulation" of beliefs becomes part of one's strategic concern. Thus, if we allowed multiple ballots in agendas, everyone must be concerned with what interpretation others will give to one's actions, and they must be concerned as well with the interpretation that should be given to the actions of others—all with the understanding that everyone is trying to take account of such matters simultaneously, while making decisions that

---

[6]The exact function is

$$v > \frac{(p_1+p_4)^n - p_4^n}{(p_1+p_2+p_3)^n - p_4^n}.$$

Notice that the right side of this inequality necessarily tends to 0 and *n* goes to infinity as long as $p_2 > 0$. For the derivation of this result and the source of our example see Joon Pyo Jung, "Condorcet Consistent Binary Agendas under Incomplete Information," in P.C. Ordeshook, ed., *Models of Strategic Choice In Politics*, Ann Arbor: University of Michigan Press, 1989.

	b_2	b_3	b_4
a_1	$7.5-C$, 15	$20-C$, 5	$7.5-C$, 15
a_2	7.5, 15	7.5, 15	20, 5
a_3	$7.5-3C/4$, 15	$18.75-3C/4$, 3.75	$8.75-3C/4$, 16.25
a_4	$7.5-C/4$, 15	$8.75-C/4$, 16.25	$18.75-C/4$, 3.75

Figure 5.9   Legislator-Lobbyist Game With Costs

lead to the best possible outcome under the circumstances. It is perhaps for this reason that we see multistage voting in committees even when, after the fact, there is an evident Condorcet winner.

Multiple ballots, then, open the door to a new possibility—deception. However, rather than explore the issue of deception in the complex context of n-person agendas, let us return to our legislator-lobbyist example, except that now we suppose that the legislator incurs a cost, C, if it asks for a favor. Because this cost assures the lobbyist that a request for a bribe is no longer *cheap talk*, both the lobbyist and the legislator may want to evaluate their strategies more carefully. Hence, looking back at Figure 5.5, notice that the lobbyist's payoffs (column chooser) are unaffected by the cost, and so we needn't concern ourselves with the strategy b_1. Thus, constructing the 4×3 strategic form in the usual way, we get Figure 5.9.

The inclusion of these costs has clearly destroyed one equilibrium, (a_1,b_2), but it has left the remaining pooling equilibrium, (a_2,b_2), intact. However, no new pure strategy equilibria are introduced, with the possible exception of (a_2,b_3) if C is sufficiently great, although this equilibrium produces the same outcome as (a_2,b_2). What is interesting about this example, though, is that we now have a mixed strategy equilibrium involving the pure strategies a_1 and a_4 for the legislator and b_2 and b_3 for the lobbyist. Such a mixture does not exist if $C = 0$, since if the lobbyist gives b_4 zero weight, a_1 dominates a_4. But with $C > 0$, some messy algebra establishes that

$$((1/9,0,0,8/9),(1-C/15,C/15,0))$$

is an equilibrium.

In this equilibrium the legislator will most probably choose a strategy, a_4, that would otherwise reveal its type. However, by placing some probability on a_1, which requires that the legislator ask for a bribe even if he or she doesn't need to be induced to vote for the bill, the lobbyist must give some weight to offering bribes when asked. In this example, though, the mixed strategy (as some additional algebra reveals) is not beneficial to the legislator, who now receives a payoff of $7.5 - C/6$. This fact, however, is largely a consequence of parameter values and the fact that the interests of the legislator and the lobbyist are not diametrically opposed—the lobbyist, after all, wants to induce the legislator to vote for the bill when constituents oppose it, and the legislator wants to be thus induced. So, with situations such as the relationship between Taiwan and mainland China or between competing states in the Middle East in mind, let us consider a second example.

Example: There are two countries B and L. B is a big country that can almost certainly defeat L, a little country, in any military confrontation. However, although it probably can't win even if it resists an attack, L can impose a heavy cost on B. Assume B chooses first (between Attacking and Not Attacking) and that L chooses second (between Resisting and Capitulating). Clearly, if B knows L's preferences, we have described a rather uninteresting situation—certainly one that does not leave much room for what people find interesting about strategic deterrence in international affairs—namely, uncertainly and the possibility of deception. So suppose that B is uncertain whether L will resist (if it is "strong") or capitulate (if it is "weak") in the event of an attack, and that it associates the probabilities p and $1-p$, respectively, with these two possibilities. In addition, suppose country L can make an initial move, which consists of signaling or not signaling its resolve to resist B if attacked. Finally, to make matters more interesting, suppose this signal is costly. Of course, we should not expect this signal to convey information if it is costless, so suppose that if L signals its intention to resist, the cost C is subtracted from its final payoff.

The issue is not simply whether L should send a costly signal, but whether the opportunity to signal can improve L's welfare. We are interested in such matters because it is not uncommon, for example, for people to question the value of some weapons system, especially if that system seems overly costly given its ostensible strategic mission. But consider this possibility: By building such a system, can a country communicate its willingness to fight if attacked? Can a country say, in effect, something like the following to an enemy:

Outcome	B	strong L	weak L
status quo	0	0	0
B attacks, L resists	U_r	u_r^s	u_r^w
B attacks, L capitulates	U_c	u_c^s	u_c^w

Table 5.3

"Although you may be able to defeat me in a war, I can punish you severely if attacked. And although you might question my resolve, I would certainly punish you; otherwise, I would not have built such a costly weapons system in the first place."

To see whether this argument makes any theoretical sense in the context of our example, consider the outcomes and payoffs in Table 5.3, where we assume the following general relationships: First, the big country prefers that L capitulate if it is attacked, i.e.,

$$U_c > 0 > U_r,$$

and, second, that what differentiates a strong from a weak Little country is these two inequalities:

$$0 > u_r^s > u_c^s \text{ and } 0 > u_c^w > u_r^w.$$

Figure 5.10 portrays this situation's extensive form by assuming that L but not B knows L's type. First, since L will not resist if it is weak or capitulate if it is strong, the X'd branches in Figure 5.10 can be deleted. This reduction of the extensive form allows us to simplify our notation by deleting the superscripts on the u's (i.e., only a strong L resists, and only a weak one capitulates).

To solve for equilibria we next construct a strategic form using the following strategies for B and L. First, for B

B_1: *Attack regardless of whether or not L signals.*
B_2: *Attack if L signals, don't attack if it doesn't.*
B_3: *Don't attack if L signals, attack if it doesn't.*
B_4: *Don't attack, regardless of whether or not L signals.*

and for L

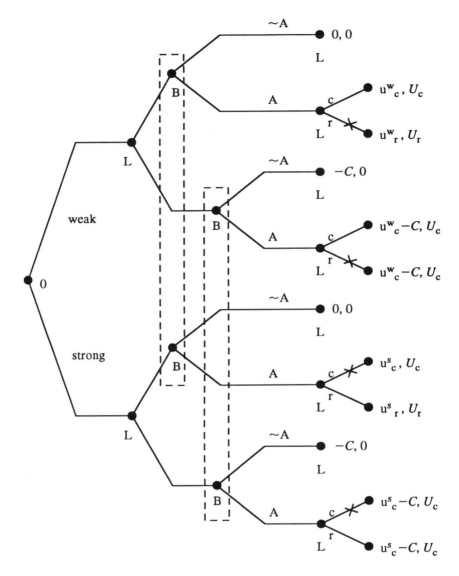

Figure 5.10 A Deterrence Signalling Game

	B₁	B₂	B₃	B₄
L₁	$pu_r+(1-p)u_c$ $pU_r+(1-p)U_c$	0 0	$pu_r+(1-p)u_c$ $pU_r+(1-p)U_c$	0 0
L₂	$p(u_r-C)+(1-p)u_c$ $pU_r+(1-p)U_c$	$p(u_r-C)$ pU_r	$-pC+(1-p)u_c$ $(1-p)U_c$	$-pC$ 0
L₃	$pu_r+(1-p)(u_c-C)$ $pU_r+(1-p)U_c$	$(1-p)(u_c-C)$ $(1-p)U_c$	$pu_r-(1-p)C$ pU_r	$-(1-p)C$ 0
L₄	$pu_r+(1-p)u_c-C$ $pU_r+(1-p)U_c$	$pu_r+(1-p)u_c-C$ $pU_r+(1-p)U_c$	$-C$ 0	0 0

Figure 5.11   The Strategic Form of Figure 5.10

L_1: *Don't signal regardless of type.*
L_2: *Signal if strong, don't signal if weak.*
L_3: *Don't signal if strong, signal if weak.*
L_4: *Signal regardless of type.*

To see how we determine the payoffs in the game's strategic form, shown in Figure 5.11, suppose B chooses B_3 and L chooses L_2. So L signals with probability p, B doesn't attack, and the outcome is $-C$ for L and 0 for B; and L doesn't signal with probability $1-p$, B attacks, and the outcome is u_c for L and U_c for B. Thus, with (L_2,B_3), the expected payoff for L is $-pC + (1-p)u_c$, and for B it is $(1-p)U_c$.

Regardless of the numbers we assign to payoffs, we can see that there are no *separating equilibria*—equilibria in which the little country behaves according to its type by signaling when it is strong and not signaling when it is weak, or vice versa. That is, neither the strategy L_2 nor L_3 is involved in any pure strategy equilibria. This follows from the fact that if L chooses L_2, then B prefers B_3, but if B chooses B_3, then L prefers L_4. If, on the other hand, L chooses L_3, B's best response is B_2; but (L_3,B_2) cannot be an equilibrium because L's best response to B_2 is L_1.

Since there is no separating equilibrium, we next look for a pooling equilibrium in which L sends the same signal regardless of its type. Ignoring the knife-edged possibility of equality, we have two cases:

$$\text{case 1:} \quad pU_r + (1-p)U_c < 0$$
$$\text{case 2:} \quad pU_r + (1-p)U_c > 0.$$

$-100, 80$	$0, 0$	$-100, 80$
$-105, 80$	$-30, -10$	$-80, 90$
$-145, 80$	$-120, 90$	$-70, -10$
$-150, 80$	$-150, 80$	$-50, 0$

Figure 5.12

If p is sufficiently large—if B initially believes that L has a sufficiently great probability of being strong and willing to resist aggression, then case 1 applies and there are at least two (pooling) equilibria: (L_1,B_2) and (L_1,B_4). In addition, if $-C > u_r$, then (L_4,B_3) is an equilibrium as well. All three of these equilibria, however, are equivalent in the sense that B never chooses to attack.

Case 2 is more interesting, because attacking L is a reasonable bet—in the absence of other considerations, B's expected payoff from attacking is greater than the status quo's value, zero, and the unique pure strategy equilibrium is (L_1,B_1). The question is whether the opportunity to signal creates any worthwhile possibilities for L. The answer to this question is, admittedly, sensitive to parameter values. So, in order to merely establish some possibilities, let $p = .10$, and

$$U_c = 100, U_r = -100, u_r = -250, \text{ and } u_c = -75/.9.$$

Since B_4 is dominated by B_1 when case 2 holds, we can eliminate B_4 from consideration. Finally, for purposes of an example assume that $C = 50$, in which case the relevant strategic form is the one shown in Figure 5.12 (country L = row chooser, country B = column chooser):

Solving for mixed strategies for a 4×4 game can be a tiresome task. Here, then, we short-circuit some details and, without explanation, focus our attention on the strategies L_2 and L_4 for L and B_1 and B_3 for B. Assuming that both players place zero weight on the excluded strategies, if we compute mixed strategies in the usual way for a 2×2 game, we get a solution of $p = (0,8/9,0,1/9)$ for L and $q = (6/15,0,9/15)$ for B. If B chooses between B_1 and B_3 with probabilities q and $1-q$, then L must be indifferent between the lotteries that L_2 and L_4 offer. In other words,

$$-105q -80(1-q) = -150q - 50(1-q),$$

which solves to establish that $q = 6/15$. Similarly, if L chooses between L_2 and L_4 with probabilities p and $1-p$, then B is indifferent between B_1 and B_3 only if $80 = 90p$, which yields $p = 8/9$.

Two tasks remain at this stage: (1) showing that this strategy pair improves L's welfare and (2) establishing that it is indeed an equilibrium. With respect to the first task, some messy algebra establishes that L's expected payoff from (p,q) is -90, which is more than what L gets, -100, if L cannot signal. Second, to see that (p,q) is in fact an equilibrium, we must show that neither B nor L has an incentive to place positive probabilities on those strategies to which p and q, respectively, assign zero probability.

> Clearly, B has no incentive to give any weight to B_2 at the expense of the other two pure strategies since B_2 necessarily gives B less than 80 as long as L mixes only between L_2 and L_4. Hence, B has no incentive to shift unilaterally from (p,q).

> Given that B is mixing between the strategies B_1 and B_3, L will not give any weight to L_1 since this strategy earns -100; nor will L give any weight to L_3 since this also earns L an expected payoff of $(-145)6/15 + (-70)9/15 = -100$.

Thus, (p,q) is an equilibrium.

Using a mixed strategy in a game that has a pure strategy equilibrium might seem strange. Nevertheless, that L can use the opportunity to signal only by implementing a mixed strategy makes sense. The pure strategies L_1 and L_4 convey no information and, thus, they cannot be used to deceive an opponent. On the other hand, using L_2 or L_3 with certainty merely signals one's type to the opponent and invites attack when one is weak. Thus, deception requires a mixed strategy—a strategy that always signals resolve when one is strong, but which leaves something to chance when one is weak.

This fact about deception is useful, at least in the context of the relatively simple game of our example. It reveals in particular that if we observe two persons playing a game that allows for the possibility of deception, we cannot come to any firm conclusion as to whether deception will or will not be attempted. Moreover, since we may only get to observe the game played once—so that we will only have the opportunity to observe a single joint choice of pure strategies—even if a player abides by a mixed strategy, we cannot determine whether that player has played well or poorly on the basis of the final outcome nor can we determine whether that player intended to deceive. In the next section we consider a game in which both players act more than once.

5.9 Rationality Reconsidered

We are now in a position to reconsider the Centipede Game offered in chapter 3 in Figure 3.13 and the contradiction that subgame perfection appears to imply with respect to the presumed rationality of players there. Actually, though, our interest in this game is not simply that we want to resolve an apparent paradox in the application of the concept of subgame perfection. We should, after all, leave such matters to game theorists. Rather, we want to confront the possibility that "irrationality" itself may be rational.

We are reminded, in this context, of the movie *The Cincinnati Kid* in which Steve McQueen, playing the role of the brash, upstart gambler, challenges the "old pro," Edward G. Robinson. After hours of endless play, Robinson's age appears to show as he seemingly wilts under the "Kid's" assault of tactical skill and luck. The dramatic end to their game of five-card stud has McQueen an almost certain winner with a full house against Robinson's flush—a flush with but only a small chance of becoming a royal flush. In what appears to be a desperate attempt at bluff, Robinson ups the ante before the fourth card is played and bets the pot on the fifth card. Robinson, of course, wins and McQueen is busted, confused, and humiliated—to which Robinson adds the admonition that poker oftentimes involves making the wrong move at the right time. Robinson's seeming irrationality has suckered McQueen into losing it all.

Our Centipede Game has nowhere near the excitment of this scene, but it too may require "irrational" action on the part of rational decision makers. To see what we mean by this, recall that the particular difficulty we confront with this situation centers on this question: Subgame perfection requires that we determine what a player should choose in the initial stages of the game on the basis of what rational players choose subsequently in later stages. But if reaching those stages requires that players choose irrationally in earlier stages, then what is the basis for supposing that players choose rationally in these later stages? Successive pruning of the game's extensive form, then, seems to make sense only if we allow a contradiction of the notion of rationality that underlies the idea of subgame perfection. Put differently, a player at something other than an initial decision node of the extensive form could reason: If everyone is rational, then I should choose . . . But wait a minute . . . if everyone is rational, then I wouldn't have the opportunity to choose at this node in the first place!

Players can reach successive decision nodes in our example, then, only if one or both of them are irrational, or at least only if one or both of them find it rational to *appear* irrational. So consider the possibility that each player selects a strategy under the hypothesis that there is some small probability that the opponent is in fact irrational. We can model this irrationality in any number of ways, including letting people have utility functions that differ from the ones we otherwise specify for them (for example, we could suppose that irrational people dislike money and that the utility of x dollars equals $-x$). Equivalently, we can suppose that there is some small probability that a player, for whatever reason, simply cannot make a choice that is otherwise optimal.

For the game in Figure 3.13, then, we can assume that there is some probability that, in lieu of picking the money up off the table, any particular player is incapable of such an action and passes at every opportunity. In the Bayesian game format, this means each player knows that it is rational, each knows that there is some probability that its opponent is irrational, each knows that the opponent believes that there is some small probability that it is irrational, and so on. The game-theoretic question, then, becomes: Is there an equilibrium in which two players, both believing that the other might be irrational, make the "irrational" decision of waiting until the game's final stages before opting to take the money offered? Is it sometimes rational to act "irrationally"?

To evaluate this possibility, consider the extensive form in Figure 5.13, which takes the game in Figure 3.13 and assumes that each player has some probability of being unable to do anything except pass. Information sets are drawn, however, to indicate that each player knows its own type but is uncertain about the "rationality" of the opponent.

Because we exclude the possibility that an irrational player can do anything but "pass," each player has three strategies that take account of their type:

s_1: *If rational, then "take" on the first opportunity (which ends the game); but "pass" if irrational.*

s_2: *If rational, then "pass" on the first opportunity, "take" on the second (which ends the game); and always "pass" if irrational.*

s_3: *If rational, then "pass" on both opportunities; and "pass" if irrational,*

To construct a numerical example, let $q = .97$, so each player has a .03 chance of being incapable of taking. Figure 5.13 shows the corresponding strategic form. For example, if both players choose s_1, then 1 receives a payoff of 40 [if 1 and 2 are both rational] with probability $(.970)^2$, a payoff of 40 [if 1 but not 2 is rational] with

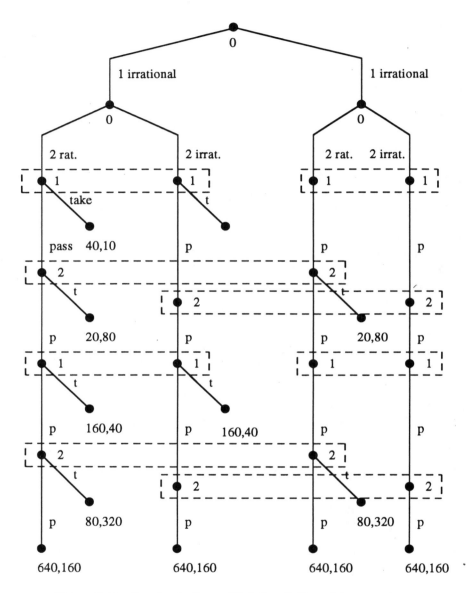

Figure 5.13 Centipede Game With Possibility of Irrationality

	s_1	s_2	s_3
s_1	40, 12.2	41.7, 19.2	58, 14.5
s_2	24.6, 78.9	158.1, 48.3	17.4, 43.6
s_3	38.2, 82.4	96.8, 315.2	640, 160

Figure 5.14 Strategic Form of Figure 5.13

probability (.970)(.030), a payoff of 20 [if 1 but not 2 is irrational so that 1 passes but 2 takes] with probability (.030)(.970), and a payoff of 640 [if 1 and 2 are both irrational and always pass] with probability $(.03)^2$. Thus, we enter a payoff to 1 of

$$40[(.970)^2 + (.970)(.030)] + 20(.030)(.970) + 640[(.03)^2] = 40$$

in the (s_1, s_1) cell. The remaining cells are computed in a similar fashion.

Notice that s_3 is dominated for player 2 by s_2, which makes sense since s_3 requires that 2 pass at the last branch even if rational, rather than simply take the larger payoff. Checking the other cells of the game reveals that this game does not have a pure strategy equilibrium, so mixed strategies must be considered. At this point, however, we must proceed carefully in order to compute this mixed solution, because we do not yet know whether player 1 should mix over all three pure strategies or over some subset of these strategies.

We begin by supposing that player 2 mixes between s_1 and s_2 with probabilities r and $1-r$. Then player 1's pure strategies each yield the following expected payoff (after some algebraic manipulation):

$$E(s_1) = 41.7 - 1.7r,$$
$$E(s_2) = 158.1 - 133.5r,$$
$$E(s_3) = 96.8 - 58.6r.$$

We know, of course, that if strategies s_i and s_j each have nonzero probability associated with them in player 1's mixed equilibrium strategy, then it must be the case that $E(s_i) = E(s_j)$—otherwise player 1 would prefer to unilaterally alter his or her mixed strategy by shifting probability from one pure strategy to the other. However, Figure 5.15, which graphs each of the preceding expected value

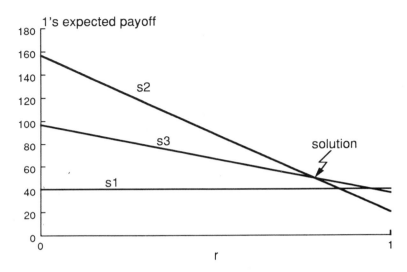

Figure 5.15 Finding a Solution to the Game in Figure 5.14

equations against r, reveals that only two expected values can be equal simultaneously, and that there are three possible pairings. This figure also reveals, however, that player 1's expected payoff is greatest if he or she sets $E(s_2)$ equal to $E(s_3)$—if player 1 chooses a mixed strategy that assigns positive probability only to s_2 and s_3. Hence, setting $E(s_2) = E(s_3)$ gives $r = .814$—that is, player 2's mixed equilibrium strategy is $(.814, .186, 0)$.

We can solve now for 1's mixed equilibrium strategy $(0, p, 1-p)$ by using the fact that 2 must be indifferent between s_1 and s_2 whenever 1 abides by $(0, p, 1-p)$. For player 2,

$$E(s_1) = 82.4 - 3.5p$$
$$E(s_2) = 315.2 - 266.9p$$

Setting these two equations equal to each other and solving for p gives $p = .884$. Thus, player 1's mixed equilibrium strategy is $(0, .884, .116)$.

Although this particular solution depends on our initial assumption that each player's probability of "irrationally" is .03, what we want to emphasize is that this irrationality is now a self-fulfilling prophesy. Both players, even if they are rational in a traditional sense, have nonzero equilibrium probabilities of passing rather than taking at any decision node. Appearing to be irrational is now rational and is sustained on the part of both players by the initial assumption that each person has some small probability of actually being (as opposed to appearing to be) irrational.

There are other models that we could use to "explain" any observed irrationality, models that do not require players knowing with such specificity the probability that the other is irrational. For example, we could suppose that each player's probability of irrationality is itself a random variable drawn in accordance with some commonly known probability density. The important point, however, is that we can now begin to study "irrationality" empirically to see if our models can account for it in the framework of the rational choice paradigm.

The implication of such models in political science is that barring some complicated measurements that are allowed only if we observe the same game played many times (in which case we must be concerned about the supergame that participants might perceive), there is no way for us to determine whether any observed irrationality is "real" or strategic. Thus, debates in both the academic and popular literature over the meaning of rationality or which pertain to some evidence we assume supports the contention that someone is irrational ought to be seriously scrutinized with our example in mind. If we observe some national leader pursuing policies that make little sense to the rest of us, our first instinct as analysts should not be to presume irrationality; instead, we should examine the nature of the uncertainty that confronts us and try to determine whether those actions are consistent with some strategic imperative.

It may be true, of course, that we will learn eventually that these policies were dictated by poor information on someone's part. But an appearance of "irrationality" may also be merely part of the deception that incomplete information allows, and it may follow a logic that is readily understood by supposing that people are rational and strategic.

5.10 Reputation and the Chain-Store Paradox

We conclude this chapter with an example that is sufficiently complex that we can only outline the general nature of its solution—the Chain-Store Paradox. Although originally formulated in a purely economic context, this game is important because of the lessons it teaches us about a variety of more general matters such as the optimal responses to terrorist threats. Briefly, the scenario of the Chain-Store Paradox is as follows:

> *A large retail store chain with, say, an outlet in each of n markets,*
> *denoted 1, 2, . . ., n, enjoys a monopoly in those markets and, ac-*
> *cordingly, charges a monopoly price for what it sells. However, the*
> *store faces potential competitors in these markets. A single small com-*
> *petitor "waits in the wings" of each market, and beginning with mar-*
> *ket 1, each must decide one at a time whether to compete against the*
> *chain. If a competitor enters a market, the chain store must decide*
> *whether to appear "weak" by adjusting its prices so as to charge the*
> *competitive market price or whether to try to establish a reputation for*
> *toughness by slashing prices drastically in that market to the point*
> *that neither it nor its competitor can earn a positive profit.*

The potential advantage of appearing tough, then, is that the chain can try to dissuade future competitors from entering its markets. On the other hand, acting tough can cost the chain considerably in terms of lost profits.

Assuming that it is a different potential competitor with whom the chain must content in each market, we have here an "$n + 1$ person" game. Without incomplete information, we can solve for subgame perfect equilibria in the usual way and conclude that competitors should enter in all markets, and the chain should always capitulate. This situation, then, is like the finitely repeated Prisoners' Dilemma in that the chain, preferring to avoid negative profits, will capitulate in the nth (last) market so a competitor enters there; similarly, competitors enter and the chain capitulates in markets $n-1, n-2, . . . 1$.

Such a prediction seems counterintuitive to the extent that we frequently see people in similar circumstances attempting to gain or to maintain reputations for toughness in order to forestall future competition. For example, it is convincingly argued that we should not negotiate with terrorists even if failing to do so results in a loss of life among hostages, because displaying a willingness to compromise merely encourages future terrorists. Similarly, mainland China breaks diplomatic relations with those states recognizing Taiwan as an independent entity in order to maintain its reputation for diplomatic toughness, thereby hoping to keep other states from establishing formal diplomatic ties with its rival.

What allows for the establishment as well as the dissolution of a reputation in each of these situations is some incomplete information about preferences. Terrorists are uncertain about our willingness to abandon hostages, and countries are uncertain about mainland China's willingness to further isolate itself from the world and the economic gains that accompany relations with other states. Thus, if we allow some uncertainty about the chain's preferences by supposing that there is some small chance that the chain actually prefers to slash prices when challenged in a market, then the chain may be able to establish a reputation for toughness—for a willingness to incur short term losses (punishing early competitors) in order to realize long term gains (keeping others from entering later in its other markets).

The analysis of this game when no competitor knows for certain whether the chain is "tough" or "weak" is challenging. In fact, additional refinement of the Bayesian-Nash equilibrium concept is required in order to restrict predictions and to contend with the possibility that the players must decide what to do if they find themselves at a decision node that is otherwise regarded as being impossible to reach. Nevertheless, if we assume that once the chain fails to "act tough," everyone thereafter knows that the chain is weak, then the general form of the solutions to this game from the perspective of the chain store is as follows:

> *The chain begins by acting tough against any early entrant. Although it incurs a short term loss by doing so, it gains because one or more potential competitors in the future are scared away. As the game progresses, the chain switches to a mixed strategy between being tough and letting competitors in. Once it acts weak, it acts weak thereafter, and as the last market is approached, the chain, because there are no longer enough markets for it to secure sufficient rewards from its reputation, allows entrants to compete at market prices.*

This solution is like the one we deduce for the Centipede example. There, the general form of the solution is for both players to "pass" in the early stages of the game, to abide by mixed strategies in subsequent stages, and (if we allowed a longer Centipede Game) to "take" in the final stages. In this way both players maintain and take mutual advantage of their "reputations" for being irrational. Of course, just as the details of this solution depend on parameters (initial prior probability beliefs, utility numbers, and the number of moves), the actual solution in the chain store example depends on these same parameters. Our analysis also changes if we suppose that the series of potential competitors is, in fact, a single decision maker who, like the chain, can choose strategies that coordinate its actions over all markets.

Suggestions for Further Reading

The discussion in section 5.2, taken from Richard D. McKelvey and Peter C. Ordeshook, "Rational Expectations in Elections: Some

Experimental Results Based on a Multidimensional Model," *Public Choice*, 44 (1984): 61–102, illustrates a growing literature that seeks to determine the robustness of the Median Voter Theorem in the face of imperfections in the information of voters and candidates. The technically advanced reader can also consult Jeffrey Banks, "A Model of Electoral Competition with Incomplete Information," *Journal of Economic Theory*, 50 (1990): 309–25.

If there is a "growth industry" in political theory it is the application of games of incomplete information, and the beginning reader should consult Eric Rasmusen, *Games and Information*, Cambridge: Basil Blackwell, 1989. Insofar as the limited examples that we consider in this chapter are concerned, the discussion from section 5.6 is taken from Thomas Palfrey and Howard Rosenthal, "Voter Participation and Strategic Uncertainty, *American Political Science Review*, 79 (1985): 62–78, and our discussion of agenda voting with incomplete information in section 5.7 is taken from Peter C. Ordeshook and Thomas Palfrey, "Agendas, Strategic Voting, and Signalling with Incomplete Information," *American Journal of Political Science*, 32 (1988): 441–66 and Joon Pyo Jung, "Condorcet Consistent Binary Agendas Under Incomplete Information," in the previously cited volume edited by P.C. Ordeshook. Other applications include the previously cited essay by Palfrey on the tendency for plurality rule systems to generate two parties.

Outside of election models, the most extensive application of such games to politics is in the area of strategic deterrence. Of course, the first application of game theory to the analysis of deterrence, threats, and deception is Thomas Schelling, *The Strategy of Conflict*, NY: Oxford University Press, 1960. A full treatment of deception and deterrence, however, requires the assumption that information is asymmetrically distributed, and current research is summarized in Robert Powell, *Nuclear Deterrence Theory: The Search for Credibility*, New York: Cambridge University Press, 1990; Bruce Bueno De Mesquita and David Lalman, *War and Reason*, New Haven: Yale University Press, 1991; Marc D. Kilgore and Frank C. Zagare, "Uncertainty and Deterrence," *American Journal of Political Science*, 35 (1991): 305–34; and George W. Downs and David M. Rocke, *Tacit Bargaining, Arms Races, and Arms Control*, Ann Arbor: University of Michigan Press, 1990. The appendix to Powell's book contains a readable summary of the basics of game theory, including some topics on incomplete information games that we do not cover here.

The reanalysis in section 5.9 of the Centipede Game is taken from R.D. McKelvey and T. Palfrey, "An Experimental Study of the Centipede Game," mimeo, California Institute of Technology, 1989. Our discussion of the Chain-Store Paradox is from David M. Kreps and Robert Wilson, "Reputation and the Chain Store Paradox," *Journal of Economic Theory*, 27 (1982): 253–79. For a specific political example, though, see James E. Alt, Randall L. Calvert, and Brian D. Humes, "Reputation and Hegemonic Stability: A Game Theoretic Analysis," *American Political Science Review*, 82 (1988): 445–66.

Exercises

1. Suppose three candidates, A, B, and C, are competing in a plurality-rule election and that an initial poll of the electorate's preferences reveals the following information:

    31% prefer A to B to C with $u(A) = 10, u(B) = 9, u(C) = 0$,
    29% prefer B to A to C with $u(B) = 10, u(A) = 9, u(C) = 0$,
    40% prefer C to A to B with $u(C) = 10, u(A) = 1, u(B) = 0$.

    a. If the pollster accurately reports the poll result, and if all voters assume that those who hold the same preferences vote in the same strategic way, who wins the election in equilibrium?

    b. Suppose the pollster misrepresents the poll and announces that 40% prefer A, 31% prefer B, and 29% prefer C. Who wins?

    c. Suppose the pollster instead announces that 40% prefer B, 31% prefer A, and 29% prefer C. Who wins?

    d. Will the pollster "be found out" in any of the preceding three scenarios when people later compare his prediction as to who will win to the final outcome?

2. Consider the following strategic form game:

0, 0	−K, 5
K, 10	5, 0

    Suppose only person 1 (row chooser) knows K with certainty, which nature has set equal to 10 and −10 with equal probability (a fact that is known to column chooser, person 2). Solve for this situation's Bayesian equilibrium strategies.

3. In his unsuccessful surgeries (those in which the patient dies)

Dr. Ian Competent has only a fifty-fifty chance of not being at fault. With this in mind, the relatives of his latest victim have asked for compensation—$1,000,000. If Competent (who has already had his insurance policy revoked but who as a shareholder in a local savings and loan association is quite wealthy) refuses to settle, the relatives can take the matter to court (or they can forget it). Once in court assume that justice is done. (This is not an exercise that concerns the competence of lawyers.) So if Competent is innocent (and only he knows for sure), he loses nothing and the relatives loose $1,000,000 (attorney's fees being what they are). On the other hand, if he loses, then he loses $3,000,000 and the victim's relatives gain $2,000,000 (again, lawyers take their cut).

   a.   Portray this situation's extensive and strategic forms.

   b.   Determine the game's equilibrium.

   c.   Interpret this equilibrium.

4. Country 1 has secretly approached country 2 with a disarmament proposal that focuses on a new weapons system developed by 2. However, this system has only a seventy percent chance of being effective, although 2 knows the system's capabilities with certainty. Country 2 can ignore 1 proposal and allow the arms race to continue; alternatively, it can publically make the same proposal, at which time country 1 must "fish or cut bait" by formally accepting 2 public offer. Associate what you regard as reasonable payoffs to the outcomes, portray this situation's extensive and strategic forms, and find any pure-strategy equilibria. Interpret these equilibria, if any exist.

5. Construct the strategic form of our reanalysis of agendas with three allowable types of preferences in Section 5.5, assuming a committee of three voters. Compare your answer to the one offered in the text and show that it is consistent with that one.

6. Consider the following *sequential elimination* agenda: "Alternatives A and B are first paired. If A wins it is the outcome; but if B wins, B is paired against C and the winner of this vote is the final outcome." Suppose that only these three preferences types are possible (ranked from first preference to last):

t_1:	A	B	C
t_2:	B	A	C
t_3:	C	B	A

a. Assuming that a person has type t_i preferences with probability p_i, that the p_i's are common knowledge, and that a person knows his own preferences, show that the selection of a Condorcet winner corresponds to an equilibrium.

b. Is it the unique equilibrium?

c. Do your answers to parts (a) and (b) change if we add a fourth preference type, "B preferred to C preferred to A"?

7. The professor asks the TA to give the next lecture, and preparing a lecture is done only the day before class. Knowing that the TA is lecturing, attendance will be 100%, but the class does not know the TA's type, which can be of two sorts. If the TA is Responsible, he will gain considerably from efficiently preparing his lecture in his Office. But if the TA is the Surfer type, he would much prefer to prepare his lecture at the Beach, where he works inefficiently but with considerably greater enjoyment. There are three states of the world, each known to the TA: (1) TA is type R(esponsible); (2) TA first chooses his location, then flips a fair coin to determine his type; and (3) TA is type S(urfer). The class does not observe the state of the world, but it has prior probability beliefs on what the true state of the world might be:

> State of the world "1" occurs with probability .5.
> State of the world "2" occurs with probability .2.
> State of the world "3" occurs with probability .3.

Using its priors and the TA's action (the class observes where it is that the TA prepares his lecture), the class chooses to "Sleep" or to be "Awake" in class. Given this description, the class confronts two alternative strategic forms, depending on the TA's type: If the TA is of type R, then

	Office	Beach
Awake	10, 10	−10, 0
Sleep	−1, 2	8, 3

whereas if the TA is of type S, then

	Office	Beach
Awake	10, −2	−10, 1
Sleep	−1, −10	8, 5

a. Portray this situation's extensive form.

b. Specify the pure strategies available to each player.

c. Determine which of the following four strategy combinations are Bayesian-Nash equilibria:

Strategy pair #	Strategy for TA	Students' Strategy
1	If state a or b, choose "Office," but if state c, choose "Beach"	If "Office," choose "Awake," but if "Beach," choose "Sleep"
2	Choose "Office" with probability .95 if state a, 1.0 if state b, 0.0 if state c	If "Office," choose "Awake," but if "Beach," choose "Sleep"
3	Choose "Office" with probability 1.0 if state a, .95 if state b, 0.0 if state c	If "Office," choose "Awake," but if "Beach," choose "Sleep"
4	Choose "Beach" regardless of type	If "Office," choose "Awake," but if "Beach," choose "Sleep"

8. Consider the following two-person, zero-sum game. Nature first chooses player 1's type. Player 1 knows his type and chooses "Yes" or "No." After player 1 chooses, player 2 chooses "Yes" or "No." Player 2, whose type is common knowledge, does not observe 1's type, but does observe 1's choice of "Yes" and "No." Player payoffs are determined according to the following table:

1's type	1's choice	2's choice	1's payoff
L	Y	Y	1
L	Y	N	2
L	N	Y	4
L	N	N	3
C	Y	Y	3
C	Y	N	7
C	N	Y	9
C	N	N	7
R	Y	Y	3
R	Y	N	4
R	N	Y	2
R	N	N	1

a. Draw the game's extensive form.

b. Identify the pure strategies available to each person.

c. Portray the situation's strategic form.

b. Give an example of a Bayes equilibrium. Use Bayes's rule to support your example.

c. Provide a solution to the game if 2 knows 1's type when making his choice.

9. Reproduce our analysis of the Centipede Game assuming that each player's probability of irrationality is .3 rather than .03.

10. In an upcoming election on insurance rate reform, it is common knowledge that you will cast the decisive vote. You are uncertain about the identity of the reform's sponsor but have (correct) beliefs that there is a 7-in-10 chance that the reform is pro-insurance (INS) and as a consequence will raise your insurance rates (making you poorer) and that there is a 3-in-10 chance that the reform is pro-Consumer (CON), in which case the reform will keep your insurance rates at their present level. A campaigner, who knows whether the reform is the insurance type or the consumer type, and, in either case, is paid only if the bill passes, must decide whether or not to go to your House to tell you to vote for the bill. (Campaigner chooses "House" or "No.") On election day, you must decide whether to vote "Yes" or "No" on the reform. The payoffs are determined as follows: It costs the campaigner $5 to go to your house. The campaigner gets paid $15 if the reform passes and $0 if the reform fails. If either an insurance-type reform passes or a consumer-type re-

form fails your rates go up—you lose $10. If either a consumer-type reform fails or an insurance-type reform passes your rates stay the same—you get $0.

   a. Draw the game's extensive form.

   b. Specify the pure strategies available to each player.

   c. Portray the situation's strategic form.

   c. Which of the following five strategy pairs are Bayesian equilibria?

strategy pair #	Campaigner's strat.	Your strategy
1	if INS, then HOUSE if CON, then NO	vote YES
2	if INS, then HOUSE if CON, then NO	if HOUSE, vote YES if NO, vote NO
3	if INS, then $p(HOUSE\|INS) = .5$ $p(NO\|INS) = .5$ if CON $p(HOUSE\|CON) = .8$ $p(NO\|INS) = .2$	if HOUSE then $p(YES\|HOUSE) = .5$ $p(NO\|HOUSE) = .5$ if NO, vote NO
4	go to HOUSE	if HOUSE, vote NO if NO, vote YES
5	if INS, then NO if CON, then HOUSE	vote YES
6	if INS, then $p(HOUSE\|INS) = .5$ $p(NO\|INS) = .5$ if CON $p(HOUSE\|CON) = .2$ $p(NO\|INS) = .8$	if HOUSE, vote NO if NO, vote NO

11. The political philosophy—authoritarian or democrat—of President Bulsky of Lower Slobovia is unknown to everyone but himself, including his chief rival, Drinksalotov. So people assume that Bulsky values democratic principles with probability q, $.5 < q < 1$. Seeking favor with the members of NUKE

(Nations United for Kapitalist Expansion), Bulsky has pledged to allow a national election for president—an election that can go either way with equal probability if Drinksalotov runs against him. Presently, Bulsky must decide whether to use recent ethnic unrest as an excuse for reneging on his pledge. If he reneges, he retains his position but his wife cannot anticipate an invitation to shop on Rodeo Drive at the next summit whereas Drinksalotov wins international sympathy and an appearance on Nightline. If Bulsky commits to an election, Drinksalotov must decide whether to challenge. An unchallenged Bulsky wins by a slim margin in an uncontested election. If Drinksalotov challenges and loses, he is revealed as someone who cannot defeat an incumbent who has steered his country to 40% unemployment and a -20% GNP growth rate. This outcome's valuation depends also on Bulsky's commitment to democracy, since losing elections has been a "very bad thing" in Lower Slobovia historically. Drinksalotov adheres to democratic principles, but a loss by a like-minded Bulsky is a crushing psychological blow that leads to his semiretirement as assistant director of the Crapski Tractor and Screen Door plant. We have, then, these outcomes:

O1: Bulsky cancels the election.
O2: Bulsky allows the election, but Drinksalotov declines to compete.
O3: Bulsky allows the election; Drinksalotov opposes him but loses.
O4: Bulsky allows the election; Drinksalotov opposes him and wins.

In terms of the world's foremost hard currency—Disney Dollars—suppose valuations, conditional on Bulsky's philosophy, are as follows (with payoffs to Bulsky and Drinksalotov respectively and assuming, as has always been the case in Lower Slobovia that Disney Dollars and utility are equivalent):

	Authoritarian	Democrat
O1	$(-1, 1)$	$(-1, 1)$
O2	$(0, 0)$	$(0, 0)$
O3	$(2, -6)$	$(2, 0)$
O4	$(-2, 4)$	$(-8, 4)$

a. Portray this situation's extensive and strategic forms.

b. Describe the players' equilibrium strategies as a function of q.

6

Cooperation and Coalitions

6.1 The Concept of a Coalition

Of all the different processes that we have thus far considered or have argued can be modeled by using game theory, there is one in particular that seems central to politics but which we have not yet discussed—coalitions. Briefly,

> A **coalition** corresponds to an agreement on the part of two or more players to coordinate their actions so as to bring about an outcome that is more advantageous to members of the coalition than the outcome that prevails from uncoordinated action.

The concept of a coalition encompasses a great many things in politics, and studying them includes studying the processes whereby governments are formed and prime ministers are chosen in Parliaments, alliances are formed and maintained in international affairs, and legislators maneuver together in order to pass mutually beneficial legislation. Indeed, given the generality of our definition, nearly any organization designed to facilitate the objectives of two or more persons simultaneously can be interpreted as the manifestation of a coalition. Thus, a political party, a legislative caucus, a Soviet cooperative, a labor union, and a citizen's interest group all represent coalitions. More fundamentally, a constitution that establishes and defines a state is the consequence of a coalition among citizens who choose to give up some degree of individual sovereignty in order to secure the gains that ostensibly flow from forced collective action.

Of course, no one disputes the fact that coalitions are an important part of politics. However, rather then proceed into a substantive discussion of their content, let us take the more abstract view suggested by our definition and consider at least these four general questions about processes of coalition formation:

1. What coalition structure is likely to prevail—which players will coordinate their actions and with whom will they co-ordinate?

2. What will be the extent of this coordination—will they agree to coordinate on all decisions or on only some subset of decisions?

3. What will be the specific intent of coordination—what outcomes will they seek to realize or avoid?

4. How will the members of a coalition enforce the agreements they reach?

Although we cannot answer any of these questions in isolation from the rest, our answer to the last one sets the stage for how we approach the first three. Taking an extreme possibility, consider a circumstance in which no agreement can be enforced, so that in principle every person is free to renege on any agreement he or she might reach with anyone else. In this event, the concept of a coalition adds little to our underscanding of events, because all action is necessarily noncooperative and our explanations for outcomes that "appear cooperative" must be formulated in terms of the ideas set forth in the preceding chapters. Of course, even if no agreements are enforceable, the negotiations that lead to them might signal something about preferences and intentions, in which case they can assist people in coordinating to a particular equilibrium, or they can affect beliefs in such a way as to influence the character of equilibria. But beyond this they cannot affect future actions, because such actions are necessarily dictated by the individual strategic imperatives we outline in previous chapters.

If we view the sale of a house as a coalition between buyer and seller, then the "glue" that holds this coalition together and that makes such activity worthwhile for both participants is not only a mutual interest in the exchange, but also the courts and a body of contract law that protect the seller against theft and the buyer against fraud. This glue keeps both buyer and seller from unilaterally reneging on their contract, because without it the buyer prefers to halt mortgage payments after taking possession of the property and the seller prefers to retain control of the property after receiving a down payment. Remove the legal mechanisms for enforcing contracts and one also takes away the basis on which such markets are built. Take away or modify the mechanisms of enforcement that define property rights in markets and you change the character of markets, including what it is that will be bought and sold in them, or whether anything will be bought, sold, or produced for sale at all.

To the extent that the various mechanisms of enforcement render some but not all types of agreements workable, identifying which coalitions might form and specifying the agreements they might implement depends critically on our understanding of these mechanisms and of the opportunities for participants to alter them as a game proceeds. At this point, however, the astute reader might want to interject with the observation that, regardless of whether or not agreements are enforceable, no new theoretical baggage is required to understand the processes whereby coalitions form. If coalitions are agreements to coordinate choices in some extensive or normal form game, then saying that a coalitional agreement is enforceable is equivalent to saying that once we include the enforcement mechanisms as part of our description of the game, the individual components of that agreement correspond to a (Nash, subgame-perfect, perfect, Bayesian, etc.) equilibrium of the extended game.

The perspective taken in the major part of this chapter, though, is that, just as we commonly ignore the details of the judicial system when studying the general forces of markets, it is sometimes better to focus on some simple possibilities and to postpone seeking answers to all questions. Consider vote trading in legislatures. We know that we are unlikely to witness the signing of legal documents when two legislators agree to support each other's bills, despite the fact that there are incentives for defection—if legislation is considered sequentially, then once one legislator votes for a bill that he otherwise prefers to see defeated, his partner in the trade prefers to renege on the agreement when the second bill (on which he must now vote against his preference) comes up for a vote. Nevertheless, enforcement mechanisms exist that render abiding by the trade a noncooperative equilibrium. That mechanism is the shared knowledge that, if such an agreement is broken without mutual consent, the defecting legislator's reputation will be damaged and his or her subsequent participation in advantageous vote trades will at best be problematical.

How we approach matters, then, depends on our research goals and on our beliefs about the enforceability of agreements. If we are not primarily interested in, say, the evolution and maintenance of legislative norms, but if we nevertheless believe that any vote trade can be accomplished, then it is more convenient to ignore those questions pertaining to enforcement, to assume that any agreement is enforceable, and to focus instead on explaining and predicting agreements. If, on the other hand, we believe that the available technology of enforcement is critically important to the determination of what agreements can be reached and implemented—if some agreements are enforceable while others are not—then we must include an analysis of those mechanisms in our models.

In this chapter we will first concentrate on trying to learn what agreements people might reach when any and all agreements are somehow enforceable. Later we will turn our attention to situations in which the subject of enforcement cannot be divorced from the study of potential coalitional agreements. In particular, we will look at an issue that has confounded students of international politics for years, determining whether a balance of power can ensure stability in systems that are otherwise anarchic—that have no exogenous enforcement mechanism other than that countries or alliances with more power can defeat those with less power.

6.2 Coalitions and Condorcet Winners

The simplest situation that we might consider that has political content is a committee that abides by simple majority rule—where by "abides" we mean that any agreement supported by a majority is somehow enforceable. But even if we thus ignore the issue of enforcement, the discussion in previous chapters warns us that we must consider the institutional structure surrounding the use of majority voting. At one extreme we can suppose that majorities must operate within prespecified rules. Thus, if parliamentary procedures are binding, majorities may have to contend in debate and in voting with rules that disallow joint consideration of more than one issue or topic. At the other extreme, we can view even the rules of a committee as the product of some majority decision—as a mechanism that, perhaps, has been left standing by tradition but is ignored by that majority. For example, because our analysis of agendas assumes that the extensive form summarized by an agenda tree is the only relevant aspect of the situation, that analysis assumes implicitly that collusive agreements are not enforceable—we do not allow voters the option of coordinating their actions with each other. However, any majority coalition can coordinate so as to move along any path of the agenda tree, in which case the agenda becomes irrelevant to the final outcome—as long as an outcome appears somewhere on the tree (as long as the outcome is feasible), a majority coalition can decide beforehand to select that outcome and can dictate a path along the agenda that yields it as the final outcome.

This fact suggests that if simple majority rule is the final arbitrator of decisions, then the details of institutional structure matter only insofar as there are frictions—transaction costs—impeding the strict enforcement of coalitional agreements or impeding the negotiation of those agreements. Without frictions, if the "institution" of majority rule is otherwise adhered to (if, for example, the participants do not revert to physical coercion), then a majority can override any procedure such as an agenda that tries to direct its actions. Indeed, we might even prefer to view institutional details of such things as agendas as merely part of some majority's plan to implement a particular outcome.

One example of procedures being part of the package that a majority coalition imposes is the debate that arose within Congress in 1981 over President Reagan's first proposed budget. Seeking to cut appropriations for a variety of domestic spending programs, Reagan's legislative strategists sought to treat his proposed cuts as a package, whereas his opponents sought to consider those cuts on a case-by-case, program-by-program basis. Reagan's side prevailed and the cuts were implemented, with the general understanding that the initial procedural decision was the critical determinant of the final outcome. Specifically, everyone assumed that it would be easier to maintain the majority coalition under one procedure and to disrupt it under the other. Thus, because a majority favored the proposed budget cuts, it was able to implement a procedure that was best suited to its ultimate purposes.

This example suggests that if we want to understand the imperatives of coalitions in frictionless majority rule committees, it is oftentimes appropriate to ignore the details of committee procedures and to focus instead on hypotheses about coalitional preference. In order to pursue this suggestion further, however, we require a modest amount of notation and new definitions. Thus, consider a committee of n members in which we denote a **coalition** with the notation C and in which the set of all **feasible outcomes** is X. Assuming that minority coalitions are powerless to affect matters, we assume that the particular outcome x is feasible if and only if any majority coalition can collude to secure x. Suppose we now allow ourselves the luxury of being anthropomorphic about coalitions by saying that

> The coalition C prefers x to x' if and only if the members of C **unanimously** prefer x to x'.

If some members of C prefer x while others prefer x', we say that C is indifferent between x and x'. We also say that C is indifferent if, regardless of the preferences of the other members of C, one or more members are indifferent between x and x'.

Having thus extended the notion of preferences from individuals to collectivities, imagine treating coalitions as individuals, where majority coalitions can alter the status quo at will, where minority coalitions have no power whatsoever, and (in the event that n is even) where blocking coalitions (those controlling precisely half the vote) can only secure the status quo. Consider now the special property of Condorcet winners. Making the bold assumption that such a winner exists, we know that regardless of the status quo's identity, a majority coalition can, if it so chooses, move to any other feasible alternative. The special property of a Condorcet winner, however, is that if it is the status quo, then no majority coalition prefers to move anywhere else. Thus, we can think of a Condorcet winner as a Nash equilibrium to the noncooperative game played among majority (winning) coalitions. Moreover, since such a winner defeats every other feasible alternative in a majority vote, it must be a unique equilibrium. Thus, quite directly, we can conclude that

> *Frictionless majority rule committees select Condorcet winners as final outcomes.*

Our argument loses its relevance if there is no Condorcet winner, but before we generalize our analysis to accommodate this possibility, suppose there is more than one feasible alternative that cannot be defeated in a majority vote. Such outcomes are not Condorcet winners (because individually they cannot defeat everything). Nevertheless, they share the special property that no majority coalition has a positive incentive to shift from such outcomes to anything else (because the members of no such coalition have a unanimous incentive to shift). Clearly, these outcomes should also be thought of as equilibria, except now equilibrium outcomes are not unique.

Without a plethora of new concepts, then, we have extended our game-theoretic understanding of politics to include coalitions—albeit for the special case of simple majority rule. Moreover, we can glean some substantive lessons from this discussion. First, consider the issue of predicting the coalitions that form. Such predictions are important since in many circumstances coalitions are more readily observable than outcomes. In parliamentary bodies, for example, we can easily see which parties coalesce to form a government, but eventual outcomes—agreements among coalition partners to share ministerships, patronage, and policy domains, and the policies the government implements—may be more difficult to detect and measure. Indeed, a government may fall before the agreements that ostensibly led to it are implemented, and political scientists have long believed that the preeminent objective of the study of parliamentary systems is an ability to predict what coalition will eventually emerge to form a government. Similarly, journalistic accounts of legislative deliberations explain the passage of some bill by using language that commonly can be reexpressed as "legislators . . ., after negotiating an agreement over the bill's content, formed a majority coalition in favor of its passage." However, the preceding discussion implies that

> *If the set of feasible outcomes and the individual preferences over them yield a Condorcet winner, then it may not be possible to predict which majority coalition will form—indeed, we may observe no explicit co-alition whatsoever.*

The rationale for this assertion is that the particular coalition that forms to upset a status quo in favor of a Condorcet winner need not be unique and generally will depend on the properties of the status quo. If the status quo is onerous to many voters, then any number of winning coalitions might form to displace it. On the other hand, if the Condorcet winner itself is the status quo, then it should be common knowledge that no alternative outcome can displace it, in which case the futility of forming coalitions should itself be common knowledge. Inaction on the part of a legislature, then, with respect to some issue may indicate merely that the status quo is majority preferred to all other possible policies.

Example: Consider Figure 6.1, which portrays the same single-peaked preferences as Figure 2.11 shows, so that the ideal of the median voter—x^*_2—is a Condorcet winner. But consider the four alternative status quos portrayed in that figure—x°_1, x°_2, x°_3, and $x^\circ_4 = x^*_2$. If x°_1 is the status quo, then the members of every two-person (majority) coalition unanimously prefer changing things to x^*_2. Thus, we cannot say whether we will see all three people move unanimously to upset x°_1, or precisely which two-person coalition will do so. If x°_2 is the status quo, then only the coalition {2,3} unanimously prefers a move to the Condorcet winner, whereas if x°_3 is the status quo, then only {1,2} would vote for a change to x^*_2. Finally, if the status quo is x°_4, which corresponds to the Condorcet winner, then no coalition should form.

This last possibility—that we will see no explicit coalitions—can occur in other contexts.

Example: Consider the vote-trading scenario in Table 6.1, which shows the payoffs that each of five legislators associates with

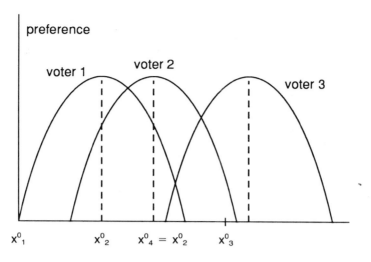

Figure 6.1

Legislator	Bill A	Bill B	Bill C	Bill D	Bill E
1	10	−2	−5	4	−5
2	−2	10	−5	−5	4
3	4	−8	−5	3	−8
4	−8	5	3	−5	−8
5	−5	−5	4	−10	4

Table 6.1   Vote Trading With Status Quo as Condorcet Winner

the passage of each of five bills. If the payoff to each legislator from a bill's failure is zero and if payoffs are separable—if each bill has nothing to do with any other bill so that the payoff from the passage of, say, two bills is simply the sum of the payoffs associated with the passage of each—then failing all bills is a Condorcet winner: No combination of pass-fail across the five bills can secure majority approval over the status quo. Notice, though, that legislators 1 and 2 have an incentive to trade votes on A and B, because doing so secures the passage, *ceteris paribus*, of A and B, which increases the payoffs to them from zero to eight. It is the *ceteris paribus* condition, however, that causes difficulty, because legislators 3 and 4 have an incentive to trade in the opposite direction so as to cancel the effect of the trade between 1 and 2 (indeed, 5 has an incentive to bring this possibility to 3 and 4's attention). Because failing all bills is a Condorcet winner, any trade that any pair of legislators might contemplate will be opposed by the remaining legislators so as to preserve the status quo.

This example, then, illustrates a situation in which the status quo is a Condorcet winner and no set of trades can be sustained by a majority. If all legislators understand this fact (which is what is implied by common knowledge), the legislature can avoid time-consuming negotiation and coalition formation by the simple expedient of allowing these bills to remain buried in committee. And as to the issue of whether we might anticipate maneuvers to bring only some subset of bills to the floor, if all legislators are fully cognizant of strategic possibilities, then no such maneuver can succeed since, if such a maneuver threatened to yield an outcome different from the status quo, a majority of legislators would block the attempt. Thus, if a Condorcet winner exists and if that winner corresponds to the status quo, then, at least for the case of complete information environments, using data drawn from actual votes poses a selection problem for empirical research—the only data that will be observed will involve situations in which there is not such winner (unless, of course, legislators choose to vote on various measures in order to publicly affirm a position on an issue for the benefit of their reputations among constituents).

Our example also illustrates an interesting general fact about vote trading scenarios. Specifically,

> If the payoffs from individual legislation are separable, and if a Condorcet winner exists, then that winner is the outcome that prevails when everyone votes sincerely on each bill.

In our example, the Condorcet winner is the status quo—no bills pass—and this winner prevails when every member votes for a bill when he or she associates a positive payoff with its passage and against when he or she associates a negative payoff with passage. Thus, if we observe vote trading in a legislature, we should infer either that there is no Condorcet winner among the feasible outcomes, or that information is not complete, or that our common knowledge assumption does not apply. Moreover, this conclusion is not dependent on selecting an example in which the Condorcet outcome is the status quo—our analysis holds regardless of what combination of passage and failure is Condorcet winning.

> **Example:** For another example of the relevance of the concept of a Condorcet winner to committee deliberations, consider the problem that confronted the Jet Propulsion Lab (JPL) of the California Institute of Technology in 1973 in determining trajectories for NASA's two Jupiter/Saturn (Voyager) space probes (launched in 1977). Ten teams of scientists were involved with experiments on the probes, and each team had specific preferences over alternative pairs of trajectories. A special committee at JPL "narrowed" the list of alternative trajectory pairs from 105 to 35 and sought a procedure for "fairly" choosing a specific pair. At this point information about the ordinal and cardinal preferences of each team was collected with the idea of comparing the alternatives by using three 'normative' criteria: choosing the alternative that maximized (1) the sum of ordinal ranks; (2) the sum of cardinal utilities; and (3) the product of cardinal utilities. Trajectory pair 31 "won" on two of these criteria whereas pair 26 won on criterion (2). After some additional modifications, however, trajectory pair 26 was selected as the final outcome. Interestingly, this pair "won" by a fourth criterion—it was the Condorcet winner among all pairs.[1]

6.3 A Generalization—The Core

We now know that there are a variety of voting mechanisms that ensure the selection of Condorcet winners under complete information—2-candidate elections, binary agendas, and cooperative majority rule committees with no impediments to coalition formation and the enforcement of agreements. However, although the preceding discussion is useful, it does not provide a general analysis of coalitional processes. Two questions in particular come to mind:

> *What can we say about processes that are not dictated by majority rule?*

---

[1]James S. Dyer and Ralph E. Miles, Jr., "An Actual Application of Collective Choice Theory to the Selection of Trajectories for the Mariner Jupiter/Saturn 1977 Project," *Operations Research*, 24 (March 1976): 220–44. Dyer and Miles note, however, that if pair 31 had been similarly improved, it might have been selected in place of 26.

> *What predictions about outcomes and coalitions can we offer if there is no Condorcet winner?*

Answering the first question requires that we restate the theoretical structure of the preceding section in a way that admits generalization. We begin thus:

1. Let the elements of X, the feasible set of outcomes, correspond to vectors that denote the utility each player associates with each substantive outcome, and let $u = (u_1, u_2, \ldots, u_n)$ be a specific vector in X.

2. As before, assume that the coalition C prefers u to u' if and only if $u_i > u'_i$ for all i in C.

3. Define the coalition C to be **effective** for u in X if the members of C can coordinate their actions so as to ensure that each member, i, of C receives a payoff of at least u_i. Let $v(C)$ denote the set of all utility n-tuples for which C is effective.

4. Say that u **dominates** u' if there exists at least one coalition that is effective for u and which prefers u to u'.

Our final step is to define the concept of a cooperative game's core:

> *The* **core** *of a cooperative n-person game is the set of undominated elements of X.*

More formally, let $v^*(C)$ correspond to those outcomes from which we cannot move so as to make **all** members of C simultaneously better off.[2] Thus,

> *The utility n-tuple* u *is in a game's core if and only if it is in* $v^*(C)$ *for all coalitions C.*

If u is not a member of $v^*(C)$ for some coalition C and if u is feasible, then, by definition, we can find a utility n-tuple in $v^*(C)$ that dominates u, thereby prohibiting u from being an element of the core.

Example: Consider Figure 6.2, which shows the same single-peaked preferences of three voters that Figure 6.1 illustrates. Recall that our discussion of the Median Voter Theorem revealed that such preferences occasioned a Condorcet winner and an

---

[2]Because we require that outcomes in the core be merely undominated rather than requiring that they dominate things not in the core, we include a broader range of outcomes in $v^*(C)$ than strict Pareto optimality allows. Even if it is possible to move from u to u' so as to improve the welfare of some members of C, u remains a candidate for inclusion in $v^*(C)$ if there are some members of C who are indifferent between u and u'.

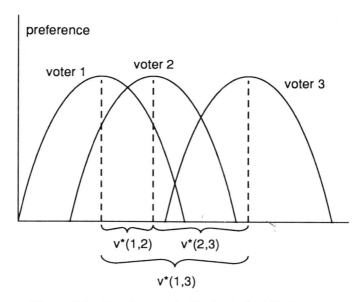

Figure 6.2 The Core with Single-Peaked Preferences

election equilibrium, which corresponded to the median voter's ideal—voter 2. However, rather than interpret these voters as an electorate, suppose they are a committee that must choose a policy through negotiation and majority rule. Notice now that all points lying between voter 1 and 2's ideals correspond to the outcomes that are Pareto optimal for the coalition {1,2}, all points between 1 and 3's ideals are Pareto optimal for {1,3}, and all points between 2 and 3's ideals are Pareto optimal for {2,3}. Thus, since voter 2's ideal is common to all three sets of Pareto optimal outcomes, that ideal is the game's core, which illustrates the fact that

> *If a majority-rule cooperative game has a Condorcet winner, that winner corresponds identically to the core.*

A Condorcet winner defeats everything in a majority vote, so no other alternative dominates it; and no other alternative can be in the core since it is defeated (dominated) by the Condorcet winner.

However, we have introduced the concept of the core to treat situations other than majority rule committees, so consider what happens when we apply this idea to a cooperative Prisoners' Dilemma:

Example: Consider the two-person Prisoners' Dilemma por-

	don't cooperate	cooperate
don't cooperate	0, 0	7, −3
cooperate	−3, 7	4, 4

Figure 6.3a Prisoners' Dilemma

trayed in Figure 6.3a. Notice, first, that although cooperation can yield a player a payoff of −3, a player can be certain that he or she does no worse than 0 by refusing to cooperate. Thus, we say that each player, acting alone, is effective for any outcome that yields that player a payoff of 0 or less. So $v(i) = \{u : u_i \leq 0\}$, and $v^*(\{i\})$ corresponds to all feasible utility 2-tuples in which $u_i \geq 0$. On the other hand, the coalition of both players, {1,2}, is effective for all feasible outcomes. Hence, the core of the corresponding cooperative game is any feasible outcome in which both players receive at least 0, and is Pareto optimal for {1,2}. As Figure 6.3b shows, the only such outcome that does not entail lotteries is (4,4), which is what prevails if both players cooperate.

This example reveals what we can and what we cannot learn from our analysis thus far. Played noncooperatively, the unique Nash equilibrium yields the outcome (0,0), whereas played cooperatively, we avoid the dilemma. What our analysis fails to specify, however, is the mechanisms these two players might use to enforce the joint installation of pollution control devices. Thus, we learn what outcomes will prevail if enforcement is feasible, but we do not learn how to ensure that feasibility.

The issue of enforcement is, as we have already indicated, profoundly important theoretically. But it is also important substantively—a fact illustrated by an important argument about the role of the courts in the adjudication of property rights, called the **Coase Theorem**.[3] This theorem asserts that

> *If transactions costs are zero, if there is a mechanism for enforcing contracts, if there is a freely transferable numeraire (money), and if there is an unambiguous specification of property rights, then everyone involved in a situation in which the actions of some hurt or benefit*

---

[3]Ronald Coase, "The Problem of Social Cost," *The Journal of Law and Economics*, 3 (1960): 1−44.

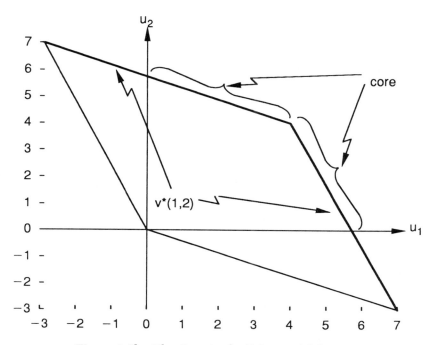

Figure 6.3b The Core in the Prisoners' Dilemma

others can reach mutually beneficial bargains without government intervention. Furthermore, if a unique outcome maximizes social wealth, then the parties will attain that outcome regardless of the prior assignment of property rights and liabilities.

Recast in the terminology of our discussion of the Prisoners' Dilemma, the Coase Theorem counters the argument that the inefficiencies occasioned by public goods and externalities justify government action, and in particular, government regulation. Instead, governments ought simply to ensure the enforceability of contracts, thereby guaranteeing legally defensible and alienable property rights. If one can receive compensation for the benefits that one's actions bestow on others, and if an institutional arrangement can guarantee such a right, then the public-goods problem dissolves. Political debate would then focus on the allocation of those rights rather than on decisions about what levels of various goods, services, and regulations to supply. For example, an industry might have a property right to pollute, which the "victims" could buy away from it if they value clean air more than the industry values the use of the ambient air as a sink. Alternatively, the victims might have a property right

outcome	person 1	person 2	total
o_1	$ 0	$12	$12
o_2	4	10	14
o_3	6	6	12
o_4	7.5	4	11.5
o_5	12	0	12

Table 6.2 Illustration of Coase Theorem

in clean air, which the industry might buy away from them. And if victims (industries) are willing to pay more for clean (dirty) air, then the same outcome, clean (dirty) air, prevails no matter what the prior assignment of property rights has been.

Example: Suppose persons 1 and 2 must choose an outcome from the set $O = \{o_1, . . ., o_5\}$, where their payoffs are as shown in Table 6.2.

Suppose person 1 has the legal right to decide which outcome is chosen—person 1 has control of the relevant property right—and suppose money and utility are equivalent. Because 1 is effective for all outcomes, he can select outcome o_5 and secure a payoff of 12. Thus,

$$v(1) = \{u : u_1 < 12\}.$$

Person 2, on the other hand, cannot guarantee receiving more than 0, so we set

$$v(2) = \{u : u_2 < 0\}.$$

Persons 1 and 2 can secure any feasible outcome, including the one that yields a total payoff of 14. Since we have assumed that money and utility are equivalent for both persons, exchanging money is equivalent to transferring utility, and since money, presumably, is freely transferable, persons 1 and 2 can thereby secure any utility 2-tuple in which the sum of u_1 and u_2 does not exceed 14. That is, 1 and 2 together can select outcome o_2, realize a combined payoff of 14, and trade money to achieve any outcome in which $u_1 + u_2 \le 14$. Hence,

$$v(1,2) = \{u : u_1 + u_2 \le 14\}.$$

Since no outcome in which 1 receives at least \$12, 2 receives at least 0, and 1 and 2 together receive at least \$14 can be dominated by $\{1\}$, $\{2\}$, or $\{1,2\}$, it follows that the core to this game is the set of 2-tuples $\boldsymbol{u} = (u_1, u_2)$ such that

$$\text{core} = \{\boldsymbol{u} : u_1 \geq 12, u_2 \geq 0, u_1 + u_2 = 14\}.$$

Alternatively, suppose 2 has the right to decide the outcome, so $v(1)$, $v(2)$ and $v(1,2)$ become

$$v(1) = \{\boldsymbol{u} : u_1 \leq 0\}; \qquad v(2) = \{\boldsymbol{u} : u_2 \leq 12\};$$
$$v(1,2) = \{\boldsymbol{u} : u_1 + u_2 \leq 14\},$$

in which case the core becomes

$$\text{Core} = \{\boldsymbol{u} : u_1 \geq 0, u_2 \geq 12, u_1 + u_2 = 14\}.$$

Thus, the specification of a property right dictates the eventual distribution of payoffs between 1 and 2, but o_2 prevails regardless of who controls the decision.

The policy implications of this example are viewed as important by scholars who criticize the expanding role of government. Instead of becoming directly involved in the production of commodities and the delivery of services, instead of establishing specific clean-air and safety standards with which businesses must comply, and instead of centralizing decisions about the resources people should allocate to each of these activities, the example suggests that governments ought simply to assist in reducing transaction costs among relevant parties and in establishing and enforcing property rights. That is, if transaction costs can be reduced to zero so that individuals can efficiently negotiate among themselves, then, while ensuring the enforceability of agreements, the state can establish property rights in such a way as to effect whatever redistribution of income is somehow deemed appropriate.

Reality, of course, is far more complex than our example, and the presumption that transaction costs can be set to zero is utopian. However, our intent is simply to show how a simple game, in conjunction with the concept of the core, leads to a discussion of important political matters.

6.4 The Politics of Redistribution

Earlier we note that a state's functions can be divided into two broad categories—regulating those Prisoners' Dilemmas that markets cannot resolve (including the implementation of mechanisms for enforcing those contracts that are an essential part of markets) and the redistribution of wealth. Our discussion in the previous section of the Prisoners' Dilemma played cooperatively reveals that the central problem with respect to the first function is enforcing decisions that yield outcomes in the core. Hence, governments are necessarily coercive entities. Our discussion of the Coase Theorem, on the other hand, suggests that if government can ensure the implementation of effective enforcement, then its primary function should be that of determining the form of redistribution—determining who wins and who loses via the specification of property rights.

This argument, however, should not be interpreted to mean that dictating the eventual form of redistribution is a straightforward task for a democratic state. Both chapters 2 and 3 illustrate electoral instability in redistributive elections, where the source of that instability is the fact that such situations do not have Condorcet winners. To see this problem using the definition of the core, consider a game of pure redistribution in which

1. Outcomes are defined in terms of a transferable commodity, such as money. Thus, every outcome in the feasible set X is characterized by the distribution of money among the players.

2. Each person's utility for this commodity is linear. So if the commodity is money, then money and utility are equivalent and utility is transferable among people. If, for example, players 1, 2, and 3 can secure the payoffs x_1, x_2, and x_3, then they can also secure the payoffs y_1, y_2, and y_3, provided that $y_1 + y_2 + y_3 = x_1 + x_2 + x_3$.

3. The transferability of utility allows us to summarize the utility outcomes that a coalition can secure, $v(C)$, more conveniently as a single number, with the understanding that the coalition C, if it forms, can secure any feasible allocation in which the sum of payoffs to its members does not exceed $v(C)$.

4. No resources are created as a function of the way players play the game, so $v(C) + v(N\text{-}C)$ equals a nonnegative constant for all C; nor are resources destroyed by the process of

coalition formation, so if C' and C'' are two disjoint coalitions, then

$$v(C' + C'') \geq v(C') + v(C'').$$

5. Strict inequality must hold in the preceding expression for at least two disjoint coalitions; otherwise no coalition is worthwhile. In particular, individual players can get as much acting alone as they can get by coalescing, so there is no need to form a coalition.

A game of pure redistribution, then, models a legislature contemplating a revision of tax codes under the constraint that the total revenues to be collected are constant. Equivalently, such games correspond to those legislative deliberations in which, after the revenues are collected, the issue is how to allocate them across the population in the form of various subsidies and transfer payments. Notice, moreover, that if the constant to which condition 4 refers is zero, then the pure redistribution game corresponds to a situation in which one coalition expropriates from another, whereas if the constant is positive, then the game is one in which some specific total of resources is to be allocated across the players.

That games of pure redistribution do not have cores—that they share the instability of majority rule games without Condorcet winners—can be established with the following somewhat fanciful example:

Example: Suppose there are n clans, each living on its own part of the "Valley of the Dump." The valley is totally walled in by the surrounding cliffs that tower above it. Everyday, each clan produces precisely one bag of garbage, but the cliffs prevent exporting the valley's garbage. Thus, each clan faces a solid waste disposal problem. The legal code of the valley, strictly enforced, allows clans to dump their garbage in their own back yards or the yards of others, but it also permits coalitions. Assume that each clan evaluates the outcome of the garbage problem solely in terms of the number of bags dumped in its yard. More precisely, each clan has a linear utility function in bags, preferring fewer bags to more, and that the utility for having one bag dumped on one's yard is -1. To see that this game of redistribution has no core, suppose to the contrary that the payoff vector $\mathbf{x} = (x_1, x_2, \ldots, x_n)$ is in the core. Then, since any n-1 clan coalition can dump all of its garbage on the excluded clan and, presumably, will have one bag of garbage spread across its yards, it must be that

$$x_2 + x_3 + \ldots + x_n \geq -1$$
$$x_1 + x_3 + \ldots + x_n \geq -1$$

$$\cdot$$
$$\cdot$$
$$\cdot$$

$$x_1 + x_2 + \ldots + x_{n-1} \geq -1.$$

Since there are n such equations, if we add them up, we have

$$(n-1)(x_1 + x_2 + \ldots + x_n) \geq -n.$$

But since there are precisely n bags produced per day, it must also be true that $(x_1 + x_2 + \ldots + x_n) = -n$. So **x** is in the core only if $-(n-1)n > -n$, which requires that n $\leq$ 2. That is, the redistributive game in the valley has a core only if there are not more than two clans.

That games of pure redistribution do not have cores helps explain a great many things. We have already argued in an electoral context that to the extent that the policies with which an incumbent must deal are redistributional, a challenger in the next election can always find some coalition of voters that can be made better off with some alternative policy and pattern of redistribution. The task for the challenger, then, is to find such a coalition and to convince its members that, were he or she in office, an appropriate redistribution would prevail. The incumbent's task, on the other hand, is to convince voters that politics is not purely redistributional or, as in the U.S. Congress, that the incumbent's seniority is critical in keeping the federal government's largesse from being redistributed away from the constituency in question. Incumbent presidents seeking reelection will tend to portray themselves as statesmen who are leading the nation to more Pareto efficient outcomes, whereas especially attractive platforms for those who challenge such incumbents will consist of populist appeals identifying the incumbent as an enemy of "us" (a majority) and an ally of "them" (some sinister, easily identified, "overfed," minority). Within Congress itself, redistributional politics is equally unstable since our formal analysis applies to majority rule committees as well as elections. Indeed, some scholars have argued that the U.S. Congress's propensity to form overly large coalitions that grant special benefits to a great many constituencies derives from the inherent risk aversion of legislators with respect to the prospect of finding themselves in a losing coalition. The alternative to a norm of "universal inclusion" is the instability and uncertainty associated with a majority rule game without a core.

6.5 The Core and Spatial Issues

It is a mistake to conclude on the basis of the preceding discussion that the nonexistence of the core is a problem that arises only in the context of redistributional politics. The fact that cores and Condorcet winners are nearly equivalent in majority voting games and the fact that Condorcet winners are rare in spatial voting games tell us that cores are rare in such voting games if played cooperatively. To see this directly, consider again the three-voter configuration of spatial preferences, which is shown in Figure 6.4. Rather than assume that these preferences refer to voters in some mass electorate, suppose instead that they pertain to members of some committee, and, rather than have the eventual policy correspond to the position chosen by a successful election candidate, suppose that policy is the one agreed to by some majority coalition.

Our earlier discussion of these preferences in an electoral context led to the conclusion that the ideal point configuration in Figure 6.4 does not yield a Condorcet winner. Hence, the cooperative majority rule coalitional game cannot have a core. To see this using the core's definition directly, recall that an outcome is in the core if and only if it is Pareto optimal for every coalition. In this instance, the Pareto optimal policies for any two-person coalition (a majority) corresponds to the line connecting their ideal points. (A simple paper-and-pencil exercise should convince the reader that we can move closer to the ideal points of any two persons whenever we are off the line connecting their ideal points.)[4] Clearly, there is no policy that is Pareto optimal for all three 2-person coalitions simultaneously—the three lines describing the Pareto optimal outcomes for the three 2-person (majority) coalitions do not have a common intersection. Thus, the disequilibrium that pervades a 2-candidate

---

[4]The Pareto optimal outcomes for a two-person coalition correspond to the line connecting their ideal points only if indifference contours are circles or if these contours are ellipses and the major and minor axes of the two persons align identically. More generally, these outcomes correspond to the locus of tangencies of the two sets of indifference contours. We note also that if larger coalitions are considered and if contours are circles, the outcomes that are Pareto optimal for that coalition correspond to the convex hull of the ideal points of the coalition's members plus all points inside that hull.

spatial election does not disappear if we assume that the electorate is a committee.

Clearly, we can extend this argument to assert that when a Condorcet winner exists in an election, it exists also if that electorate acts as a majority rule committee. In this way, then, we can view a two-candidate election as a device for achieving the same outcomes that would be achieved in a "New England town meeting model" of democratic processes, except that the election has the advantage of easier implementation in large electorates, whereas the town meeting has the advantage of ensuring that the members of the electorate can inform each other directly about their views.

This discussion also reveals a useful tactic for moving a committee (as well as an electorate) away from an outcome that one prefers to avoid but that otherwise seems inevitable because it corresponds to a core. If a committee's deliberations can be characterized as a debate over a single issue (that is, if everyone's preferences are single peaked over some discernable dimension so that a Condorcet winner exists), then a useful tactic is to introduce a new issue into the debate. If done with skill and with an eye to the possibilities of manipulating the committee's procedures (e.g., the order in which motions are brought to the floor for debate and a vote), this new issue should destroy the core's existence and allow for the strategic manipulation of outcomes so as to secure a more favorable result. Indeed, in one of the more challenging applications of this idea, William Riker has argued that just such a tactic allowed opponents of the Seventeenth Amendment to the U.S. Constitution (popular election of Senators) to postpone the eventual approval of this amendment in Congress by the timely introduction of the issue of states rights (federal supervision of elections) into the debate. In addition, Riker has argued that the infusion of the issue of slavery into national debates on policy in the 1830's and 1840's, which up to that time had been dominated by antimercantilist issues, set the stage for a grander form of political instability that led eventually to the division of the Democratic Party, to the election of Lincoln, and, ultimately, to the American Civil War.

6.6 Institutional Impediments to Disequilibrium

The fact that neither games of pure redistribution nor spatial games have cores is important. Both types of games are central to politics and, thus, we should assume that the instabilities associated with cooperative games without cores necessarily pervade our subject. In

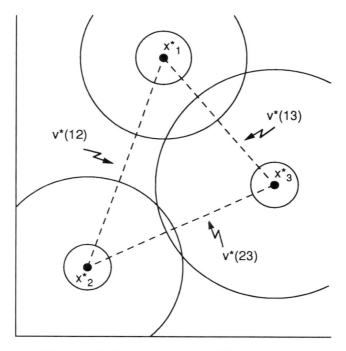

Figure 6.4 An Empty Core With Two Issues

fact, it is not unreasonable to suppose that the realization of this theoretical proposition explains some of the structure that the Framers of the U.S. Constitution imposed on our political system.

Any student of American politics knows that our constitution establishes a federal government that hardly matches the idea of direct democracy. Among the provisions that place distance between governmental officials and the mass electorate are the facts that the connection between president and electorate is made indirect by the electoral college, that the unamended constitution made no provision for the popular election of the Senate, that Senators are appointed or elected in staggered terms so that a majority of the Senate is not subject to electoral evaluation in any given election year, that an unelected court oversees the constitutionality of legislation, and that the legislative branch itself is divided into two chambers.

At least one of these constitutional provisions can be interpreted as an attempt to mitigate against the instabilities of simple majority rule. Specifically, consider the bicameral structure of our national legislature. It is generally assumed that this division accomplished a compromise between "big" states, that sought representation on the basis of population, and "small" states, that were concerned that their interests would be overridden with any representation scheme based solely on population. Although this concern may have dictated the ultimate form of compromise, that compromise had another important effect that bears on the stability of the American political system.

First, consider a single legislature operating under majority rule, where each representative in the legislature responds to the majority will of his or her constituents, and imagine that only two positions are possible—for or against changing the status quo. The interesting fact is that only a majority of constituents in a majority of legislative districts is required to ensure approval of a change. Thus, it is possible to imagine a circumstance in which only slightly more than one quarter of the overall electorate prefers to change the status quo, yet that change prevails in the legislature. Thus, although simple majority rule guarantees instability whenever purely redistributional issues are considered, we should anticipate instability encompassing a broader range of issues in unicameral majority rule legislatures, because if legislators merely record the preferences of their constituents, then something less than a majority of constituents can upset any status quo. And in this context, we can easily imagine circumstances in which the legitimacy of political institutions is undermined as minorities continually thwart the will of majorities.

It is not unreasonable to suppose that designers of political institutions prefer to avoid such instability since it can lead to even more profound instabilities. One expedient is to raise the vote quota within the legislature to something greater than a majority. However, although imposing such a quota seems prudent when we are concerned with constitutional changes, imposing them generally poses a dilemma for designers of constitutions who do not want to appear to be "undemocratic." In this context, we can interpret the invention of the bicameral legislature as an imaginative and democratically acceptable device for raising quotas. To see what we mean by this, let us turn to a simple example:

Example: Consider a bicameral legislature in which voters 1 through 9 are represented by legislators L_1, L_2, and L_3 in the first legislature and by legislators l_1, l_2, and l_3 in the second legislature. Suppose that L_1 represents voters 1, 2, and 3, legislator L_2 represents voters 4, 5, and 6, and so on as shown in Figure 6.5. Notice first that if voters 1, 2, 5, and 7 prefer upsetting the status quo and if legislators l_1, l_2, and l_3 alone are empowered to effect

L₁	voter 1	voter 2	voter 3
L₂	voter 4	voter 5	voter 6
L₃	voter 7	voter 8	voter 9

l_1 l_2 l_3

Figure 6.5 Bicameral Legislature

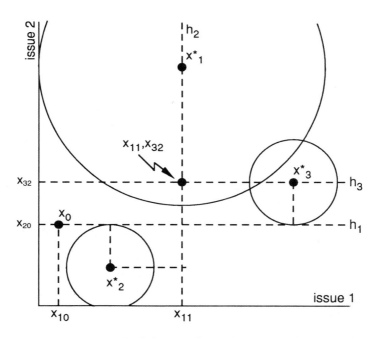

Figure 6.6 Stability With Issue-By-Issue Voting

a change, then the change passes. But if legislators L_1, L_2, and L_3 must also pass the measure in a majority vote, the measure fails. It will pass both houses only if a fifth voter is added to the list of those who prefer changing the status quo. Thus, a bicameral legislature is more inherently conservative than a unicameral one. Put differently, bicameral legislatures generally increase the domain of the core over its domain in a unicameral legislature.

Changing vote quotas is only one route to muting the instabilities inherent in majority rule. Another route is to impose constraints that preclude a committee from voting to change the status quo on several issues simultaneously. Previously, of course, we argued that majority coalitions in a legislature can, in principle at least, impose rules to their own liking, and indeed, the U.S. Constitution empowers each chamber of the national legislature to determine its own rules. However, it is frequently the case that specific rules cannot be so easily changed because they serve a purpose larger than the issues confronting a legislature at any point in time, in which case rules have a permanence that transcends any specific vote. (One of the ongoing avenues of legislative studies is understanding the source of rules such as seniority and committee structure.)

To see, then, how one rule in particular can induce stability in an otherwise unstable context, consider Figure 6.6, which approximately reproduces the three ideal points from Figure 6.4. Suppose that the outcome $X_o = (X_{1o}, X_{2o})$ is the status quo, and suppose that this three-person committee must abide by a parliamentary procedure that "divides the question" in the sense that the committee must consider the issues one at a time. That is, suppose proposals to change X_o that correspond to diagonal moves are necessarily ruled out of order. Such a restriction might appear in a committee when it imposes parliamentary rules of issue relevance in its deliberations; alternatively, something similar to this procedure in larger legislatures results if the legislature divides into subcommittees, where each subcommittee must consider only one issue of this multidimensional legislation.

Assuming that the committee considers issue 1 first and that everyone temporarily ignores the possibility that what they do on this issue might influence their actions on the second, our analysis proceeds in five steps:

1. With voting limited to changing the status quo on issue 1, the committee is, in effect, choosing a point on the line h_1. Each voter's preferred policy on h_1 corresponds to the tangency between this line and an indifference curve: however, because we have drawn all indifference curves as circles, this preferred policy is found by simply dropping a perpendicular from the voter's ideal to h_1. (Thus, each voter's preference on issue 1 is independent of where we place the status quo.)

2. Notice that not only is voter 2's ideal on h_1 the median preference, but everyone's preferences on h_1 are single-peaked—

as we move along h_1 away from any voter's ideal, we move to lower indifference curves (circles of greater radius) for that voter. Thus, the median ideal point, x_{11}, is the committee's decision on issue 1.

3. With (x_{11}, X_{2o}) the new status quo, the committee considers issue 2 and, using the same reasoning as above, chooses a point on the line h_2. In this instance, voter 1's ideal is the median, so the tentative final outcome is $x^* = (x_{11}, x_{32})$.

4. Consider the possibility that after having voted on issue 2, the committee reconsiders its decision on issue 1, which is in effect a vote over the outcomes on the line h_3. But again voter 2's ideal remains the committee's median preference on this line. Hence, reconsideration of issue 1 cannot upset the outcome $x^* = (x_{11}, x_{32})$.

5. Finally, notice that our conclusion about the final outcome is unaffected by voters who look ahead to issue 2 before they vote on issue 1. Owing to the fact that our example uses circular indifference contours, the same policy on issue 2 (voter 3's preference) will prevail regardless of what is chosen on issue 1. Thus, voters might as well vote sincerely on issue 1 since this decision cannot effect what happens on issue 2.

This example reveals how voting on a proposed change in the status quo one issue at a time generates stability. However, we perhaps should anticipate that some majority coalition will try to resist x^* later in the legislature's deliberations—despite this rule, there is no core and more than one majority coalition can gain if it can successfully upset the issue-by-issue procedure. Stability, then, depends on the extent to which majorities cannot upset a rule dictating that the committee must consider the issues separately. Any explanation for a rule's effect on outcomes must ultimately explain why that rule was chosen in the first place. Indeed, just as we can cycle over outcomes, it is possible to imagine circumstances in which, if there are more than two possible rules, cycling occurs over the selection of a rule. That is, while each rule may yield a determinate outcome, the necessity for selecting a rule merely pushes the cycle back one step to this selection process.

The consequences of a rule such as the one we have just considered depend also on whether it makes "substantive sense" to consider issues separately. The critical feature of our example is that with circular indifference contours, preferences are separable and a person's ideal preference on one issue does not depend on what prevails

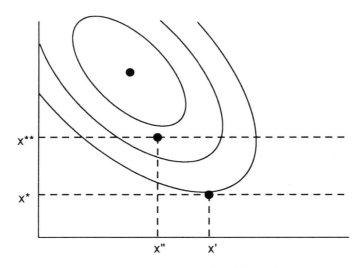

Figure 6.7   Non Separable Spatial Preferences

on the other issue. (For example, the policy voter 2 most prefers on issue 2 does not depend on the committee's decision on issue 1—on where we draw h_2.) But suppose that preferences on issues interact so that what a legislator most prefers on one isse depends on the resolution of other issues. Figure 6.7 shows such a set of indifference contours, so that, for example, if the status quo is x' on issue 1, this legislator most prefers x^* on issue 2; however, if x'' prevails on issue 1, then this legislator's preference changes to x^{**} on issue 2. And in general, if issues are not separable, then issue-by-issue voting cannot induce stability.

> **Example:** To see the effect of nonseparability on issue-by-issue voting, consider the three-member committee in Figure 6.8, with ideal points at x_1, x_2, and x_3, each of whom perceives some relationship between the issues. Suppose the committee votes first on issue 2, then issue 1, and consider what eventually prevails as a function of what the committee agrees to on issue 2. For instance, if they choose x^* on issue 2, then they must vote subsequently on the line h_1, in which case x' ultimately prevails, because x' is the median preference on h_1. On the other hand, if the committee chooses x^{**}, then, B is the median on the line h_2. And if the committee initially agrees to x^{***} on issue 2, then the final outcome is x''. The curve S, then, maps all such outcomes and tells us what prevails as a function of what is chosen on the first ballot over issue 2.

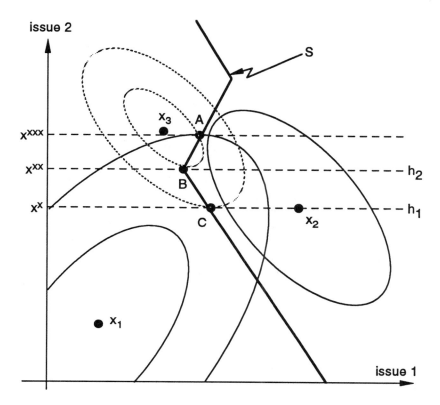

Figure 6.8 Disappearance of Stability Without Separability

To this point matters seem unexceptional, but consider the significance of S and its shape. S tells us what eventually prevails on both issues, given a specific decision on issue 2. Thus, when evaluating how to vote on issue 2, committee members should look ahead and evaluate the outcome on S implied by their initial decision. However, because S is not a straight line (which it is with circular indifference contours), committee members can have preferences that are not single-peaked along it. For example, voter 2's ideal preference on S is the point A, but notice that the point C lies on a higher indifference curve for 2 than does B. Thus, it is not the case that preferences decline monotonically as we move away from a person's ideal—voter 2's utility declines as we move from A until we get to B, and then it increases until C is reached.

The fact that a committee member does not have a single-peaked preference on S means, of course, that a cycle can develop when evaluating what to do on issue 2. Indeed, A, B, and C cycle in our example. (Voter 3 most prefers B and least prefers C, voter 1 most prefers C and least prefers A, and voter 2 most prefers A and least prefers B—which occasions the usual Condorcet cycle.) Thus, issue-by-issue voting fails to induce a stable outcome.

In this example, then, although the committee's procedure seeks to enforce a separate consideration of the issues, this separation does not exist in the minds of the committee's members. So if those members anticipate the consequences of their actions on one issue, procedures alone cannot ensure stability. Hence, the extent to which rules induce stability depends on many things, including, as our examples show, the extent to which the rules themselves are subject to revision and whether issues take a special, separable form.

This discussion does not mean, however, that rules are unimportant. Indeed, if we take the previous example and suppose that the committee votes first on issue 1, rather than issue 2, then the reader should be able to confirm that an equilibrium exists (provided that the committee does not allow a reconsideration of the issues). Thus, even a simple rule such as one that designates the voting order has a profound effect. We are, then, emphasizing two things. First, in determining the influence of a rule or institution, we should suppose that people react strategically to its imposition, with the understanding that all others are trying to do the same thing. And second, to reiterate a lesson learned from the analysis of agendas, those who wish to study legislative outcomes must understand legislative procedures and the opportunities for individuals and majorities to manipulate those procedures for their own purposes.

6.7 Majority Rule Games Without Cores

Although we might interpret parts of the preceding discussion to imply that institutional procedures can induce stability, the fact that the details of those procedures also influence the selection of a final outcome implies the existence of higher orders of instability—instability in the selection of rules themselves. For example, if we take the usual three-voter example of the Condorcet cycle of the three alternatives A, B, and C (in which A defeats B, B defeats C, and C defeats A), we now know that the agenda

"A versus B, the winner against C," yields B,

"A versus C, the winner against B," yields A,

"B versus C, the winner against A," yields C.

So, although a specific agenda yields a determinate outcome, a cycle reappears if the committee is asked to vote on the agenda.

This example illustrates a principle we might call *the unavoidability of cycles*:

> *Unless individual preferences over the basic outcomes themselves occasion a Condorcet winner, we cannot escape the fact that at some point in the process of selecting rules or voting on outcomes, alternatives will cycle, and opportunities will present themselves for people to try to manipulate the process to their own advantage.*

This principle tells us that it is imperative that we say something general about majority rule games without cores. Saying something about coalitions and outcomes when there is no core, however, requires an adjustment in our thinking about the nature of prediction. Accustomed as we are to assuming that, except for the chance events of nature, outcomes follow a definitive logic, we commonly overlook the possibility that there may be fundamental indeterminacies in politics. When we observe and attempt to understand the formation of a particular legislative or parliamentary coalition, we generally approach matters with the implicit supposition that we should attribute an inability to explain why a particular coalition formed as against some other to our failure to measure some relevant parameter such as the complex details of the personalities of the participants. This may be true, but generally such refined measurement is impractical; moreover, we have little theoretical guidance in determining what ought to be measured and how measurements and prior observations relate to subsequent events. A similar problem, of course, confronts those who wish to predict whether a tossed coin will land heads or tails. In principle, precise measurement of all physical characteristics of the coin toss will allow a prediction to some refined degree of accuracy. But such measurement is impractical, and, thus, we find it more convenient to treat the outcome as a random event.

In a similar spirit, imagine that three people, who are identical in every respect, must use majority rule to divide $1,000. If utility and money are equivalent, the corresponding pure redistribution game has no core. But because they abide by majority rule, we might be willing to utter the tentative prediction, based on the assumption that they are "sufficiently avaricious" so as to be unconcerned with "fairness," that two people will coalesce to divide the money evenly between themselves, excluding the third from any payment. Notice, though, that we cannot say which coalition will form—from our view, all three 2-person coalitions are equivalent. Indeed, in this circumstance, the only reasonable prediction (aside from the possibility that all three members coalesce to choose a "fair" outcome) is that some two-person coalition will form.

We have, of course, encountered indeterminacy in games with multiple equilibria. But recall that whether a particular n-tuple of strategies is or is not an equilibrium depends solely on the properties of that equilibrium's component strategies—we do not say that some n-tuple is a Nash or subgame perfect equilibrium because some other n-tuple is or is not an equilibrium. In the context of cooperative games without cores, on the other hand, things may be quite different. Specifically, in the cyclic bargaining that seems inevitable in pure redistribution games, we might speculate that the participants will be especially attracted to specific proposals and that these proposals will achieve special significance **as a set**. For example, for the case of three people negotiating to divide $1,000, the set of outcomes $\{(500,500,0), (500,0,500), (0,500,500)\}$ comes to mind. First, no outcome advantages either member of the corresponding winning coalition in such a way as to give a partner an incentive to switch to another proposal in the set. Second, all other feasible outcomes are dominated by at least one proposal in the set.

Although this reasoning is not yet precise, what we want to emphasize is this: we do not focus on the set $\{(500,500,0), (500,0,500), (0,500,500)\}$ because each of the outcomes in it satisfies some property that renders it an equilibrium; rather we focus on these outcomes because they satisfy certain properties taken together as a set. Thus, although we do not attempt to predict which of the three outcomes eventually prevails, our identification of the set as an equilibrium corresponds to the prediction that some outcome in the set will prevail. Consider the implications of this perspective. For example, although recognizing that an understanding of why one coalition rather than another forms in a Parliament or a legislature may require a detailed analysis of personalities and chance events, even without such measurements, we may be able to exclude a great many coalitions as feasible merely on the basis of the participants' general policy preferences. It is in this spirit that we consider the hypothesis that a general abstract characterization of situations allows us to identify sets of feasible outcomes as predictions.

To make this reasoning more precise, we proceed by first trying to generalize the definition of the core. There are several possibilities to consider. First, we could simply play with the component parts of the core's definition, weakening one or more of those parts. Second, using some general ideas about how bargaining might proceed, we could specify "reasonable" properties that a predicted set ought to satisfy. Finally, we could attempt to describe an explicit extensive form model of bargaining and thereby deduce an appropriate solution as a Nash equilibrium to the corresponding noncooperative model of the coalitional game. Traditionally, game theory focuses on the first two avenues, but some progress has been made recently with respect to the third. For the moment, though, let us focus on the first avenue.

Recall that the elements of a core share two properties:

1. The core is **internally stable** in the sense that no outcome in it dominates another outcome in it.

2. The core is **externally stable** in the sense that outcomes in it are undominated by the feasible outcomes that are not in the core.

The problem in games without cores is that everything is dominated—there is no externally stable set. However, looking back at our example in which three people must use majority rule to divide $1,000, one feature of the set of outcomes $V = \{(500,500,0), (500,0,500), (0,500,500)\}$ that we find especially attractive is that coalition partners do not have any apparent incentive to switch from one coalition to another within this set. Maintaining this requirement (which is admittedly arbitrary at this point), we know, of course, that feasible outcomes outside the set dominate outcomes in it (otherwise, the set is a core, which we know to be empty). But in this pure redistributional example, we can readily verify that every outcome outside of V is dominated by some outcome in V. Thus, even if bargaining "wanders out of V," there is a pairing of alternatives that takes negotiators immediately back to this set. So if we modify only the definition of external stability, we arrive at the following characterization of a stable set:

1. V is **internally stable** in the sense that no outcome in it dominates any other outcome in it.

2. V is **externally stable** in the sense that every feasible outcome not in V is dominated by some outcome in V.

Sets of feasible outcomes that together satisfy internal and external stability are called **von Neumann and Morgenstern solutions**, or **V-sets**. Thus, V-sets are like cores except that their definition imposes a slightly weaker definition of external stability. The core requires that every outcome in it be undominated by every outcome outside of it; the *V*-set requires that every outcome outside of it be defeated by **something** inside of it.

Although we will argue shortly that the *V*-set is deficient as a general hypothesis, we want to reemphasize the important perspective that it takes with respect to prediction—a perspective that is not familiar to the general character of political analysis. Specifically, if we predict outcomes in *V*, we do so not merely because of the properties of those outcomes taken one at a time, but rather because of the properties of the set, *V*, to which they belong. Thus, our explanations for legislative or parliamentary outcomes can no longer take the form "outcome . . . prevailed because the majority . . . preferred it to all other outcomes and because this majority had sufficient skill in forming before any opposition could materialize." To this explanation we must append such statements as "and because that outcome was among a set of outcomes, consisting of . . ., that could prevail in this way." The V-set, then, requires that we diminish somewhat our focus on the particular character of victorious outcomes and coalitions and that we pay greater attention to the general characteristics of such outcomes and to the other outcomes that share these characteristics.

Aside from its innovative perspective, the notion of the *V*-set is attractive because it seems to be a mathematically straightforward generalization of the core. However, its definition occasions certain problems, the most important of which is that for a great many games *V*-sets are not unique. Indeed, the set of outcomes in some *V*-set typically includes nearly all feasible outcomes. For example, in the divide-the-thousand-dollars game, the set

$$\{\boldsymbol{u} : u_i = c, u_j + u_k = 1{,}000 - c, c \leq 1{,}000/3\}$$

satisfies both internal and external stability. A second difficulty is that as a generalization of the core, *V*-sets are wholly ad hoc and without behavioral justification. For this reason game theorists have sought to narrow the *V*-set's predictions with additional refinements and to associate it with some notions of bargaining process. One such refinement is the **main-simple V-set**, which treats majority rule games.

> A V-set is **main simple** and is denoted V_m if we can associate each outcome in it with a minimum winning coalition so that every member of that coalition prefers the corresponding outcome at least as much as any other outcome in V_m.

The important property, now, of main-simple *V*-sets is that they are unique for a game. Also,

> *if utility in a majority rule game is like money and is perfectly transferable among the players, then that game has a unique main-simple V-set in which each minimum winning coalition is represented by an outcome in V.*

For example, in the divide-the-thousand-dollars game, V_m is the set {(500,500,0), (500,0,500), (0,500,500)}. More generally, if the game is perfectly symmetric in the sense that each player has one vote and if each minimum winning coalition can win the same amount, *X*, as any other, then the elements of *V* take the form $(2X/(n+1),\ldots,2X/(n+1),0,\ldots,0)$. Thus, main-simple *V*-sets rationalize the prediction that, in majority rule pure redistribution games, some minimum-winning coalition will form to divide the spoils evenly among its members.

Example: A seemingly disquieting note with respect to the main-simple *V*-set's predictions is the fact that in the U.S. Congress we oftentimes observe nearly unanimous agreement to pass legislation that is redistributive because the component parts of that legislation benefit only specific constituencies. One explanation for this phenomenon is that legislators choose beforehand between being "competitive" or "cooperative," where being cooperative means to avoid forming a minimal winning coalition in favor of a more universally acceptable result; being competitive means seeking to form a minimal winning coalition that expropriates from a maximal minority. The advantage of being competitive is that it maximizes one's gains whenever one is included in the winning coalition, but the disadvantage is that one takes the chance of being excluded from the majority. Being cooperative ensures against losing, but one cannot win a great deal. For example, in the divide-the-thousand-dollars game, each person in a minimal winning coalition gains $1,000/[(n+1)/2]$ whereas excluded players gain nothing. The probability that person *i* is included in a minimal winning coalition equals the proportion of such coalitions that includes *i*, $(n+1)/2n$, so the expected gain in a noncooperative legislature is

$$\left[\frac{2,000}{n+1}\right]\left[\frac{n+1}{2n}\right] + 0\left[1 - \frac{n+1}{2n}\right] = \frac{1,000}{n},$$

which is what one earns if everyone plays cooperatively and

simply divides the thousand dollars among all players. Thus, even a modest degree of risk aversion or a sense that outcomes ought to be "fair and equitable" is sufficient to explain unanimity among legislators.

Example: Figure 6.9 reproduces once again the preferences illustrated in Figure 6.4, but now let us focus on the three outcomes A, B, and C formed by the simultaneous tangencies of person 1 and 2's indifference contours, 1 and 3's contours, and 2 and 3's contours. Notice first that in this game, because the players are assumed to be able to bargain only over policy, utility cannot be transferred among the players—one player cannot transfer x units of utility to some other player, because there is no commodity like money in the game. However, this game does have a main-simple V-set. First, to see that {A,B,C} is a V-set, notice that since A and B both lie on the same contour for person 1, 1 is indifferent between these two outcomes. Persons 2 and 3, on the other hand, hold opposite preferences with respect to A and B, so A does not dominate B nor does B dominate A. A similar argument holds for B and C and for C and A, so the set {A,B,C} is internally stable. To show, then, that {A,B,C} is a V-set, notice that the two hatched "petals" in Figure 6.9 correspond to the set of outcomes that defeat A. A simple paper and pencil exercise, though, reveals that B or C defeats any outcome in this set, while those outcomes that defeat B are defeated by A or C and that those that defeat C are defeated by A or B. Hence, {A,B,C} is a V-set. The reader should be able to confirm now that this set is a main-simple solution, although as we show later, there are majority rule spatial games without main-simple V-sets.

The impetus for the development of the main-simple V-set lies not only with the necessity for refining the V-set but also with the view that in a competitive coalitional environment, minimal winning coalitions somehow play a special role. Thus, the definition of a main-simple V-set adds some seemingly reasonable conditions to those of internal and external stability in the hope of generating a more refined prediction. Unfortunately, although its predictions seem reasonable within its domain, important problems remain. First, its definition pertains only to majority rule games, and, second, its definition, like that of the V-set itself, is ad hoc. Thus, the logical connections of this idea to the general perspectives of game theory are unclear. For this reason two related alternatives to the V-set have been offered—the bargaining set and the competitive solution.

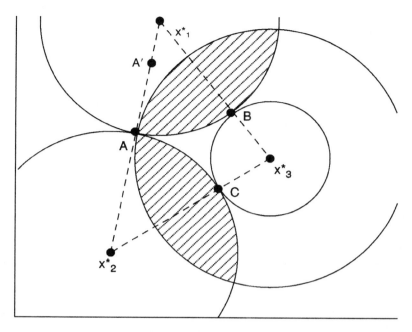

Figure 6.9 A *V*-Set

The **bargaining set** is based on the idea that if a coalition can form around a specific outcome, then each member of that coalition should be able to defend what he or she receives from the outcome which the coalition proposes against the possible objections of other members of the coalition. If a person is getting "too much" —if he or she cannot defend a payoff—then we ought not predict that outcome. But if each person can mount a defense against every conceivable objection, then that outcome is "stable" and it should be included in the set of predicted possibilities. Put differently, members of a coalition should be able to offer legitimate **counterobjections** to any **objection** against what they are getting in that coalition; and if they cannot formulate such a defense, then either the coalition must adjust the payments to its members or that coalition cannot ultimately form.

Example: Consider again the divide-the-thousand-dollars game, and the outcome (500,500,0) supported by the coalition {1,2} against 3—denoted by the **proposal** ((500,500,0), {1,2}). Suppose person 2 seeks a greater share. Person 2, then, might **object** against 1 with the proposal ((0,550,450), {2,3}), which he and his coalition partner prefer to the original proposal. However, 1 can defend his payoff of 500 in the original proposal by **counterobjecting** with ((500,0,500), {1,3}), because this counter gives him 500 as well and is preferred by 3 to the objection. Indeed, every objection by 2 against 1 (as well as every objection by 1 against 2) can be countered, so ((500,500,0), {1,2}) is in the bargaining set. Alternatively, consider (600,400,0). In this instance, 2 can object with ((0,500,500), {2,3}) and 1 cannot counter—person 1 cannot give 3 as much as 500 and at the same time defend his or her original payoff of 600. So the proposal ((600,400,0), {1,2}) is not in the bargaining set.

The bargaining set clearly provides a more reasonable basis for analyzing political coalitions than the *V*-set, but like the *V*-set, it is not without difficulties. First, there are several variants to its definition, and there is no clear reason to choose one variant over another. For example, can several persons object simultaneously against more than one person? If an objection can be directed against more than one person, must the targets of the objection all counter simultaneously with the same proposal, or can they counter individually with different proposals? Must those who are included in the counter strictly or weakly prefer the counter to the objection? To the original proposal? Must the counter itself be stable (in the bargaining set) and, thus, be believable? (Bargaining sets satisfying this property are called **strong bargaining sets**.) A more serious problem, however, is that this idea is designed for pure redistribution games and not for spatial policy games. In a pure redistributional game there is a commodity (money) that can be traded among the players so as to transfer utility, so if a player is "getting too little" in a coalition, a transfer is feasible from those who are getting "too much." But such transfers are generally impossible if only policy represented by spatial preferences is considered. If the only way to adjust a coalition partner's payoff is to alter the coalition's policy proposal, then we may be unable to transfer utility to one or more coalition partners without fundamentally undermining the coalition's viability.

With the bargaining set's limitations in mind, another idea is the **competitive solution**, *K*. Briefly, this hypothesis is based on the suggestion that coalitions, in order to form, must compete successfully with other coalitions for critical—pivotal—members. If two coalitions, *C* and *C'*, are to be simultaneously viable—if they are both capable of forming in a competitive environment—then it must be the case that the players who pivot between *C* and *C'* (the members who are common to both coalitions) cannot all prefer the proposal of one coalition to the proposal of the other; otherwise these pivotal players would block one coalition in favor of the other.

Referring to the three-person game in Figure 6.9, suppose, for whatever reason, that voters 1 and 2 do not appreciate the potential value of their coalition. Since player 3 is temporarily the sole pivot between the coalitions that might form—{1,3} and {2,3}—we can imagine a bargaining process in which voters 1 and 2 begin offering voter 3 outcomes such as B and C, but find themselves eventually "bidding up" to 3's ideal point as they each try to secure 3's loyalty. However, unless 1 and 2 are completely dense, one or the other should soon realize that they can avoid having to give in to 3's ideal point by forming a coalition of their own. With voter 3 no longer enjoying the position of sole pivot, and finding it necessary to compete with 1 and 2 as potential pivots as well, we can expect 3 to begin proclaiming, "Honest, I was only kidding in asking for my ideal. I'll settle for B or C as originally discussed." The competitive solution tries to formalize this bargaining scenario.

To define the competitive solution, we first introduce the notion of viability. Focusing on proposals that identify a payoff vector and the coalition that forms to realize that outcome (note that p does not refer here to a probability),

> If $p = (\mathbf{u},C)$ and $p' = (\mathbf{u}',C')$ are any two feasible proposals, then p is **viable** against p' if
> 1. $\mathbf{u}$ is Pareto optimal for C.
> 2. It is not the case that everyone in both C and C' prefer $\mathbf{u}'$ to $\mathbf{u}$— at least one common member is indifferent between $\mathbf{u}$ and $\mathbf{u}'$ or strictly prefers $\mathbf{u}$ to $\mathbf{u}'$.

And p is **strictly viable** against p' if all pivotal coalition members strictly prefer $\mathbf{u}$ to $\mathbf{u}'$.

The notion of domination used to define the core and the V-set focuses on all the players in a coalition that might enforce a particular outcome. The notion of viability, on the other hand, focuses only on the players that are pivotal between alternative proposals. With this difference, we then say that the set of feasible proposals K is a competitive solution if

1. *No coalition is associated with more than one proposal in K.*

2. *K is **internally stable** in the sense that all proposals in it are viable against each other.*

3. *K is **externally stable** in the sense that if some p'' not in K is*

strictly viable against some p in K, then there is a p' in K that is strictly viable against p".

Although the definition of K parallels the definition of the V-set—like the V-set, it makes use of notions of internal and external stability and it focuses on the properties of a set of outcomes rather than on the properties of outcomes taken one at a time—note the important differences. First, because it is based on the idea of coalitions competing against each other, because a coalition's strategy is its proposal, and because "players" can choose but one strategy in a game, K allows coalitions to have only one proposal. Second, as we have already noted, K uses the notion of viability rather than that of domination. Third, rather than supposing that all feasible proposals not in V are dominated by at least one proposal in V, we require that some member of K be strictly viable against those feasible proposals not in K that might upset K—that are strictly viable against something in K.

Despite these differences, there are important relationships between the V-set and K, as well as between the core, the bargaining set, and K. Specifically,

> *An outcome in the core (associated with any winning coalition) is a competitive solution. The outcomes in a main-simple V-set (associated with the appropriate minimum winning coalition) also constitute a competitive solution. Finally, the elements of the strong bargaining set are a competitive solution.*

In this way we can think of K as a generalization of the core, the V-set, and the strong bargaining set (at least for majority rule games), so in the next section we illustrate K's application to coalition formation processes in parliamentary systems. But first consider this example:

Example: In the ostensible "corrupt bargain" of 1824, in which no candidate secured a majority of the electoral college vote, John Quincy Adams was elected president over Andrew Jackson by the House of Representatives even though, following the election, Jackson controlled more electoral votes and had secured a majority of popular votes in more states than had Adams. The actual electoral college vote tabulation following the general election was

Jackson:	*99 votes and a majority in 11 states*
Adams:	*84 votes and a majority in 7 states*

Crawford:	*41 votes and a majority in 3 states*
Clay:	*37 votes and a majority in 3 states*

In the House each state has one vote, but because only three candidates can be considered, Clay was eliminated. The issue for Clay, however, was: Whom should he support? An intense series of negotiations preceded the final vote, with some of Jackson's support shifting to the other three candidates, and with Clay's support in Missouri shifting to Adams, at which time the candidates support became

Adams:	*10 states*
Jackson:	*7 states*
Crawford:	*4 states*
Clay:	*3 states*

Suppose for purposes of an example that if C is winning, then $v(C)$ equals the size of the opposition—suppose size measures resources, which a winning coalition can expropriate. For example, then, $v(\text{Adams, Crawford}) = 10$. Assume that a coalition's value can be divided in any way among its members, and let J, A, Cr, and Cl denote Jackson, Adams, Crawford, and Clay, respectively. There are three facts that we can use to find this game's competitive solution:

1. The game has a main-simple V-set, because it has only winning and losing coalitions and because utility is transferable among the players.

2. The outcomes in this set correspond to a competitive solution, and each minimal winning coalition is represented by a proposal in K.

3. If K is a competitive solution, then each proposal in it must be Pareto optimal for the respective winning coalition—otherwise that coalition has a proposal that is strictly viable against its own proposal in K and viable against all other proposals.

Consider the set of proposals $K = \{(w,\{A,J\}), (x,\{A,Cr\}), (y,\{A,Cl\}), (z,\{J,Cr,Cl\})\}$ made by the four minimum winning coalitions. Because the elements of K must be Pareto optimal for the corresponding winning coalition, we must have,

$$w_A + w_J = 7,$$
$$x_A + x_{Cr} = 10,$$
$$y_A + y_{Cl} = 11,$$
$$z_J + z_{Cr} + z_{Cl} = 10.$$

To ensure that those who pivot between the coalitions with proposals in K are indifferent—that no proposal in K be strictly viable against any other proposal in K—we must have

$$w_A = x_A = y_A,$$
$$w_J = z_J,$$
$$x_{Cr} = z_{Cr},$$
$$y_{Cl} = z_{Cl}.$$

These equalities, taken together, solve to establish that Adams receives 6 whenever included in the winning coalition, Jackson 1, Crawford 4, and Clay 6. Thus,

$$K = \{((6,1,-4,-3),\{A,J\}),\ ((6,-7,4,-3),\{A,Cr\}),$$
$$((6,-7,-4,5),\{A,Cl\}),\ ((-10,1,4,5),\{J,Cr,Cl\})\}$$

is a competitive solution. Hence, Clay could join either with Adams alone or with Jackson and Crawford. We cannot say, then, whether the bargain was indeed corrupt, but there seems ample reason for understanding why Clay secured from Adams the promise of eventual succession to the presidency—a promise that Adams was ultimately unable to deliver on owing to Jackson's victory over Adams in the next election.

6.8 Parliamentary Coalitions

One of the most widely studied coalitional processes in politics is that of parliamentary coalitions in which parties maneuver to form governments. Generally, this process assumes simple majority rule, although it is not unusual to observe minority governmental coalitions whenever a majority coalition, for various reasons, is unable to form. The usual commodities subject to negotiation are policy compromises and the allocation of ministerial positions. The fact that both policy and ministries are negotiated simultaneously presents some modest conceptual difficulties. Specifically, we should ask: Are ministerial positions valued as badges of prestige and as sources of employment for government bureaucrats or are they valued because their control also implies control of dimensions of public policy? If the primary motivation of parties is to secure prestige and jobs, then parliamentary maneuvering ought to be conceptualized as a purely redistributional game in which the parties vie for some (imperfectly) divisible commodity—the total of ministerships. On the other hand, if control of policy is the primary motivation, then we must conceptualize the preferences of political parties differently.

To take the most interesting possibility, assume that policy is the principal motivation, and to simplify matters, suppose we view a political party in a parliamentary setting as a unitary decision-making entity with a complete and transitive utility function defined over a policy space similar to the one we considered in section 6.4. Thus, we suppose that the set of all alternative governmental policies can be represented by a simple coordinate system with each dimension of the coordinate system corresponding to a specific issue, that each party has an ideal point (most preferred policy) in that policy space, and that the party's utility declines as we move away from that ideal point in any direction. We know, of course, from Arrow's Impossibility Theorem that this simplification cannot be sustained generally, and, in particular, that it glosses over the policy conflicts within parties that often manifest themselves as competitions for party leadership. Nevertheless, this simplification does allow a "first-pass" at the issue of parliamentary coalition processes.

Example: Consider once again the three policies A, B, and C in Figure 6.9, except in this instance we will associate those ideal points with parties 1, 2, and 3. Recall that the outcomes A, B, and C, which together constitute a main-simple *V*-set, are selected so that party 1 is indifferent between A and B, party 2 is indifferent between A and C, and party 3 is indifferent between B and C. What we want to establish now is that {A,B,C} corresponds to a competitive solution; that is,

$$K = \{(A,\{1,2\}), (B,\{1,3\}, (C,\{2,3\})\}.$$

First, notice that no coalition is associated with more than one outcome. Second, having associated the outcome A with {1,2} and so on, party 1 is pivotal between the two coalitions {1,2} and {1,3}—and, as required by *K*'s definition, 1 is indifferent between

A and B. Similarly, the other pivotal players are indifferent in the required way. Thus, no proposal in K is strictly viable against any other proposal in K. Finally, to see whether K can be upset with a new proposal, consider first the possibility that a coalition already represented by a proposal in K, say $\{1,2\}$, tries to upset K with a new proposal. However, referring to Figure 6.9, if $\{1,2\}$ proposes A', then although (A',$\{1,2\}$) is viable against (A,$\{1,2\}$) (because the pivots, 1 and 2, do not strictly prefer one outcome to the other) and although (A',$\{1,2\}$) is strictly viable against (B,$\{1,3\}$) (the pivot, 1, strictly prefers A' to B), the proposal (A',$\{1,2\}$) is not strictly viable against (C,$\{2,3\}$)—the pivot, party 2, strictly prefers C to A'. Similar reasoning establishes that no larger coalition—in particular, $\{1,2,3\}$—can upset K, so K is a competitive solution.

Before we consider parliamentary games with more than three parties, it is useful to pause at this moment to consider the fact that, aside from assuming that no party controls a majority of seats (a majority of the votes in Parliament), our discussion of this example makes no reference to the actual number of seats allocated to each party. Thus, subject only to the constraint that no party is a majority, the identification of $\{A,B,C\}$ as the predicted set of outcomes is invariant with the actual distribution of seats. If there are 99 seats in the Parliament, then we predict the same set of outcomes regardless of whether those seats are divided (33,33,33) or (49,49,1)—even if one party's share of the seats is considerably smaller than the other two parties, it is as essential to the formation of a winning coalition as are the two large parties. Thus, the electoral success of a party should not be measured simply by the number of seats it controls, but rather by whether it is a potentially critical member of a winning coalition.

In addition, we can use the competitive solution and the spatial representation of preferences to demonstrate the importance of the relative positioning of parties in the issue space.

Example: First, consider Figure 6.10, which shows the ideal points of four parties, and suppose that seats are allocated so that only $\{1,2\}$, $\{1,3\}$, $\{1,4\}$, and $\{2,3,4\}$ are minimal winning coalitions. Next, consider the set

$$K = \{(A,\{1,2\}), (B,\{1,3\}), (C,\{1,4\}), (D,\{2,3,4\})\}.$$

To see that K is a competitive solution, notice first that no co-

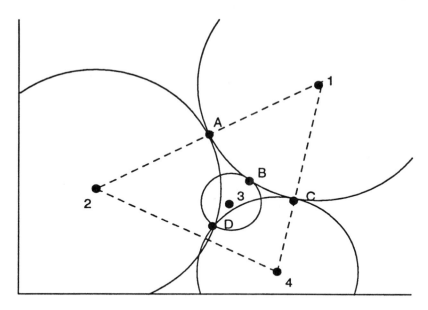

Figure 6.10 A Competitive Solution

alition has more than one proposal in *K*. Second, A, B, C, and D are positioned so that the pivots between any two coalitions in *K* are indifferent between the outcomes associated with those coalitions. Next, suppose {1,2} tries to upset *K* with the proposal (A',{1,2}). However, if {1,2} selects an A' that makes (A',{1,2}) viable against, say, (B,{1,3}), that proposal cannot be viable against (D,{2,3,4})—if we make any move from A that does not injure party 1, we necessarily make party 2 worse off. Thus, no coalition in *K* can upset *K*. And once again, a similar argument establishes that no other coalition can upset *K*.

Example: Now consider the ideal point configuration in Figure 6.11, which differs from the one shown in Figure 6.10 only in the location of party 3's ideal. In this instance, we can establish that the coalition {1,3} no longer has a proposal in *K*. Specifically, let

$$K = \{(A,\{1,2\}), (C,\{1,4\}), (D,\{2,3,4\})\}$$

and suppose {1,3} tries to enter with (B,{1,3}). Notice that to be viable against (A,{1,2})—and Pareto optimal for {1,3}—B must be located on the line between the point *q* and party 1's ideal,

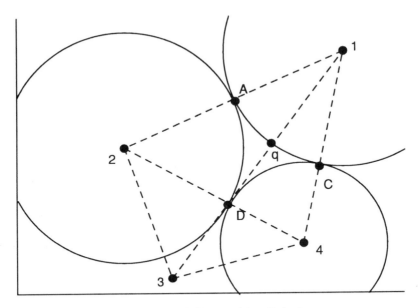

Figure 6.11 A Competitive Solution

because 1 pivots between {1,3} and {1,2}. However. if we satisfy this constraint, then party 3 strictly prefers D to {1,3}'s proposal, and since 3 pivots between {1,3} and {2,3,4}, no such proposal can be viable against D. Thus, {1,3} cannot enter the bidding to upset *K*. (Since it is not the case that all minimal winning coalitions have proposals in *K*, one implication of this example is that once we turn to a game in which utility does not act like money and is not perfectly transferable among the players, then that game need not have a main-simple *V*-set.)

The preceding examples reveal that when we attempt to predict parliamentary coalitions we should be concerned not only with what coalitions are winning and losing but also with the parties' policy preferences. This analysis also reveals that the overall policy associated with a parliamentary coalition is not some simple weighted average of the policies preferred by the member parties. Rather, it is the product of bargaining that takes into account the alternatives available to all coalition members. Closer inspection of our example reveals, moreover, that the coalitions with proposals in *K* are generally those that consist of "contiguous" parties—roughly speaking, parties with diametrically opposite preferences will not coalesce if there are winning coalitions that require less compromise. Finally, the coalitions with proposals in K generally will not contain inessential members—only coalitions just large enough to win will form, and if other parties are allowed to join in to ratify a government coalition, they may be allowed to do so but they cannot affect policy.

6.9 The Balance of Power and Self-Enforcing Agreements

Once we reconceptualize players as coalitions and strategies as the payoff vectors coalitions can secure, the concept of the core seems a natural extension of the idea of a Nash equilibrium to a cooperative context. The remaining solution concepts such as the V-set and the competitive solution, on the other hand, have a disturbing ad hoc quality to them, because the hypotheses that form their definitions are not derived from any readily identifiable postulates of rationality. Moreover, if the mechanisms of enforcement are germane to the kinds of agreements people reach, then, because these ideas sidestep the issue of enforcement, we cannot be certain they apply universally.

There is, in fact, at least one circumstance in which the task of understanding how the absence of an exogenous enforcement mechanism effects outcomes is the central research issue. Specifically, consider the view of international affairs which argues that stability in international politics, if it arises at all, arises because of a "balance of power." Without delving into the many issues surrounding this argument (such as the definition of "power" and the confusing array of definitions of "balance of power" found in the literature), this view sees international affairs as basically anarchic in the sense that whatever cooperation we observe arises and is enforced endogenously by the self-interest of relevant decision makers. Institutions and organizations such as the United Nations are regarded as largely irrelevant to the establishment and maintenance of stability because such institutions are themselves endogenous phenomena. Arguing that international institutions stabilize international politics merely pushes our explanation back a step to where we must explain why countries establish and abide by the edicts of such institutions.

The difficulty with the argument that a balance of power enforces stability is that it does not establish the circumstances under which alliances are enforceable in the sense that abiding by an agreement is an equilibrium strategy for the individual states in question. Of course, we have already seen how cooperation can emerge in repeated Prisoners' Dilemmas, but balance-of-power politics differs from such games in important ways. Cooperation in the repeated Prisoners' Dilemma arises in a game in which all players gain when cooperating as compared to when they are not cooperating. That is, cooperation moves outcomes from Pareto inefficient to Pareto efficient outcomes. However, power is presumably a relative variable and in constant supply, so unlike a Prisoners' Dilemma, balance-of-power politics is necessarily zero sum. Hence, with games like "divide-the-dollar" in mind, the question that arises in arguments over the viability of a balance of power system and international stability is the following: If power politics is like a majority rule game in which coalitions with a majority of power can defeat those with less, then why doesn't a majority coalition of countries form to eliminate the rest, with this process continuing until there are only two countries in the system?

This question is partially answered by observing that a balance of power system differs from a divide the dollar game in that even if we play divide the dollar several times in succession, we can define the game so that the players' voting weights remain constant, with each player controlling $1/n$th of the vote. In a balance of power scenario, on the other hand, a "voting weight" is presumably endogenous and equals that country's proportion of resources ("power"). That is, countries can expropriate resources from others in order to augment their ability to threaten and overcome adversaries. In a balance-of-power game, then, a country must be concerned about the possibility that if it coalesces with someone to eliminate others, it will become the next victim of its coalition partner.

To see how such a concern changes our view of coalitional possibilities, consider a system with three countries, $i = 1, 2$, and 3, and suppose country i controls r^o_i resources, which it values and which can be used to defend against or to overcome an adversary (for convenience, let $r^o_1 \geq r^o_2 \geq r^o_3$). Thus, if $r_j > r_i$, then in principle at least j can defeat i and expropriate all of j's resources. Next, assume that no country controls more than half the resources in the system, so no country can overwhelm the other two. Now consider the following extensive form game, which we denote by Γ:

1. Nature randomly picks one of the countries, say i.

2. Country i chooses whether to make a threat, $\mathbf{r} = (r_1, r_2, r_3)$, or to pass; if it passes we return to step 1.

3. If i threatens $\mathbf{r}$ and if $r_j \geq r^o_j$, j is i's coalition partner and must approve or reject i's proposal. If j rejects, we return to step 1; if j accepts, then $\mathbf{r}$ becomes the **current threat**.

4. Let k be the country threatened by $\mathbf{r}$ (which requires that r_k

$< r^{\circ}_{k}$). Country k has three responses: do nothing, in which case r becomes the status quo and we return to step 1; propose an alternative threat r'; or transfer resources to i or j.

5. If k chooses the second option, its coalition partner (i or j) must approve or reject k's proposal. If this partner rejects, r becomes the status quo and we return to step 1, whereas if it accepts, r' becomes the new current threat and we return to step 4. If k chooses the third option of transferring resources, then if the country who is a party to the transfer accepts, the transfer is consummated to form a new status quo, and we return to step 1, but if it is rejected, then the current threat r becomes the new status quo and we return to step 1.

We also impose two assumptions that help define the game's strategic character. First, we suppose that if two countries "war," then a third country that is larger than each of them can take advantage of the situation to realize some unspecified gains. This assumption has the effect of "freezing" systems in which one country controls half the resources. For example, if (150,100,50) is the status quo, then 2 will not attack 3, because 1 can use the conflict to become predominant —in which case it will eliminate both 2 and 3. Similarly, if 1 attacks 2, then 3 must come to 2's aid lest it become 1's next victim (which illustrates some of the "glue" that sustains alliances in international politics). Since 1 knows this beforehand, it will not attack 2.

Our second assumption accommodates in a modest way the costs that might reasonably be associated with conflict. Specifically, if given a choice between securing X units of resources by implementing a threat versus securing those resources via a transfer, a country prefers the transfer.

The analytic problem that confronts us now is that, in theory at least, our game can continue forever—1 and 2 could threaten 3, 3 could counter by proposing that 2 and 3 threaten 1, 1 can counter by proposing that 1 and 3 threaten 2, and so on. This fact creates two problems. First, if we once again define a strategy as a "plan of action" for the entire game, then there are infinitely many possible strategies. Thus, we may have to appeal to various intuitive criteria in order to narrow the list of possibilities we consider. Here we will initially consider only **stationary** strategies—strategies in which countries merely try to form the best available coalition, without regard to the threats or counters others have previously participated in. Stationary strategies, then, model countries that will form coalitions with whomever they can, without regard to what country might have defected from some coalition or agreement in the past. Such strategies are distinct from strategies like tit-for-tat, and instead they model a circumstance in which countries act in a pure Machiavellian fashion.

The second problem with which we must contend is that some branches of our extensive form have no end, so we cannot "work backward" from terminal nodes to deduce subgame perfect equilibria. Furthermore, it is inappropriate to suppose, as we did in the analysis of infinitely repeated Prisoners' Dilemmas, that future payoffs are discounted. All of the reasoning that our game models may merely be occurring in the heads of the participants as they contemplate strategic possibilities. Moreover, because the status quo never changes along those branches of the extensive form in which threats and counterthreats follow each other in an infinite sequence, there need not be any stream of benefits or losses to discount.

However, we can solve this game by pretending that it is finite— by supposing that we know the consequences of all branches in the game's extensive form. After postulating these consequences, a subgame-perfect equilibrium is characterized by strategies in which no one has an incentive to defect unilaterally to any choice not dictated by that player's strategy, and the postulated consequences are consistent in that they are "self-fulfilling prophesies" —the subgame perfect choices they imply must yield those consequences.

To formalize this idea, suppose, in accordance with the assumption that countries consider only stationary strategies, that all countries respond to r without regard to the histories associated with each player. Next, let Γ_r denote the subgame that follows the threat and acceptance of r. If country i associates the value $v_i(\Gamma_r)$ with playing that subgame, then $v(\Gamma_r) = (v_1(\Gamma_r), v_2(\Gamma_r), v_3(\Gamma_r))$—the **continuation value** of Γ_r—summarizes what countries 1, 2, and 3 believe follows from the approval of r. Thus, $v_i(\Gamma_r)$, when compared against whatever follows if r is rejected, determines i's preference for acceptance or rejection of r or for making this threat in the first place. Once values for all threats are specified we can assume that the acceptance of a threat or counter is a terminal node with its continuation value as the "final outcome." We then analyze Γ like a finite extensive form game of complete information, deducing the subgame perfect equilibrium strategies by working backward from the "terminal nodes" in the same way we treat finite agendas in majority voting games—we deduce what each country ought to do any time it must choose a threat, a counter, or accepting or rejecting a threat or counter. Hence,

An equilibrium is a set of continuation values—one for each threat—and a set of strategies for each country such that these values and strategies are consistent.

That is, in equilibrium, the choices implied by the continuation values—the strategies that are a subgame perfect equilibrium given the continuation values—must, in turn, imply those continuation values.

Example: Suppose $(S,r^o) = (\{1,2,3\}, (120,100,80))$, and let country 1 threaten $((150,0,150),\{1,3\})$. Limiting our discussion to threats in this form (i.e., two players threaten a third with elimination) and to transfers, consider the representation of the situation in Figure 6.12, where ● denotes a terminal node. After 1 proposes its threat, 3 must decide whether to accept or reject. If 3 accepts, 2 must then offer a counter that, given the limitations we impose on threats and counters, is either a coalition with 1 or with 3 to divide 300, or a transfer of thirty units to 1 (which, if offered, 1 accepts since this is the best possible payoff for 1 given that 2 and 3 will not allow an outcome that gives 1 more). Country 2 need not consider a transfer to 3 since, being larger, 1 can be made to prefer the transfer over the original threat with the expenditure of fewer resources. Depending on which counter 2 chooses, either 1 or 3 must decide whether to accept or reject. In the event of a rejection, the threat is implemented and 2 is eliminated. In the event of an acceptance, the counter becomes the new current threat, and the subgame that follows is denoted by Γ with an appropriate subscript. Figure 6.12 portrays the next step in this process with either 1 or 3 offering a counter.

Without concerning ourselves with how they arrive at such numbers, suppose the countries assume that the following continuation values hold for the three threats that eliminate a country (we need not consider threats that give someone more than 150 since no one will allow it to go unchallenged):

$$v(\Gamma_{(150,0,150)}) = (150,70,80),$$
$$v(\Gamma_{(0,150,150)}) = (70,150,80),$$
$$v(\Gamma_{(150,150,0)}) = v(\Gamma_{(150,0,150)})/2 + v(\Gamma_{(0,150,150)})/2,$$
$$= (110,110,80).$$

The value for $v(\Gamma_{(150,150,0)})$ is based on the assumption that country 3 counters with $(150,0,150)$ and $(0,150,150)$ with equal probability whenever it is indifferent between these two choices (or

that 3 accepts each counter with equal probability if it is indifferent). Once we have assigned values to each subgame we can
then deduce the choices they and subgame perfection imply for
the extensive form in Figure 6.12. Referring to this figure, then,
after 1 proposes a threat and 3 accept's, country 2 has three
choices:

1. Counter with the threat (0,150,150).
2. Counter with the threat (150,150,0).
3. Transfer resources to 1 so as to make 1 near-predominant
   and to freeze the system.

Consider the top-right of Figure 6.12, which assumes that 2
counters with (0,150,150), and suppose for the moment that 3
accepts 2's offer. At this point, with (0,150,150) the current threat,
country 1 must act and it has three choices:

1. Counter with the threat (150,0,150).
2. Counter with the threat (150,150,0).
3. Transfer resources to 2 so as to make 2 near-predominant
   and to freeze the system.

If 1 proposes (150,0,150), 3 rejects 1's offer because it prefers
(0,150,150) to the continuation value of $\Gamma_{(150,0,150)}$. At this point,
given our assumption about continuation values, 3 is choosing
between a payoff of 80 ($v_3(\Gamma_{(150,0,150)}) = 80$) and a payoff of 150.
We indicate this preference by an arrow. Similarly, if 1 ap-
proaches 2 by proposing (150,150,0), then 2 rejects since
$v_2(\Gamma_{(150,150,0)})$ corresponds to a lottery between 150 and 70. Thus,
1 prefers to transfer resources to 2, because each of the other
alternatives available to 1 leads to 1's elimination. (We need not
consider any other type of transfer: Transfers giving less than
150 are rejected since rejection implements the threat, and a
transfer that renders 3 near-predominant is more costly than a
transfer to 2.)

Notice, now, that the node corresponding to the point at which
1 must respond to 3's acceptance of 2's counter begins a subgame,
$\Gamma_{(0,150,150)}$, with which we initially associated the continuation value
$v(\Gamma_{(0,150,150)}) = (70,150,80)$. Since we have shown that 1 transfers
to 2, our initial supposition is sustained—to this point at least,
subgame perfection and our initial conjectures about contin-

uation values are consistent. Also, country 3 prefers not to play this subgame and instead rejects 2's offer of (0,150,150) in favor of implementing the initial threat, because it gives 3 a payoff of 150.

Next consider the lower-right part of Figure 6.12. In this instance 2 counters the initial threat with (150,150,0). Suppose for the moment that 1 accepts. This acceptance marks the beginning a subgame, $\Gamma_{(150,150,0)}$, in which it is 3's turn to respond. Notice, however, that given the continuation values, country 3 need not consider offering to transfer any portion of its resources since either counterthreat has associated with it a value of eighty for 3. However, this fact implies that 3 is indifferent between countering with (0,150,150) or with (150,0,150), so let 3 choose between these counterthreats with equal probability. Once again, then, we deduce a value $v(\Gamma_{(150,150,0)})$ that is consistent with our initial conjecture. But just as 3 rejects 2's offer of (0,150,150), 1 rejects 2's offer of (150,150,0), because 1 prefers the certainty of getting 150 units by implementing the original threat to the lottery that $\Gamma_{(150,150,0)}$ implies.

Thus, both of 2's counterthreats are rejected, leaving 2 with only one choice—transfer enough resources to 1 so as to make one near-predominant. Although we have not drawn in 1's decision as part of Figure 6.12, it is evident that 1 accepts this transfer since it knows that it can never get more than 150 and since it prefers becoming near-predominant by accepting a transfer over implementing a threat. But notice now that the acceptance of the initial threat by 1 or 3 marks the beginning of a subgame, which we have just shown leads to 2 transferring resources to 1. So as initially conjectured, $v(\Gamma_{(150,0,150)})$ = (150,70,80). A similar analysis for initial threats of (150,150,0) and (0,150,150) confirms the continuation values we posited for them.

What remains in the analysis of this example is a specification of $v(\Gamma)$—the value of the entire game—and an equilibrium identifying the initial choices and responses of countries. Suppose first that $v(\Gamma)$ = (120,100,80)—in effect, suppose that no initial threat is offered or accepted, and that the status quo prevails. This supposition is sustainable, in fact, if we characterize equilibrium strategies thus: A country does not initiate or agree to a threat unless it gains resources. Since the $v(\Gamma_r)$'s imply that countries 1 and 2 can each gain from an initial threat, whereas 3 can neither gain nor lose, 3 has no positive incentive to participate in a threat. Thus, the only threat

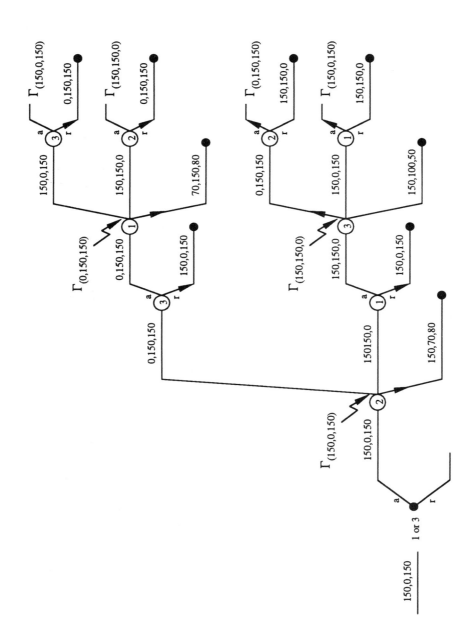

that might be approved is (150,150,0). However, 1 and 2 are essentially playing a constant-sum game since, as we have already learned, player 3 is never forced to transfer to 1 or 2. So, depending on the probability that 3 chooses one action or another when it is indifferent, neither 1 nor 2 has an incentive to threaten or to approve of (150,150,0). Indeed, 3 can counter with a threat that requires the originally threatening country to transfer resources to 3's partner in the counter. Hence, three-country systems can be wholly stable without anyone offering an initial threat.

There is, however, another stationary equilibrium that generates a reallocation of resources characterized by: Accept all initial threats if they promise no loss; otherwise reject. This equilibrium sustains $v(\Gamma) = a(150,70,80) + (1-a)(70,150,80) = (70+80a,150-80a,80)$, where a is the probability that 3 coalesces with 1 if it is indifferent between coalescing with 1 and 2. Although country 3 cannot gain resources if it abides by such a strategy (the continuation values for all threats remain as before), 3 has no positive incentive to defect unilaterally to another strategy. However, although 2 transfers to 1 or 1 transfers to 2, no country is eliminated. Thus, our conclusion about this three-country system is that if we see any coalition, it will be either $\{1,3\}$ or $\{2,3\}$, with either 1 or 2 becoming near-predominant. And since all three-country systems without a predominant player are equivalent to our example, this fact establishes the possibility of stability in anarchic international systems.

Naturally, we should extend this analysis to larger systems before inferring anything general about balance of power. Rather than consider this generalization, though, let us consider instead the possibility that there exists a "nicer" equilibrium in which no threats are ever made. Recall that as a partial justification for the Iraq war, President George Bush presented American intervention as a prelude to the formation of a "new world order" in which the confrontational style of the Cold War was to be replaced with a universal agreement among nations to eschew conflict in favor of the mutual benefits of economic cooperation. Of course, this idea met with considerable skepticism, in part because such a scheme had been attempted before in the form of the abortive League of Nations and had clearly failed. One failed experiment, however, does not invalidate a theory, because we can always appeal to the particular circumstances of that experiment to explain the failure (in the case of the League, we have the "circumstance" of the Great Depression).

The issue, then, is whether there is any theoretical basis for looking at Bush's proposal with skepticism. To address this issue, we note that this new world order in fact corresponds to the idea of

collective security, which is an international system in which all countries initially agree to refrain from making an initial threat and to refrain from accepting one in the event that it is offered. And to enforce such an agreement, countries also agree to punish, whenever possible, those who defect or those who fail to participate in the administration of punishments (regardless of whether the initially threatened states export oil or mushrooms). So the game-theoretic question that confronts us is whether states will have an incentive to administer punishments in the event that one or more other states defect from the initial agreement and whether the existence of this incentive is sufficient to preclude any initial threat.

To answer this question, notice first that a collective security equilibrium calls for strategies of a different sort than the type we have thus far considered. Specifically, it calls for an equilibrium of nonstationary strategies in which the target of threats is a function of history (defined in terms of who has defected). However, to make matters more precise, assume that if a nonpunishing threat is ever made and accepted, all countries play stationary strategies thereafter as described previously. Staying now with our three-country example, suppose country 1 defects and proposes (150,0,150). If 3 accepts, then, since all countries play as before, 2 must transfer resources to 1. On the other hand, if 3 rejects 1's overture, and if 2 then proposes to punish 1 by threatening (0,150,150), 3 accepts since it has no positive incentive to defect—as the smallest country, we already know that it can never gain resources. Similarly, if 3 has the opportunity to punish 1, it is indifferent between defecting and proposing the (0,150,150) punishing threat; thus, it has no incentive to defect from the presumed punishment equilibrium. Hence, 3 receives eighty regardless of whether it accepts 1's initial offer or rejects it in favor of administering a punishment, which is to say, as before, that 3 has no incentive to defect from the presumed equilibrium.

At this point, of course, the reader may feel a bit uncomfortable with our assumptions about 3's actions whenever it is indifferent. Indeed, because of such indifference, the presumed collective security equilibrium is weak and is vulnerable to the possibility that countries choose "erroneously." However (and we refrain from demonstrating this fact), the extension of our analysis to larger systems reveals that in such systems all countries can be targets of "profitable" threats, which thereby gives everyone a positive incentive to avoid the possibility of being the target of a punishment as well as a positive incentive to punish.

Our model, then, has at least two equilibria that are of opposite

Cooperation and Coalitions / 313

types in the sense that one predicts the eventuality of threats and the other predicts that the status quo will prevail. This model, though, is far too abstract to allow definitive statements about the viability of foreign policies based on collective security arrangements versus balance-of-power notions. We have not considered such things as uncertainty, the costs of conflict, geography, and the possible existence of more complex equilibria (as when, for example, subsets of countries form alliances and agree to play "collective security" among themselves and stationary strategies with respect to everyone else in the system). Nevertheless, this type of analysis does establish the possibility of sustaining cooperation without exogenous enforcement in a world in which "power" is the sole arbiter of disputes.

Suggestions for Further Reading

Most game theory texts contain extensive discussions of the core (e.g., the previously cited texts by Luce and Raiffa and by Moulin). However, the correspondence between the core and the Condorcet winner in a spatial context is best explored in Judith Sloss, "Stable Outcomes in Majority Voting Games," *Public Choice*, 15 (1971): 19–48. The advanced reader should also consult Richard D. McKelvey and Norman Schofield, "Generalized Symmetry Conditions at a Core Point," *Econometrica*, 55 (1987): 923–33 for the most current results.

With respect to the role of institutions in inducing stability, a large literature has developed that elaborates on the ideas we survey. The seminal essay is Gerald H. Kramer, "Sophisticated Voting Over Multidimensional Choice Spaces," *Journal of Mathematical Sociology*, 2 (1972): 165–80. Kramer's essay, however, is quite technical, and the beginning student may prefer to consult Kenneth Shepsle, "Institutional Arrangements and Equilibrium in Multidimensional Voting Models," *American Journal of Political Science*, 23 (1979): 27–59, and Kenneth Shepsle and Barry Weingast, "Structure Induced Equilibrium and Legislative Choice," *Public Choice*, 37 (1981): 503–19 for a substantive interpretation. For the particular problems that strategic voting engenders, however, see Arthur Denzau and Robert Mackay, "Structure Induced Equilibrium and Perfect Foresight Expectations," *American Journal of Political Science*, 25 (1981): 762–79. And for an assessment in a spatial context of the procedural constraints imposed by the U.S. Constitution, see Thomas H. Hammond and Gary J. Miller, "The Core of the Constitution," *American Political Science Review*, 81 (1987): 1155–74.

The seminal volume in political science on coalition formation in games without cores is William H. Riker's *Theory of Political Coalitions*, New Haven: Yale University Press, 1962. Indeed, Riker's volume is the source of our discussion of the election of 1824. However, Riker assumes transferable utility, and for a discussion of cooperative solution theory in a spatial context as well as citations to the relevant literature see Ordeshook, *Game Theory and Political Theory*, cited earlier. For a contemporary account of this theory and an attempt to overcome some of the shortcomings of bargaining sets and the competitive solution, see W.W. Sharkey, "A Model of Competition Among Political Interest Groups," 1990, mimeo, Bellcore, Morristown, New Jersey. We hasten to add that a great many ad hoc hypotheses exist in the political science literature about coalition formation in Parliaments, but only a few bear any direct relation to game theory.

Our discussion in section 6.9 of balance of power and collective security is from Emerson M.S. Niou and P.C. Ordeshook, "Stability in Anarchic Systems," *American Political Science Review*, 84 (1990): 1207–34 and "Realism versus Neoliberalism: A Formulation," *American Journal of Political Science*, May 1991. The interested reader, however, should also consult R. Harrison Wagner, "The Theory of Games and the Balance of Power," *World Politics*, 38 (1986): 546–76.

Exercises

1. Is vote trading in a legislature profitable and most likely to be observed when (a) various minorities find it in their interest to thwart the will of the majority? (b) there is no uniquely stable outcome, and it is possible for every agreement to be upset by something else? (c) congressional rules are sufficiently inflexible that only behind-the-scenes deals will accommodate the majority will? or (d) legislators are constrained by their constituents from voting sophisticatedly?

2. Suppose one of the following four payoff vectors must be chosen by three voters using simple majority rule:

voter 1	voter 2	voter 3
2	−1	−1
−1	−3	3
−1	3	−3
−3	1	1

    a.   Does this game have a core or a *V*-set?

    b.   If you assume that utility is transferable does your answer to part (a) change?

3.   Recall our example, from section 6.4, of the Valley of the Dump. Suppose, however, that there are only four clans (euphemistically named 1, 2, 3, and 4), each living on its own quarter of the valley, and that everyday, the number of bags of garbage produced by each clan equals its name—clan *i* produces *i* bags of garbage per day. As before, the legal code of the valley, strictly enforced, requires each clan to produce its allotted bags of garbage, and it allows clan *i* to dump exactly *i* bags of garbage in its own backyard or the yards of others. However, the bags must be dealt with as distinct units—no scattering of any bag's contents is permitted. (They have high standards in the valley.) Assume that each clan evaluates the outcome of the garbage problem in the same way as in our original example.

    a.   Define and interpret the conditions that must be satisfied if this game is to have a core.

    b.   Does a nonempty core exist for this game?

    c.   How do your answers change if we suppose that bags of garbage are infinitely divisible?

4.   Assume that a five-person committee uses issue-by-issue, majority rule voting, and that its members have the following ideal points on the two-dimensional issue space (let all indifference curves be concentric circles).

> *voter 1: (7,2)*
> *voter 2: (8,9)*
> *voter 3: (3,4)*
> *voter 4: (4,8)*
> *voter 5: (10,5)*

    a.   If communication and coordination are impossible, what is the outcome?

    b.   If the committee abandons its restrictive rules in favor of free and open debate, does the game have a core?

    c.   More generally, can issue-by-issue voting lead to a different outcome than the core with simple Euclidean preferences? Explain your answer.

5. Consider the following system of representative majority rule among twenty seven voters: There are three regions, each divided into three districts. Each district has three voters. There are representatives (who are computers, and are not to be considered part of the voting body) at the regional and district levels. District level representatives inherit (over any pair of alternatives) the majority preferences of the voters in their districts, and regional representatives inherit the majority preferences of the representatives in their region. A policy outcome is chosen by a majority vote of the regional representatives.

    a. What is the minimum number of voters that can form a decisive coalition (i.e. get their preferred policy positions as the outcome)? Construct an example to support your answer.

    b. How does your answer to (a) change if the district level representatives are eliminated?

    c. Assuming that all preferences are single-peaked over a single issue, does the final outcome depend on the existence of the district level representatives? Why?

6. Consider a six-person symmetric game where the value of a coalition C, $v(C)$, is given by

    $$v(C) = \left\{ \begin{matrix} 0 \\ 1 \\ 2 \\ 3 \\ 3 \\ 4 \end{matrix} \right\} \ if \ |C| = \left\{ \begin{matrix} 1 \\ 2 \\ 3 \\ 4 \\ 5 \\ 6 \end{matrix} \right\}$$

    where $|C|$ denotes the number of members of C. Assuming that what a coalition earns is infinitely divisible among the coalition's members, does this game have a core?

7. In economics, a common representation of utility for two commodities is the function $u_i(x_i,y_i) = x_i^\alpha y_i^\beta$ where both α and are positive constants. So suppose two persons are bargaining over the allocation of ten units of each of the goods, where both goods are infinitely divisible. Let $\alpha = = 2$ for both persons, and suppose that person 1's initial endowments of the two goods are 2 and 7, respectively (so that 2's initial endowments are 8 and 3, respectively). What is the core to this two-person game?

8. Using the spatial policy positions in problem 4, determine whether the coalition {1,3,4} has a stable coalition proposal in the bargaining set. (Hint: suppose players 1, 4, and 3 tentatively agree to the proposal that is Pareto optimal for them and approximately midway between 1 and 4's ideal. Now let 1 object against 3 with a proposal that is Pareto optimal for {1,2,5}, and check whether 3 can counter with any coalition that excludes 1 and with a proposal that gives 3 as much as 3 get from the original proposal with {1,3,4}.)

9. Suppose three houses, each with a large front-facing window, are arrayed in a triangle such that a person sitting in any house can see one-fifth of its own garden, all of the garden of the house on the left, and none of the garden belonging to the house on its right. Suppose each homeowner is endowed with one bag of fertilizer and is required by law to use it (suburban values being what they are). A bag of fertilizer, allocated to one garden, improves that garden so that a person having a full view of it enjoys a benefit of five units of utility, a person having only a one-fifth view enjoys a one unit utility increase, and a person with no view is not benefitted at all. Assume that the home owners can coalesce to allocate their fertilizer, and that people cannot fertilize another's garden without permission. Suppose also that if two bags of fertilizer are allocated to any one garden, then that garden is doubly beautiful.

   a. Does the game have a core?

   b. How does your answer change if we suppose that a coalition of two persons can commit itself to an action before the excluded player acts? (Hint: suppose the coalition allows the excluded player to distribute his or her fertilizer in a way that is an optimal response to the coalition's actions.)

10. For the example in Figure 6.8, determine whether the order of voting effects the existence of a stable outcome. That is, consider the possibility that the committee votes first on issue 1, then on issue 2.

11. Assume a two-dimensional policy space, assume that no two committee members share the same ideal point, and assume that all indifference contours are circles. Using the core's definition in terms of Pareto optimal policies for winning coali-

tions, what general implication can you draw about the distribution of ideal points for majority rule spatial games with cores?

12. Sketch the proof of the assertion that the core of a majority voting game, after being associated with any winning coalition, is a competitive solution. Also, sketch the proof of the assertion that the main-simple V-set, in association with the appropriate minimal winning coalitions, is also a competitive solution.

13. Suppose three people, 1, 2, and 3, must use majority rule to choose a rule for dividing $1,000 among themselves, and suppose that only two rules are available: (1) face-to-face bargaining in which persons 1 and 2 have two votes and person 3 has one vote, and (2) a procedure whereby 1 makes a proposal in which he or she receives $500 and in which 2 and 3 divide the remaining $500 in units of $250 (i.e., 2 gets either $500 or $250 or $0). If the proposal is accepted by 2 or 3, it is implemented. If it is rejected, 3 can make a similar proposal (i.e., $500 for person 2, with persons 1 and 3 receiving the remainder in units of $250). If it is rejected, the outcome (333, 333, 333) is implemented. What is the final outcome?

14. Describe the V-set and competitive solution to the following vote-trading game (excluding lotteries, letting the defeat of each bill be worth zero to each legislator, and assuming the payoffs across bills are separable):

Legislator	A	B	C	D	E	F
1	3	3	2	-4	-4	2
2	2	-4	-4	2	3	3
3	-4	2	3	3	2	-4

15. Consider the preferences of the following four-person committee over three bills, A, B, and C:

L_1	L_3	L_5	L_7	U_i
A	B	C	A	2
B	C	A	B	1
C	A	B	C	0

Suppose the committee can pass one and only one of the three bills. In order for a bill to pass, it must receive at least two-thirds of the vote. Voting is weighted so that L_1's vote counts once, L_7's vote counts seven times and so on. Legislators are strategic, vote simultaneously, vote for only one bill, and are free to communicate and form cooperative agreements. A legislator receives a payoff of 2 if his most-preferred alternative passes, 1 if his second-most-preferred alternative passes and 0 otherwise. Utility is transferable and infinitely divisible. All cooperative agreements are costlessly enforceable.

    a. Which, if any, of the bills pass?

    b. If L_1's vote is counted three times instead of once, how does your answer to part (a) change?

16. Bicameralism (a two-chamber legislature) is assumed to induce stability. Consider a spatial situation with three legislators in each of two chambers, and assume that all preferences are given by simple Euclidean distance. Indifference contours are circles.

    a. Construct a two-issue example in which, using majority rule, there is no core within each chamber, but there is a core overall if any motion to upset the status quo must defeat it in each chamber.

    b. Can Pareto inefficient outcomes be sustained as equilibria under such an arrangement?

    c. Can there ever be a circumstance in which the status quo is a core under bicameralism, but isn't if the two chambers are combined?

17. In the following two-person game in strategic form, the game ends at the assigned payoffs if the players choose anything but (a_1,b_1). However, if they choose (a_1,b_1), they must replay the game. Specify a continuation value for (a_1,b_1) that allows you to solve the game.

	b_1	b_2
a_1	replay	2,5
a_2	5,5	0,6

Index